ADVANCED GUIDE TO HYDROPONICS

Frontispiece – The author with hyacinths grown in hydroponics during winter.

James Sholto Douglas

ADVANCED GUIDE TO HYDROPONICS

[SOILLESS CULTIVATION]

PELHAM BOOKS: LONDON

By the same author:

HYDROPONICS: THE BENGAL SYSTEM
Oxford University Press, 1951 and subsequent editions.

HYDROPONICS (SOILLESS CULTIVATION)
Government of West Bengal, 1948.

THE POSSIBILITIES OF SOILLESS CULTIVATION
United Nations Educational, Scientific & Cultural Organization, 1955.

BEGINNER'S GUIDE TO HYDROPONICS (SOILLESS GARDENING)
Pelham Books, 1972.

BEGINNER'S GUIDE TO APPLIED ECOLOGY
Pelham Books, 1974.

FOREST-FARMING
Robinson & Watkins, London, 1976

First published in Great Britain by PELHAM BOOKS LTD
52 Bedford Square, London WC1B 3EF
1976

ISBN 0 7207 0830 3

Filmset and printed in Great Britain by
BAS Printers Limited, Wallop, Hampshire
and bound by James Burn

Contents

Seed germination, Plant propagation, Culling and thinning, Hardening-off, Cuttings, Other propagation techniques, Transplanting, Sowing and planting *in situ*, Spacing, Seed quantities, Pretreatment of seeds and planting material.

Illustrations

FIGURES

Three specimen record charts – on pp 228–231.

ACKNOWLEDGEMENTS

The author wishes to express his thanks and gratitude to all those individuals and organizations that have provided advice and material for this book. He is also indebted to the following for permission to reproduce illustrations and desires to record his appreciation for their interest and support:

PHOTOGRAPHS

Frontispiece *Garden News*; 1, 2, & 3 Government of Abu Dhabi and Manley Inc.,; 4 Professor G. Rivoira, University of Sassari; 5 Dr A. A. Steiner, Centre for Plant Physiological Research, Wageningen; 6 & 7 United States Department of Agriculture; 8 Hydroponics Inc., Indianapolis, Indiana; 9 J. A. Gordon & Son Ltd., Stonehouse, Glos.; 14 Mrs Grace Gericke, California; 15 & 16 Dr Cyril Pustan, Jena; 17 & 18 Professor G. S. Davtyan, Institute of Agrochemical Problems and Hydroponics, Erevan, Armenia.

FIGURES

9 A. Beltran and New American Library; 10 Hydroponics Inc., Indianapolis; 11 Professor G. Rivoira, University of Sassari; 14 Hydroculture Inc., Glendale; 23 Dr H. Filippo; 30 V. K. Chatterjee, Hydroponic Investigation Unit, Sibpur; 35 Dr Hugo Boyko, Academy of Art & Science, Rehovoth; 37 and 41 Professor Y. Hori, Tohoku University; 43 M. Ranseder.

Dedication: to Anisa

There is a procedure in every part of nature that is perfectly regular and geometrical, if we can but find it out; and the further our searches carry us, the more we shall have occasion to admire this and the better it will compensate our labour.

JOHN WOODWARD in *Some Thoughts and Experiments Concerning Vegetation*, 1699.

Preface

It has for sometime been apparent that a wide-felt need exists for a fully comprehensive and easily understood guide to the more advanced practice of hydroponics, which would cover to sufficiently high standards and with adequate technical detail all the main systems and methods of soilless cultivation. Although a number of books and many scientific papers on this branch of plant growing have been issued over the years, most of them would appear to be directed towards particular aspects of hydroponics, such as specific unit designs or modes of operation, or else they deal only with quite simple techniques or complicated laboratory and experimental work.

However, the fact is that farmers and gardeners often raise plants in differing local circumstances and situations, so consequently their individual requirements may vary greatly. A system or method of hydroponics that is well suited to one area or site may not always provide completely satisfactory growth in others. Indeed, the multiplicity of soilless cultural techniques available today bears witness to the efforts that have been put into the development and adaptation of hydroponics, based upon the desire to discover the most efficient ways of producing crops without soil in all types of contrasting conditions. In other words, the aim has been to devise different methods intended to satisfy diverse operational needs.

Nevertheless, the considerable number of hydroponic techniques may often create some difficulties. Faced with a wide and perhaps slightly bewildering choice, the commercial or professional grower, the working farmer or the more advanced amateur gardener may well wonder which system or method he or she should adopt, given a specific set of local circumstances. Frequently, the beginner in hydroponics, who has mastered the care and management of simple soilless gardens, and who wishes to undertake more advanced cultures, will want to know what options are open which offer the opportunity for useful and profitable progress in plant growing without soil.

This book is intended to provide readers with detailed guidance for the general practice of more advanced hydroponics. At the same time, every effort has been made to present the subject in a clear and straightforward manner, so that the systems and methods can be understood easily and used efficiently by the average person with basic knowledge of agriculture or horticulture, provided that he or she is prepared to study with reasonable care the particular technical skills demanded by hydroponics.

In addition, the principles upon which plant growing without soil are founded have been set out, different techniques of hydroponics are discussed, and the main aspects of practical plant physiology are presented for the reader's attention. A wide choice of unit designs and constructions are offered, with details of cultural operations. Suitable nutrient formulae are listed, as well as the modes of exercising chemical control over crops. Finally, the ecology of hydroponic units has been examined and the all-important questions of costs and returns considered.

It is the author's hope that this working guide to advanced hydroponics will serve as a practical manual to all those anxious to make further progress in soilless cultivation and constitute an effective aid to skilled and profitable cropping.

J. SHOLTO DOUGLAS

NOTE

In accordance with modern practice all weights and measurements in this book are given in the metric system.

METRIC TABLES

1 millimetre (mm)	$\frac{1}{1000}$th of a metre
1 centimetre (cm)	$\frac{1}{100}$th of a metre
10 millimetres	1 centimetre
100 centimetres	1 metre (m)
10 centimetres	1 decimetre
10 decimetres	1 metre
10 metres	1 decametre
10 decametres	1 hectometre
10 hectometres	1 kilometre

100 square metres (m²)	1 are
10 ares	1 decare
10 decares	1 hectare

1 milligramme (mg)	$\frac{1}{1000}$th of a gramme
1000 grammes (gm)	1 kilogramme (kg. or kilo)
1000 kilogrammes	1 tonne

1 millilitre	$\frac{1}{1000}$th of a litre
10 millilitres	1 centilitre
10 centilitres	1 decilitre
10 decilitres	1 litre

PART ONE

General Principles

1. Hydroponic tomato growing using sand culture and plastic lined troughs or beds with trickle irrigation of solution at Sadiyat, Abu Dhabi. (Government of Abu Dhabi and Manley Inc.).

CHAPTER 1

Growth without soil

Soilless cultivation in its broadest sense can be described as the use of any method of growing plants which does not involve the employment of natural earth or specially compounded soil-based composts and similar complexes. Several different names have been proposed for, or given to, these techniques of crop production without soil, including such expressions as *nutriculture* (a contraction of the words 'nutrient' and 'culture'), *chemiculture, artificial growth, soilless agriculture* or *gardening, aquiculture, olericulture,* and *tank farming,* but the most popular and best known of all is undoubtably the term *hydroponics.**

Hydroponics means literally 'water-working' or 'water-activation', in reference to the fact that green or higher plants growing without soil are dependent for their supplies of the essential inorganic elements upon solutions of nutrient ions in water. The term is derived from a combination of two Greek words: *hudor,* water, and *ponos,* working. Both the theory and the practice of hydroponics are based on scientific principles, involving the application of plant physiology, chemistry, horticulture and agronomy, as well as the several phases of environmental and disease control, to the production of economic and ornamental crops under appropriately regulated conditions.

Before attempting any evaluation and description of hydroponic techniques, it is necessary to remember that soilless cultivation is a specialized branch of agricultural crop production, and as such, it will serve the user either poorly or superbly, depending entirely upon whether or not it is properly carried out. The main utility of hydroponics lies in its ability to provide growers with a means of raising good quality crops in areas where there may be a shortage of suitable soil for farming or gardening or where water supplies, space, or other facilities, in the amounts needed for conventional cultivation, are lacking. In addition, several important advantages may well be secured as the result of a decision to introduce hydroponics in a particular locality.

---

*The term hydroponics has been translated into numerous languages; for example, *hidroponia* (Spanish), *idroponica* (Italian), *idporonika* (Russian), and *hydroponiques* (French). In France, the expression *cultures sans sol* is used frequently, while the Hindustani rendering *panikheti* is employed sometimes in India.

Not only is soilless cultivation the most economical way of supplying water and nutriment to plants, but it also enables growers to control the spread of various disease organisms. Other benefits frequently include a higher level of crop yields than is generally obtainable in ordinary soil culture, together with quicker growth and earlier development of fruits, vegetables and flowers. Standard methods simplify the work schedule, which is further lightened by the elimination of hard manual operations such as ploughing, digging, weeding, and sterilization of soils. The cleanliness inherent in hydroponic systems, combined with an absence of dirt and smells, is another significant factor of some importance, which assists in the maintenance of good phytosanitary conditions.

Technical ability

The profitable operation of more advanced or large-scale hydroponic units demands a degree of technical skill, combined with a basic understanding of plant physiology. The hydroponicist in business must know how to make the periodically necessary adjustments in the controllable factors of the cropping environment in order to secure maximum yields and superior quality produce. Additionally, most successful growers of commercial crops possess or acquire what may be termed 'plant sense' or 'green fingers'. This 'feel' for plants is a type of artisan skill which comes to individuals as a result of careful observation, long experience, or sometimes an inherited gift for handling crops. Growers should be able to recognise speedily any abnormalities in the plants under their charge, including symptoms of nutritional or physiological disturbances caused by changes in cultural conditions, deficiencies, environmental influences and other factors that may from time to time affect the health and yield of hydroponic crops.

It will therefore be apparent to the reader, who has perhaps already had a certain amount of experience with small-scale hydroponics, that while very satisfactory yields may be obtained from simple soilless units operated in home gardens or households, the profitability of larger commercial or semi-commercial installations must necessarily stand or fall by the amount of technical skill employed in running them. The position as far as professional growers are concerned has been summed up appropriately by W. G. Templeman of I.C.I. Ltd., in the following words: 'It cannot be overemphasised that plants grown by nutrient solutions in sand culture demand the same cultural knowledge and care and similar conditions of light and temperature as do plants grown in soil'. These remarks of course apply with equal force to all the various systems of soilless growth of crops.

Most amateur gardeners and householders obviously do not need to acquire the same degree of knowledge or technical skill in hydroponic methods as professional growers must. Many people are simply anxious to raise fresh salads or other greenstuffs at home to supplement the family diet. From the practical angle, they will not be concerned with nutritional theory, although naturally if they do have some understanding of how plants grow it will add interest to the daily routine of the garden and contribute to the success of their hobby. However, it is important that amateur hydroponicists should be prepared to carry out the procedures laid down for the satisfactory operation of home units, because unless there is strict adherence to instructions, failures may result. In devising methods of soilless culture to cater for the needs of the average gardener or householder, considerable attention has been paid to the simplification of techniques. The amount of equipment necessary and the level of skill demanded for the operation of simple hydroponic units have been reduced to the minimum. But soilless cultivation is an art as well as a science. Just as in any walk of life, there are some persons who are gifted with an aptitude for getting the best out of a task, so it is with hydroponics – certain individuals will inevitably do better than others. Nevertheless, very much depends upon diligent study of the subject and it is possible for anyone to become a good grower of soilless cultured plants if he or she is prepared to take the trouble to learn the basic rudiments to begin with. Once this elementary knowledge has been acquired a sound foundation upon which to build for the future will be available. Some extremely successful soilless gardens have been built and run by amateurs. There are in existence in the world today great numbers of small hydroponic units, maintained by housewives, flat dwellers, city residents, villagers and suburban dwellers. Surveys undertaken recently have produced estimates which indicate that there are about a half-a-million such home hydroponic gardens in the United States alone, and probably a total of two million throughout the world at the present time. Expansion is, of course continually taking place.

For more advanced amateurs and for professional and commercial growers concerned with hydroponics, the position has already been quite clearly defined. The need here is for the maximum possible utilization of technical skills and the aim must always be to seek to improve and perfect the operation of specific installations. Hydroponic crop production is not a static activity. On the contrary, new systems and applications are being evolved continually and consequently it is imperative that all growers should attempt to keep abreast of technical developments.

The question of technical ability is an important one. Put in its simplest terms, it means that every hydroponicist should try to ensure that his or her knowledge is adequate for the level of plant culture being operated. The more advanced the work or the more elaborate the system used, the greater will be the amount of skill and training needed. The best advice that can be given is to limit initial activities in conformity with the knowledge to hand and expand only as further practice is acquired. There is no substitute for diligent and intensive study combined with suitable experience in operating hydroponic units. The information contained in this book is intended to provide readers with a reliable guide to advanced techniques of soilless cultivation, whether they may be commercial or semi-commercial growers, proficient and resourceful amateurs, or professional farmers and horticulturists. The actual point at which each individual should make his or her entry to hydroponics must however depend upon the level of skill attained and the degree of competence – and confidence – achieved. It is therefore highly desirable that careful study of this book should go hand in hand with practical work in order to ensure that a full and comprehensive understanding of the technology of growing plants without soil is obtained.

Historical background

For many thousands of years civilised man has been endeavouring to safeguard his crops from the vagaries of nature, with the objects of increasing the yield and improving the quality of the produce obtained from farms and gardens. That basic principle of good husbandry – the provision of an optimal environment for growth and development – was not unknown in the ancient world, as a perusal of early historical writings soon reveals. The *Rig Veda*, a Hindu scripture, contains many references to various plants used by the Aryan conquerors of India in the 12th century B.C., while the *Yu Kung*, a book named in honour of the emperor Ta Yu, who reigned in China from 2205 to 2197 B.C., mentions certain fruits which were held in high esteem by that monarch. Theophrastus (372–287 B.C.) writing in Babylon, after the successes of Alexander the Great had opened up western Asia to Greek knowledge and influence, recorded with considerable accuracy a number of details concerning the popular plants of his day. Among the Latin authors, Virgil, Horace, Pliny the Elder in his *Natural History* published about A.D. 77, and Palladius, have dealt at some length with the problems of growing crops.

An early attempt at the culture of plants under artificial conditions was made by King Nebuchadnezzar when he built the famous Hanging Gardens of Babylon, counted among the seven wonders of the ancient world. The Romans employed various devices to shield exotic and tender crops from climatic hazards. Seneca noted, in his 90th epistle, that in his time panes of mica had come into use as a means of protecting against cold the more delicate of the plants then grown in Roman gardens. The poet Martial (circa A.D. 81–96) similarly refers to these early kinds of greenhouses. During his years of retirement at Capri, the Emperor Tiberius used to eat cucumbers daily, which had been produced out of season in cloches made of transparent material, the plants being forced into fruiting by intensive treatments.

Despite, however, the levels of technique which the early horticulturists undoubtably attained, they possessed no real knowledge or understanding of how their plants grew and of the manner in which crops obtained their nourishment. Indeed, throughout the Middle Ages and up to the 18th century A.D., it was commonly believed that ' . . . for nourishment of vegetables the water is almost all in all; . . . the earth only keeps the plant upright.' Such views were considered to have been proved experimentally by the result of van Helmont's trial with a willow tree. This tree had been grown for five years in a vessel containing two hundred pounds of soil to which nothing was added except rain water or distilled water, yet it had attained a weight of 169 pounds with an expenditure of only two ounces of earth.

The first investigator to put forward a different opinion was John Woodward, who in 1699, published *Some Thoughts and Experiments Concerning Vegetation,* an account of the growth of plants in various types of water. Woodward found that the addition of small quantities of garden soil to water resulted in improved growth, and he therefore concluded that 'earth and not water is the matter that constitutes vegetables.'

In 1772, Priestley discovered that green plants confined in an atmosphere rich in carbon dioxide, or as he called it 'fixed air', produced after some time a considerable amount of oxygen (dephlogisticated air). Two years later, Jean Ingen-Housz showed that plants were able to purify foul air in a few hours when placed in sunlight, and that sunshine itself had no effect in increasing the amount of oxygen without the action of the plant. He further noted that the absorption of air and the exhaling of oxygen were more active in bright light than in dull conditions, and that only the green parts of plants emitted oxygen. Ingen-Housz's work was followed by that of J. Senebier, of Geneva, who investigated the influence of light upon vegetation. In 1804, Nicolas de Saussure issued his classical work *Recherches Chimiques sur la Vegetation.* De Saussure's experiments, which were entirely quantitative, showed that the elements of water were fixed in plants at the same time as the carbon, and that there was an increase in weight as a result of the process. Additionally, they revealed that without absorption of nitrates and mineral substances normal nutrition of crops was impossible.

By the middle of the 19th century, Jean Boussingault had introduced controlled studies of the growth of plants in sand, quartz, and charcoal, to which solutions of known chemical composition were supplied. These methods of artificial culture were improved by F. Salm-Horstmar in 1856–60. In 1860, Julius von Sachs published the first standard formula for a cultural solution, which was followed five years later by that of W. Knop. During the period 1865–1920, many other formulae were devised, notably by F. Nobbe (1869), B. Tollens (1882), A. F. W. Schimper (1890), W. Pfeffer (1900), G. von der Crone (1902), W. E. Tottingham (1914), J. W. Shive (1915), and D. R. Hoagland (1920).

Laboratory techniques

It was the work of Julius von Sachs and his pupils that really laid the foundations for the eventual emergence of the modern technique of hydroponics. For over half a century, the discoveries made by Priestley, Ingen-Housz, and de Saussure, had been either ignored or misinterpreted by botanists, who at that time were completely absorbed in the description and classification of plants, to the exclusion of virtually all else. By developing a method of growing plants in a dilute aqueous solution of various salts, however, Sachs provided investigators with the means through which the nutritional needs of crops could be studied in the laboratory. He connected the appearance of starch in the green plant with the fixation of carbon, as well as showing that chlorophyll is generally formed only in the presence of light. He wrote: 'In the nutrition of plants it is only necessary in the first place to decompose carbon dioxide under the influence of light in the cells containing chlorophyll, with the co-operation of certain mineral matter absorbed by the roots and to produce at the cost of its carbon an organic substance — starch (carbohydrate) which then represents the starting point, so to speak, from which all the organic substances of the plant proceed by progressive chemical changes.'

During the period 1860 to 1900, the preparation of laboratory water cultures became more or less standardised, and the methods of using them in experimental studies were well established. It was ascertained that the concentration of the nutrient solution used might vary from 0.1 to 0.6 per cent, yet still produce optimal growth. At the same time, ten of the elements essential for healthy development were identified.

Sachs' standard formula (1860) was made up of the following salts:

SACH'S SOLUTION			*gm*
Potassium nitrate	KNO_3		1.00
Calcium phosphate	$Ca_3(PO_4)_2$		0.50
Magnesium sulphate	$MgSO_4$		0.50
Calcium sulphate	$CaSO_4$		0.50
Sodium chloride	NaCl		0.25
Ferrous sulphate	$FeSO_4$		Trace
Water	H_2O		1 litre

The composition of Knop's solution (1865) differed in choice of some chemicals:

KNOP'S SOLUTION			*gm*
Potassium nitrate	KNO_3		0.20
Monopotassium phosphate	KH_2PO_4		0.20
Magnesium sulphate	$MgSO_4$		0.20
Calcium nitrate	$Ca(NO_3)_2$		0.80
Ferric phosphate	$FePO_4$		Trace
Water	H_2O		1 litre

This was later (1868) amended to read:

		gm
Potassium chloride	KCl	0.12
Monopotassium phosphate	KH_2PO_4	0.25
Magnesium sulphate	$MgSO_4$	0.25
Calcium nitrate	$Ca(NO_3)_2$	1.00
Ferric chloride	$FeCl_3$	Trace
Water	H_2O	1 litre

Pfeffer's two formulae (1900) were similarly constituted:

PFEFFER'S STRONGER SOLUTION

		gm
Potassium nitrate	KNO_3	1.00
Potassium phosphate	KH_2PO_4	1.00
Potassium chloride	KCl	0.50
Calcium nitrate	$Ca(NO_3)_2$	4.00
Magnesium sulphate	$MgSO_4$	1.00
Ferric chloride	$FeCl_3$	small amount
Water	H_2O	3 litres

PFEFFER'S WEAKER SOLUTION

		gm
Potassium nitrate	KNO_3	0.20
Potassium phosphate	KH_2PO_4	0.20
Potassium chloride	KCl	0.20
Calcium nitrate	$Ca(NO_3)_2$	0.80
Magnesium sulphate	$MgSO_4$	0.20
Ferric chloride	$FeCl_3$	small amount
Water	H_2O	1 litre

In 1902, von der Crone recommended the use of another formula for laboratory water cultures:

VON DER CRONE'S SOLUTION

		gm
Potassium nitrate	KNO_3	1.00
Calcium phosphate	$Ca_3(PO_4)_2$	0.25
Calcium sulphate	$CaSO_4$	0.25
Magnesium sulphate	$MgSO_4$	0.25
Ferrous phosphate	$FePO_4$	0.25
Water	H_2O	1 litre

All these nutrient solutions varied appreciably in their total concentration, as well as in the proportions of the ions present. After the turn of the century, however, more attention was paid to the physical effects of artificial cultures upon plant growth, with especial consideration being given to the osmotic properties of the different solutions. Such factors as the relationship between development and the proportions of salts present, and the influence of light and heat upon the relative value of the numerous formulae proposed, became the subject of extensive studies, while the question of the reaction of the nutrient solution as affected by the unequal absorption of particular ions received much attention.

In 1914, W. E. Tottingham published the results of his investigations as a quantitative chemical and physiological study of the various water culture solutions. Using Knop's 1865 four-salt solution as a basis, Tottingham found that a total concentration of 0.6 per cent (or 2.5 atmospheres osmotic pressure) produced the best growth. Out of 84 possible combinations in that series, he selected T3R1S4 as superior. The salts in this formula were distributed in the following way:

TOTTINGHAM'S T3R1S4	KNO_3	0.0049 M
SOLUTION	KH_2PO_4	0.0130 M
	$Ca(NO_3)_2$	0.0144 M
	$MgSO_4$	0.0145 M
	$FePO_4$	2 drops of a suspension containing 0.0024 gm of ferric phosphate per cc added to each 1 litre of solution as renewable.

In order to reduce the number of components in a formula, J. W. Shive in 1915 introduced the three-salt solution. His experiments indicated that an osmotic pressure of 1.75 atmospheres was the most favourable for good plant growth. The production of dry matter by plants growing in Shive's R5S2 solution exceeded that obtained with Tottingham's four-salt mixture.

SHIVE'S R5S2 SOLUTION	KH_2PO_4	0.0180 M
	$Ca(NO_3)_2$	0.0052 M
	$MgSO_4$	0.0150 M
	$FePO_4$	0.0044 gm per litre of solution.

Further studies were made by D. R. Hoagland (1919–1920), who discovered that solutions with total concentrations ranging from 0.48 to 1.45 atmospheres gave similar results, if renewed frequently.

Experimental cultures

Although Boussingault had used sand as a growing medium in the laboratory, the employment of inert aggregates was not favoured by Sachs and Knop. The aim of these investigators, and of their followers, was to eliminate sand entirely, and to grow their test plants in solution only. Water cultures held the field from 1860 until the early part of the twentieth century. It was then found that a sand culture encouraged better growth of roots, due to the improved aeration provided. Furthermore, the setting up of sand cultures was simpler in practice, since the plants were supplied in advance with a natural anchorage, whereas with water cultures it was necessary to incorporate special supporting devices in the design of the containers, in addition to artificial aerators.

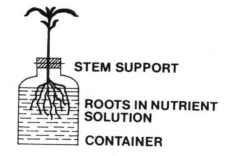

STEM SUPPORT

ROOTS IN NUTRIENT SOLUTION

CONTAINER

FIG. 1.
Early water or solution culture experiment in hydroponics by J. von Sachs and W. Knop in 1859–65. Plants were grown in jars or containers, fitted with supports for the stems and partially filled with nutrient liquid.

Nevertheless, it was still widely contended that water culture produced the best growth of tops. This was well illustrated by the work of A. L. Bakke and L. W. Erdman (1923), which showed that in the case of wheat a greater dry weight of grain and straw resulted when the plants were raised in solutions, but that better root growth occurred in sand beds. The comparative trials conducted by these investigators also indicated that the amount of water transpired was, generally speaking, higher in the solution cultures than it was with the sand techniques.

Until 1925, both water and sand cultures were used solely as laboratory techniques for the study of plant nutrition. The methods evolved during the past seventy-five years were not supposed by scientific workers to have any potential value other than as standard experimental usages in plant physiology. It was considered that for successful growth without soil rigidly controlled and exact conditions were essential. In fact, the aim of artificial culture then was to investigate the life processes of vegetation.

Commercial applications

The first suggestion that artificial cultures might have some commercial application came from the greenhouse industry in the United States. Growers situated near the large cities and towns of America were experiencing great difficulty in obtaining adequate supplies of manure and suitable soil for use in their beds and benches, due mainly to the rapid development of motor transport which was taking place in the mid-nineteen-twenties, and the consequent elimination of the big urban stables of former times, as well as the spread of housing schemes. With the object of solving this problem, research workers in certain experimental stations began to consider the possibility of substituting modified forms of sand and solution culture for growth in soil under commercial conditions. Between 1925 and 1930, extensive development took place in adapting the laboratory methods of the plant physiologists to large scale crop production.

In 1928, W. R. Robbins, working at the New Jersey Experimental Station, reported encouragingly upon the prospects of sand culture for commercial horticulture, following numerous trials with vegetables and fruit tree seedlings. At the same time, H. M. Biekart and C. H. Connors gave it as their considered opinion that 'the possibility of growing carnations commercially in sand is not remote.' These announcements were followed by the preliminary studies of W. F. Gericke, of the University of California, who in 1929, succeeded in devising a practical system of solution culture. Two years later, A. Laurie, at Ohio Agricultural Experiment Station, issued a description of the use of washed sand as a substitute for soil in greenhouse culture of carnations.

FIG. 2.
W. F. Gericke's original water or solution culture system. The waterproof basins or tanks contained the nutrient solution and the plants grew in a litter tray or bed placed on a wire mesh screen through which the roots descended into the liquid fertilizer below.

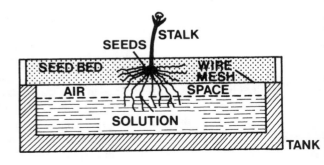

At first, public interest was concentrated upon the Gericke method of water culture, soon to be named 'hydroponics.' In 1936, Gericke, in conjunction with J. R. Travernetti, published an account of tomato production by this technique, in which they stated that in a basin of 9.2 square metres in area one tonne of good quality tomatoes could be grown in a year, provided that ample room was provided for upward development. The method required a series of waterproof tanks, surmounted by mesh screens and layers of bedding material. The tanks were filled with nutrient solution to within 2.50 to 5 centimetres of the top. Each plant was allowed an area of 11.60 square decimetres. With a constant temperature of between 22° and 25°C, the plants attained a

height of 7.5 metres within twelve months. Despite the obvious success of these experiments, however, and the initial flush of enthusiasm that followed, the method did
not become as popular as might have been hoped. This was mainly due to the high
degree of technical skill and practical experience that were found to be needed for the
economic operation of the apparatus.

FIG. 3.
Sand culture. The con-
tainers are filled with clean
sand, the nutrients being
applied in liquid form by
pipes, sprays or sprink-
lers. Some experimenters
spread the formulae dry
over the surface of the
growing medium and then
watered it in.

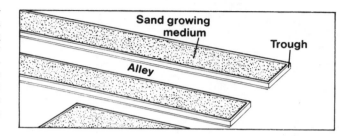

In order to overcome the difficulties inherent in the daily working of the water culture methods, and to improve upon the production output of sand cultures, R. B.
Withrow and J. P. Biebel, of Purdue University Agricultural Experiment Station
devised in 1936 the original mechanics of the automatic sub-irrigation method. A
similar technique was soon afterwards introduced by C. H. Connors and V. A. Tiedjens.
In 1937, a further advance was made when workers at Ohio University, following the
mechanical set-up of Withrow and Biebel, substituted coarse aggregates for sand in the
beds, so initiating gravel cultures.

By 1938, hydroponics had entered the field of practical horticulture. Many big
commercial growers in the United States had installed soilless culture beds, and a
number of organisations and private individuals were making use of the technique in
one form or another to produce both ornamental and edible crops. But despite this display of interest, its progress had by and large been disappointingly slow, due in the
main to inertia on the part of the horticultural industry, lack of easily obtainable information about specific problems, and extravagant propaganda by unscrupulous
persons who attempted to exploit the gullibility of the public by selling worthless
chemicals and equipment at exorbitant prices. Had it not been for the continued
research into the adaptation and modification of the various methods of soilless growth
of crops carried out by scientific workers at different institutions, not only in the
United States, but also in England and in France, hydroponics would possibly have
been discarded eventually by all but a few initiates.

During the period 1938 to 1947, R. H. Stoughton, of the University of Reading,
undertook a series of trials with tomatoes and other crops, using cascade tanks, sub-
irrigation, and also surface watering. Both clinkers (cinders) and sand were employed

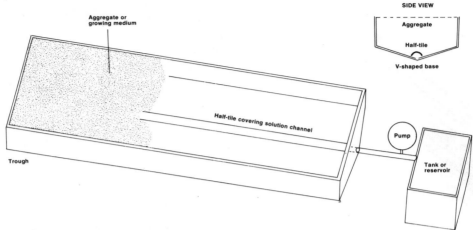

FIG. 4.
Automatic sub-irrigation hydroponic unit. The nutrient solution is pumped from the tank or reservoir into the aggregate-filled growing trough at regular intervals and then allowed to drain back slowly.

as growing media. The object of these experiments was to adapt the American techniques to English conditions. Tests were, in addition, carried out at Jealott's Hill Research Station by W. G. Templemann and N. Pollard, and by a number of professional growers. In France, P. Chouard (1940) paved the way for the introduction of hydroponics, which has today become popular amongst rose growers in that country. J. Sholto Douglas (1945) investigated the possibilities of soilless cultivation in India, and, in 1946, started, under the auspices of the Government of Bengal, a research centre at the experimental station at Kalimpong. In 1947, the Bengal method of hydroponics was introduced, and this technique has since spread to many other parts of the world.

The outbreak of the Second World War in 1939 stimulated interest in soilless culture as a means of providing beleaguered countries with extra supplies of home grown

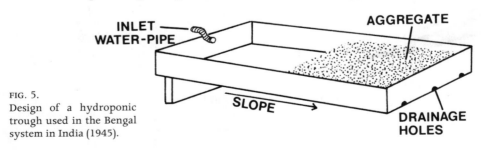

FIG. 5.
Design of a hydroponic trough used in the Bengal system in India (1945).

foodstuffs, but little in the way of practical effort could be attempted at first, owing to a shortage of nutrient chemicals. In England, a few individuals did succeed in raising useful crops of vegetables by means of hydroponics, but as the technique was then virtually unknown to the British public, no general adoption of the methods occurred. In 1944, however, General H. H. Arnold, Commanding General, United States Army Air Forces, decided to utilise soilless culture for supplying AAF personnel stationed at isolated bases with regular quantities of fresh vegetables. The first air force hydroponic installation was established at Ascension Island early in 1945. This consisted of twenty-five beds each 122 metres long and nearly one metre wide, irrigated with distilled sea water. During the first year of operation, the yield of salad vegetables, such as tomatoes, cucumbers, lettuces, radishes, and green peppers, amounted to 94,000 pounds.* In the summer of the same year, seventy-five hydroponic troughs were laid down at Atkinson Field, British Guiana (now Guyana), yielding in 1946 a total of 234,337 pounds* of greenstuff, while in the following November a third unit was opened on Iwojima. Two further hydroponic projects were constructed in Japan by the Quartermaster Corps at Chofu, near Tokyo, and at Otsu, amounting to a total area of about 31 hectares. The Japanese units were in operation, under the control of the respective theatre commanders, during the period of the American occupation of the country following World War Two.

The standard unit of the American Armed Forces hydroponic installations consisted of a ten-bed layout, occupying approximately ¼-hectare of ground space. This is considered to be capable of supplying one large salad per diem for 400 men. Ordinary fertiliser grade chemicals were used to make up the nutrient formulae, and a representative list of salts would read as follows:

	%
Potassium nitrate	19.8
Potassium sulphate	17.8
Monocalcium phosphate	11.2
Calcium sulphate	27.3
Magnesium sulphate	18.7
Ammonium sulphate	5.1
	100.0

In addition, traces of ferrous sulphate, ferric ammonium citrate, manganese sulphate, manganese chloride, boric acid, borax sodium tetraborate, copper sulphate, and zinc sulphate, are incorporated in the solutions.

*One pound = 0.4536 kilogramme (kilo).

Alternative nutritional methods

Until 1947, plants growing in hydroponic units had been provided with their supplies of the essential elements by the admixture of certain fertilizer salts with water to form a nutrient solution. In that year, however, D. I. Arnon and K. A. Grossenbacher published an account of the artificial culture of crops by means of the use of synthetic ion-exchange materials. Although this technique was not a new development, it had not previously been employed in practical work. As far back as 1933, H. Jenny and E. W. Cowan grew soyabeans in different systems containing calcium as the only ion. In one case it was adsorbed on colloids, while in another it was fixed in the interior of crystals. It was found that with high concentrations of calcium, plants did better in the adsorbed system than in the control-free solution. Further work on these lines continued, and was followed by the publication in 1942 of the details of an experiment on the availability of adsorbed ions to plants growing in quartz sand substrate.

The object of these studies was to try and reduce soilless culture to the relative simplicity of soil management. In cultural solutions the nutrient ions are free to move, and normally the concentrations used are far higher than may be found in the natural soil. This means, of course, that the safety margin is appreciably lower, necessitating much greater care in day-to-day operation. The conditions of restraint which exist in soil, where the nutrient ions are adsorbed on colloidal particles or fixed in crystals, do not occur in liquid cultures. If, however, the essential elements could be supplied to plants growing in hydroponics in adsorbed form, then several practical advantages would result. In particular, sufficient nutrients could be incorporated in the media at the beginning of the season to last all through the crop growth period. This would obviate the need of periodic mixing of cultural solutions, or frequent spreading of dry salts over the beds, since only regular irrigations with ordinary water would be required. Then again, many of the complications of nutrient solution management would be eliminated, and there would also be reduction of losses from leaching during rainfall in the case of open air troughs.

Successful results have followed from the use of synthetic ion-exchange resins in hydroponics, notably in the cultivation of tomatoes. G. Rivoira, working in Sicily, has reported excellent growth in 1972–74. Sand and gravel cultured plants have responded well when grown in beds containing clay colloids or artificial zeolites with adsorbed cations, and adsorbed anions on aniline material. Unfortunately, these slow release synthetic fertilizer substances, especially the amberlites and equivalent materials are still expensive, and are therefore generally out of the question for large scale commercial work at the present time, unless of course regeneration *in situ* can be practised.

In order to overcome objections on the score of cost, E. L. Schioler in 1955 developed a material known as *sustanum,* which would act as a carrier for the nutrient ions. This is a spongy substance, containing silica and diatomaceous earth, which is capable of absorbing essential elements and releasing them gradually thereafter to the plant roots. Sustanum has proved a satisfactory carrier for nutrients in hydroponics, and it has the advantage of being less expensive than synthetic resins.

The sequestrated or chelated compounds have also been shown to be good sources for the supply of available iron to crops. L. Jacobson (1951) noted that the necessary iron could be supplied as ferric potassium ethylenediamine tetra-acetate to plants growing in cultural solutions. Another interesting development has been the introduction of the glass frits. In this case, the nutrients are mixed with glass so that subsequent leaching and chemical action are impossible. Although supplied in a non-water-soluble form, the fertilizing elements still become available to the plants, due to the action of minute quantities of ascorbic acid released by the roots which in course of time dissolve the matrix. F. E. Johnstone Jr., of the University of Georgia, reported in 1953 that it was possible to provide all the essential trace elements by means of glass frits.

Practical developments

Probably nowhere in the history of technological development is there another instance similar to the case of hydroponics in which principles so widely used in experimental work have not sooner provided a practical approach to the problems of field production. In the early days of the laboratory water and sand cultures, it was the scientists themselves who failed to realise the true value of the methods they had discovered. At a later date, when the potential utility of the hydroponic technique had, at last, been fully appreciated, and it was announced to a wondering world, hostile groups and circles denounced it with scepticism and ridicule. In numerous instances, it was exploited unscrupulously, so that but for the painstaking efforts and the continuous research of those devoted persons who really believed that it had a useful future, soilless cultivation might have disappeared back into the obscurity from which it had only just emerged.

The social implications of hydroponics have always been thoroughly understood by the disinterested discoverers of the different techniques. Thus, W. F. Gericke wrote in 1940: '. . . the wage earner with a small plot of ground at his back door may regain a measure of economic independence. His food supply will be more under his own control so that his livelihood will no longer depend solely upon national philanthropy or the weekly pay check. As a means of providing subsistence to those thrown out of employment by recurring economic depressions, hydroponics deserves the utmost consideration from government.' These opinions were fully shared by many other scientists. J. Sholto Douglas commented in 1949: 'Multiple cropping and intensive culture by hydroponic means will effect profound changes in the social life of the world. A worker may hope to regain some measure of that economic independence that his peasant ancestors possessed. With a permanent food supply at his back door, the fear of unemployment will be considerably lessened . . . States lacking in soil resources would find soilless culture ideal . . . Unfortunately, the world food shortage shows no sign of abating at any time in the predictable future, and urgent steps are needed to save millions from semi-starvation. By bringing cheap and nourishing foodstuff within the reach of all, hydroponics offers something of real value to humanity. As a Grow-More-Food device there can be few things more worthy of national recognition and official encouragement.'

The commercial application of hydroponics, as already noted, was first attempted in the United States, mainly by professional horticulturists in Ohio, Illinois, Indiana, Pennsylvania, and New York State, where growth under glass is essential during winter, as well as in the warm, sub-tropical areas of Florida, California, and Texas, which are admirably suited to out-of-doors work throughout the year. Later on, Pan-American Airways established a soilless garden on Wake Island, a small United States colony in the Pacific Ocean, for the purpose of providing the passengers and crews of transit aircraft with fresh vegetables. The experience gained through the operation of these installations was at a subsequent date to prove of very considerable importance, particularly in the field of logistics. The question of provisioning large bodies of troops quartered at isolated bases, or stationed in countries where the locally produced foodstuffs are either inadequate in quantity or unsuitable for consumption, has always been a particularly difficult one. During the Second World War (1939–45) the United States Army was able to solve this problem by the construction at various strategic points of large hydroponic farms. So successful were these units in practice that their operation has, in certain cases, been continued as a permanent feature of the Quartermaster Corps. The War Department officially described soilless culture as 'a distinct contribution to the science of supply'.

Authority for the establishment of new hydroponic gardens may be granted by the American Army when the following conditions subsist:

(a) No soil is available in which vegetables can be grown safely in the normal agricultural manner;

(b) The installation is so located that no fresh vegetables can be supplied by shipping in adequate quantity or at reasonable cost;

(c) The post camp or station is permanent or is expected to be in existence for a considerable period;

(d) There is at least a four-month growing season each year;

(e) There is an adequate supply of suitable water.

From 1941 onwards, the section working with floriculture and ornamental horticulture of the Division of Fruit and Vegetable Crops and Diseases, Bureau of Plant Industry, Soils, and Agricultural Engineering, at Beltsville, Maryland, undertook studies in soilless culture. These investigations, conducted mainly by N. W. Stuart, resulted in the accumulation of a mass of significant data. The section maintained about 550 square metres of concrete troughs, divided into eighty-eight parts, each of which was provided with a solution tank and pump for sub-irrigation, so as to give control of experimental treatments. These beds were used for growing plants in phytopathological, genetic, and physiological investigations. The last named included studies on nutrient balance and absorption, as well as the effects of temperature, light, and the growing medium upon crop development. This section was probably the first to test the use of urea-form materials in hydroponics.

In 1944, both the Shell Oil Company (C.P.I.M.) on the island of Curacao, and the Lago Oil and Transport Co., Ltd., at Aruba, commenced the operation of soilless culture units. The purpose of these gardens was to supply their respective staffs with fresh salads. The two localities were situated in the Netherlands West Indies (Lesser Antilles), and were barren in the extreme. An account of the progress of the work was compiled by T. Eastwood in 1947. It contains an extremely valuable study of the application of hydroponics to tropical conditions. During the period 1946–1957, further extensive work was carried out in India. This resulted in the establishment of a number of new gardens in different areas, notably in Tanganyika (now Tanzania), where in 1955, a series of trials was initiated by L. Dobson at Geita. Using the water from Lake Victoria, a wide range of vegetables was grown successfully, many of them out of season. The South Pacific is another region where hydroponics has attracted much attention. The well known Compagnie Francaise des Phosphates de l'Oceanie, at Tahiti, has stated: '. . . we have no soil available, our people are living on sand and coral rock, so hydroponics is the obvious way for us too'.

A noteworthy contribution to the development of soilless cultivation under sub-tropical conditions has been made by V. K. Chatterjee (1956) who, working near Calcutta, successfully introduced certain technical modifications, mainly in the con-struction of the beds and the preparation of nutrient mixtures under practical condi-tions in Bengal. The experiments conducted by Dr Sampurnanand, former Chief Minister of Uttar Pradesh, India, are also of much interest. Using both sand and gravel cultures, as well as the solution system, Dr Sampurnanand has grown several different crops in hydroponics. He is reported as being conservative in his reluctance to discard what is old and has withstood the test of utility (soil), but once convinced of the superiority of scientific methods (hydroponics), he is ready to abandon the beaten track. The Chief Minister said: 'the method can be applied successfully by any intelligent person . . . the cost will be small, and the psychological satisfaction and relief to the eye by growing green things round a house will be invaluable'. Dr Sampurnanand is gratified with his results. These comments are not dissimilar to those made in a report entitled *Soilless Cultivation on Desert Airstations* prepared in 1945 for the British Air Ministry. Considering the question of the establishment of hydroponic units at Habbaniyah, and along the Persian Gulf, this document concluded: 'The psychological implications of creating vegetation where none was are clearly of immense importance . . . and soil-less cultivation methods offer the only present hope of production'.

An extremely simple and practical system of hydroponics has been developed by L. Erikson, of Hamilton, New Zealand. In his particular area, there is a yearly rainfall of some 1050 mm mostly as light drizzle and well distributed. In consequence, Erikson decided that troughs were not necessary for soilless culture in Hamilton, as this rainfall was sufficient for almost continuous moisture. He spread fine creek gravel 31 centimetres deep over his harder ground, and planted seedling tomatoes about 22 centimetres high in this aggregate in 1955. A complete fertilizer mixture was then applied at the rate of 56 grammes per plant to the beds, followed by watering in of the salts. Further dressings were given fortnightly throughout the growing period, with enough water to keep the gravel damp, in the intervals between rain showers. Good crops, of excellent size and free from disease, were produced from both trellised and untrellised plants. Such methods are especially suitable for use by the farmer, amateur grower, or the house-holder, particularly where installation expenses have to be considered carefully.

The use of the hydroponic technique has become popular in many countries with a wide range of climatic conditions. In England, it is mainly employed by tomato and salad growers under glass, or by producers of ornamentals, like carnations and dahlias. In Canada, much work has been done with chrysanthemums, especially at the Central Experimental Farm, Ottawa, by H. Hill and M. B. Davis. Extensive out-of-doors culture is practised in Puerto Rico. M. Bentley, in South Africa, has achieved good results with potatoes, tomatoes, and other vegetable crops grown in a vermiculite aggregate. In the Netherlands, the National Council for Agricultural Research has set up a special department of soilless culture, while in Belgium the Agricultural Ministry takes an active interest in hydroponic developments. The cultivation of vegetables without using soil has even been employed on the Antarctic continent, in the first instance by the various expeditions located there during the geophysical year of 1957–58, and again in 1961–62.

Under temperate zone conditions, such as prevail in the northern United States, Canada, parts of Europe, including Russia, Japan and China, and some areas of New Zealand and Australia, as well as the southern Argentine, soilless culture occupies an important place in glasshouse crop production, particularly in the heavily industrialised areas, where labour is expensive and difficult to obtain. The fact that hydroponic units can be operated by means of automation may well become a factor of considerable importance in reducing the ultimate cost to the consumer of essential foodstuffs. At the present time, labour charges are usually the biggest single item in the commercial horticulturist's budget in industrial countries. Any method which offers growers an opportunity of substantially cutting them down is worthy of careful study. The application of hydroponics to large scale greenhouse work has reached its widest extent in the Middle West, chiefly in Illinois, Ohio, and Indiana. It is also quite popular in southern England, but expansion there has been handicapped by a shortage of supervisory staff with the necessary training and experience.

The growing of high priced vegetable crops in sub-tropical and tropical regions, like Cuba, Puerto Rico, the Bahama Islands, Florida, and the East African littoral, using the hydroponic technique, has developed considerably during recent years. Commercial units have been set up in many of these places, notably near Miami, in Florida, on Puerto Rico, and adjacent to Dar-Es-Salaam in Tanzania. Both local markets and distant customers are supplied. In Colorado, Arizona and Utah there are several large commercial producers.

It is often stated that as the humid areas of the tropics are so luxuriant in plant life, the employment of an artificial and specialized system of cultivation for vegetable production is quite uncalled for. The fact is, however, that in such regions there are no periods of cold weather corresponding to the freezing winters of northern latitudes which serve as limitary agents to the populations of various fungus and soil-borne diseases. The high rainfall in the tropics produces conditions of excessive humidity which are extremely favourable for the development of moulds and similar diseases of leaves. In addition, it also causes leaching of nutrients from the soils, resulting in a low level of fertility, with consequently poor crop yields under natural conditions. These drawbacks often make it very difficult, indeed at times impossible, to grow good vegetables in tropical areas, using ordinary methods. The native vegetation has become adapted to the prevailing situation and is able to exist as a result of long periods of natural selection, but cultivated plants which are entirely dependent upon man for their survival do not generally make satisfactory headway for any appreciable space of time. Hydroponics is, on the other hand, especially suitable for the growth of economic crops in hot countries, since it provides the grower with the means of controlling every detail of the plants' environment.

In arid zones, such as deserts or barren districts, soilless culture holds out good promise for food production. In these regions there is usually a very limited supply of water available for irrigation, and it is therefore a matter of the greatest importance to ensure that the most efficient use is made of it. The advantage of piping water into controlled hydroponic beds rather than wastefully dissipating it over the fields, where a large part is soon lost through evaporation is too obvious to need reiteration. Valuable work on the application of hydroponics to desert conditions has been undertaken by the Israeli authorities at Eilat and other areas in the Negev; as well as in Kuwait and Abu Dhabi, by the governments of those countries.

The taste of vegetables grown in hydroponics differs in no significant way from that of crops raised from soil. Flavour, in any case, is largely conditioned by climatic factors and the nutritional conditions obtaining during the growth period. The mineral and vitamin contents of soilless cultured plants and fruits are essentially the same as those of very high quality soil crops. Here, again, it is possible to raise or lower the mineral content of vegetables by making appropriate adjustments in the cultural solution.

Tests with fibres, such as jute, flax, and cotton, grown in hydroponics have proved encouraging. Although barely out of the experimental stages yet, the soilless culture of natural fibres is a matter of great interest and importance to the textile and cordage industries, both for economic and strategic reasons. Rising wages on estates and plantations have pushed up the production costs of the raw material, while there is a constantly increasing level of competition from synthetic substitutes. Cost factors have also been the main consideration behind the recent adoption by many growers of tea, tobacco, coffee, citrus fruits, and sisal, of hydroponic techniques for propagation work. For forestry, the sand culture system is frequently utilised as a quick way of raising seedlings in nursery beds. Trials have shown that the incidence of mortality, due to disease, failure of cuttings to strike, and delayed germination, can be greatly reduced in soilless beds.

The artificial culture of algae, using hydroponic nutrient solutions and special apparatus, has assumed some prominence within recent years. The need of the world for additional sources of high protein food is so great, especially in overpopulated areas, that very serious efforts have been made to bring the commercial growth and processing of algae to a point where the technique could serve a most useful purpose. The Carnegie Institution of Washington's project on the mass culture of these tiny plants, a preliminary account of which was published in 1953, constitutes a distinct advance in this direction. Regarding these possibilities, Dr Vanhevar Bush has written:

'Such great advances in technology have already come from the coupling of engineering with biology that it seems inevitable that the production of food, at least in certain areas, will eventually be carried out by ''process'' industries. The large scale culture of algae may well become the first of them. In regions of the world where population is especially dense, and fertile land is limited, it is entirely possible that process-industry methods of producing food may furnish a respite from the threat of famine and so contribute toward more salutary conditions for civilized living. If algal culture can serve such a purpose, it is well worth development for that reason alone. It is hoped that such a development may take the form ultimately of a multitude of individually owned, relatively small establishments, combining the culture of algae perhaps with utilization of the product for animal feeding on the spot. The new industry that would result would thus enter into our economic life in such a manner as not to produce disruption, but rather to strengthen individual enterprise.'

Further progress

The past twenty years have witnessed many important new technical developments and considerable general progress in the extension of hydroponics. Notable amongst these activities has been the creation of the International Working-Group on Soilless Culture (I.W.O.S.C.) an independent organization of scientists and practical growers, with members in nearly one hundred countries throughout the world. The secretariat of I.W.O.S.C. is located at Wageningen in the Netherlands. In co-operation with the Spanish authorities, this body has established an International Hydroponic Institute at Las Palmas in the Canary Islands, where research studies and trials in soilless cultivation can be carried out on a permanent basis and where courses of training and instruction will be available for students and horticultural workers interested in growing crops without soil. I.W.O.S.C. has sponsored three world congresses, attended by numerous participants from many countries, the most important being those held at Las Palmas in 1969 and at Sassari in Sardinia in 1973. A further meeting is scheduled for 1976.

It has been pointed out that hydroponics, by means of its capacity to grow fresh food in problem areas, can play an important role in epidemiological control through ensuring local sufficiency in agriculture on a global basis. Epidemiology is the science of epidemics, relating to diseases that attack great numbers of individuals in one place and which travel in the form of widespread outbreaks from one area to another. Malnutrition is a very frequent first cause of epidemics, for when people or livestock are unhealthy and ill-nourished they are in no condition to ward off the assaults of epidemic diseases. So to be able to stop epidemics, or inhibit epidemic conditions from existing, due to malnutrition, is vital.

The construction of geodesic hydroponica or soilless megafarms, together with their systematic utilization on a three-dimensional pattern, that is to say for the culture of plants, the feeding of utilitarian animals for meat, dairy and other production, and the provision of nutriment and raw materials for human beings, combined with tidal and/or solar heating and power, environmental controls to regulate temperature, humidity, and light, for maximum and consistent crop output, is a practical proposition. Such installations could assure a continual supply of fresh food in adequate quantities in the regions where it is needed. Furthermore, portable hydroponic units, built from plastics, could be airlifted at short notice into famine or drought-stricken areas, or places devastated by natural or man-induced calamities, to provide succour for whole populations very quickly.

Significant advances have been made recently in the utilisation of automatic equipment in soilless cultivation, including the sprinkling of nutrients, micro-fine and filtered screening, use of saline waters, and related techniques. These are additional to the general developments in standard horticultural and controlled environment agricultural methods, a great proportion of which are applicable to hydroponics. Another field of activity that has been the subject of investigation is that of lightweight substitutes, such as polyurethane foam and other expanded plastic substances for use as growing media in place of heavy gravels or sands. It has been found that healthy, vigorous and active root development occurs in such substrate materials. In fact, the whole concept and practice of soilless cultivation is undergoing a marked transformation and techniques are becoming increasingly sophisticated.

In British Colombia, E. F. Maas and R. M. Adamson, working at the Saanichton Research Station of the Canada Department of Agriculture, developed a method of tomato growing in sawdust. The nutrient solution was supplied semi-automatically through a proportionating system utilising perforated thin-walled plastic tubing laid between each double row of plants. Individual fine-bore tubes conveyed the liquid feed to each specimen, delivering it to the bases of the stems so that it was absorbed quickly by the growing medium and thus became available speedily to the roots. Following on successful trials with sawdust, experiments were commenced using ground bark, local peat material and expanded shale in hydroponic units.

Considerable attention has been paid by investigators in different areas into the employment of calcareous aggregates in soilless culture, especially in Israel, the West Indies, and parts of Africa. Volcanic ash and tuff—a rock composed of fine volcanic fragments and dust—has also given good results in the Middle East and the Canary Islands. Saline or brackish waters, which may often be the only sources of supply for irrigation purposes in certain regions, have been the objects of studies and experiments in North Africa, India, western Asia and several other places and notable successes have been achieved with plants grown in such waters, particularly by H. Boyko in Israel, F. Penningsfeld in Tunisia, J. Sholto Douglas in India, and S. R. Victor in the Bahama Islands. In Italy, the use of a technique called *aeroponics* was evolved at the University of Pisa in the Institute of Agronomy by F. Massantini. This method involves the cultivation of crops in vertical or horizontal closed containers, through which jets force sprays of nutrient solution. The plants are inserted into the aeroponic units through holes or apertures in the sides or tops of the containers. A similar device is utilised for the soilless mist propagation of cuttings in hydroponics.

The problems of disposing of sewage and effluents from modern towns, as well as of slurry or semi-fluid mixtures of water and dung from 'factory-farms', have engaged the ingenuity of environmental and agricultural scientists and planners for some time. However, these materials can be employed profitably to irrigate and feed crops growing in different types of hydroponic units. Waste water can also be utilised without great difficulty.

Fodder production is another area in which soilless cultivation is expanding rapidly. Cereal grasses and other green crops can be grown very rapidly, within a week or ten days, in specially designed units, to heights of up to 20 or 22 centimetres, and then fed direct to farm livestock. Provided that temperature and light needs are adequate, regular output of such forage is possible all the year around, whatever local weather conditions may be.

At the present time, the main countries where hydroponics is receiving particular attention are the United States, the Soviet Union, Japan, and some lands in the West Indies, Africa, and the Middle East. In North America and Japan, efforts are concentrated on high quality fruit and vegetable or salad species, while in Russia the emphasis is not only on these crops but also on other economic plants, such as essential oils in Armenia. Protected and heated housing is provided at Moscow, Kiev, and other centres for out-of-season growth of greenstuff during the severe Russian winters. At Erevan in Armenia, there is an active Institute of Agrochemical Problems and Hydroponics. Soviet scientists have described hydroponics as a biological industry, falling midway between manufacturing and agriculture as a production technique. In Poland, strenuous efforts have succeeded in improving water culture and the University of Wroclaw has developed new methods of growth in tanks filled with nutrient solutions. The work of G. S. Davtyan at Erevan and that of Z. Guminska at Wroclaw have resulted in striking advances during recent years, especially in the mechanical control and the operation of soilless installations.

Large hydroponic farms exist in Kuwait and in Abu Dhabi. In the latter country, the Arid Lands Research Centre at Sadiyat has carried out trials under exacting desert conditions. Work on soilless cultivation is also in progress in India, France, Germany, Spain, Austria, the Netherlands and Belgium, Great Britain, Sweden, Mexico, and many other lands. In Australia and New Zealand, the South Pacific regions, Brazil, and the Philippines additional studies have been undertaken. Commercial application of the different systems, with adaptations of the various methods to local conditions, have followed the research trials in most cases.

Investigations into hydroponic techniques are currently concentrated on two main aspects: first, studies of the nutritional needs of crops in soilless cultures, and secondly, the development of improved mechanisms for solution application, rooting of plants, and the management of units. In addition, the place of hydroponics in urban planning has come increasingly within the purview of architectural projects, notably for new towns and for the amelioration of living conditions in existing cities and industrial districts. In forestry, too, hydroponic methods are being utilised for raising tree seedlings economically, particularly where labour costs for conventional nursery practice are excessive.

To conclude this necessarily brief survey of the development and utilisation of hydroponics, it is worthwhile to mention certain important aspects of the contributions that soilless cultivation is making – and will make increasingly in the future – to human living standards. Soilless culturists hold in their possession a valuable key for the survival of man in his environment. This key can open several doors, thus enabling whole populations to assure themselves of shelter, food, agreeable working conditions, and satisfactory equilibrium with their surroundings. Man and nature must co-operate, and hydroponics, by its ability to provide extra nutriment and better life styles in depressed or barren areas, offers a possible solution to the problems of malnutrition, hunger, and frustration that afflict so large a proportion of mankind today. Indeed, not only in desert and neglected regions, but also in industrial and urban districts, hydroponics has a very significant part to play in ameliorating the hardships and difficulties of daily existence. In 1969, F. Penningsfeld pointed out that 'hydroponics lends itself pre-eminently for co-ordination and it has the potency to play an active role in the fight against hunger . . .' These words are even more true today as world population continues to increase, and the coming years will only add urgency to their meaning.

From the commercial point of view, soilless cultivation is a standardized branch of agriculture and horticulture. Growers are offered the choice of many different systems and methods, fully capable of adaptation to varying local conditions as may be required, which if properly operated and managed, will give steady and consistent yields and provide good profits and satisfactory incomes for those who may decide to take up this mode of earning a living. In contemporary terms, hydroponic units fall naturally into the sphere of agri-business or as has already been mentioned, into the category of biological industry.

Finally, it must be said that hydroponics is an expanding and progressive activity. New techniques are constantly being developed; research and experiments continue throughout the world; the future holds out the promise of vastly greater efforts and achievements. The prospects are exciting, for in many ways, we are still in the infancy of soilless culture, with much intensive research ahead and the scope for hydroponic extension is virtually unlimited.

CHAPTER 2

Systems and methods

All the various systems of hydroponics which have been developed may be classified, for the sake of convenience, under four main headings. These are: *water* or *solution culture, sand culture, aggregate culture,* and finally a group of *miscellaneous cultural techniques.* Each system contains within its limits a number of sub-divisions, or methods, representing modifications or simplifications designed to improve its efficiency in certain given conditions. From a commercial point of view several different methods are practicable, but usually the choice of any particular one will be governed by such factors as climate, locality, meteorology, availability of apparatus, operating skills and financial limitations. In general, there is no 'best' system of soilless cultivation, but there should be, of course, a right technique for use in a particular area, the selection of which must ultimately depend upon the conditions prevailing there.

Water or solution culture

Plants of a great number of species have been grown successfully in water culture, and the system has been extensively employed in the laboratory for research into problems of crop nutrition. On a larger scale, it has given good results in field work.

THE STANDARD JAR.   This method is particularly suited to home use, especially for the

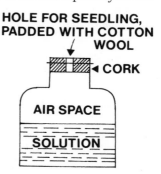

FIG. 6.
Standard jar for hydroponics. These containers are useful for house plants.

growth of ornamental plants in individual containers. Any kind of glass or porcelain vessel may be pressed into service, but the best receptacles are probably ordinary wide-mouthed jars of a half to one-litre capacity. Flat perforated corks, with wads of non-absorbent cotton, are firmly fixed in the necks of the containers and suffice to hold the plants in position. The roots are submerged in the cultural solution which fills the body of the jar to within 5 or 6 centimetres of its top. Clear glass vessels of this type need covering with dark paper or a black cloth to exclude light from the roots. In order to provide aeration, the plants have to be removed from the containers every three days for a few minutes, while the solution is vigorously shaken.

CONTINUOUS-FLOW METHODS.   The solution in which the roots of the plant are suspended is contained in a culture vessel which is supplied from a small reservoir by means of a siphon tube. An outlet pipe, bent into the form of another siphon extends from a point near the bottom of the cultural vessel to a second overflow jar, so creating a continuous flow of solution through the whole apparatus. By raising or lowering the end of the outlet it is possible to vary the level of the nutrient solution around the plant's roots. At regular intervals, air is forced under pressure into the culture. This method was evolved at the New Jersey Agricultural Experiment Station. It is quite simple to construct, as well as being compact, and inexpensive. Automatic operation is ensured, so long as the reservoir is kept supplied with solution, while that collected in the overflow jar may be re-used. The only problem is the periodical aeration that has to be carried out, but this can be most easily accomplished by employing a light bicycle pump fitted with a length of flexible rubber tubing, or by an aquarium air pump.

DRIP METHOD.   Here essentially the same apparatus as for the continuous-flow method is used, but in order to obviate the need for forced aeration, an ingenious modification has been incorporated in the technique. A gap of about 10 to 12 centimetres is left between the end of the siphon tube which conveys the nutrient solution from the reservoir and the funnel which receives it at the top of the cultural vessel. By careful adjustment of the siphon, the solution can be made to exude in slow drips, each of which collects a certain amount of air as it crosses the space between the end of the tube and the funnel. This bubble of air is carried down into the region of the plant's roots. It should, however, be noted that in practice aeration by the drip method is not as effective as it is in the continuous-flow method, where periodic forced aeration has to be carried out of necessity.

SWISS METHOD.   Another type of water culture jar has been designed in Switzerland under the name of plantanova. This consists of an egg-shaped vessel, the upper quarter of which lifts off to reveal a small detachable tray filled with stone chips, resting on a wire grid. The root crown of the plant is supported on this grid, while the stem protrudes into the air through an aperture in the removable lid, and the roots descend into the solution below. The device is obtainable in several sizes to suit different kinds of plants.

WICKS.   Cylindrical lamp wicks, as well as special ones made of glass wool, are often used in hydroponics to irrigate the roots of crops growing in trays filled with some type of litter above basins of nutrient solution. They are particularly well adapted to olericulture. Instead of the roots descending into the cultural liquid, they are kept regularly moistened by a constant flow passing up the wick.

GERICKE METHOD.   This technique was originated by Dr W. F. Gericke of the University of California. It has been used with considerable success in large scale commercial production. The method calls for waterproof basins or tanks, which may be constructed of any suitable material. A wire grid fits closely over the top of each tank in which the nutrient solution is contained. This grid serves as a support for the growing plants, whose roots descend through the mesh into the liquid below. A covering of wood wool (excelsior), peat, sawdust, rough dried hay and some other kind of litter serves to exclude light from the solution, besides giving additional support and protection to the crop. Aeration of the root system is ensured by adjusting the level of the nutrient so as to leave an air space between its surface and the base of the wire grid, although in some cases artificial aeration has been resorted to.

Excellent results have been obtained by the use of the Gericke method, but it is probably most suited to climates with strong sun and high light-intensities. Such areas are distinctly favourable to large-scale water or solution cultures. In California, yields of over 600 tonnes of tomatoes to the hectare have been obtained with these methods. When tried out by growers in the Middle West, and later, on its introduction into the United Kingdom, the Gericke style hydroponicum proved less satisfactory due to lack of aeration of the root system. While this was undoubtably due in certain cases to poor technique, it is practically certain that it was caused in some instances by the number of consecutive cloudy days in these areas. It is, of course, quite possible to aerate the solution in the tanks by artificial means, but to do that would involve extra expense.

A modification of the Gericke method of water or solution culture has, however, been developed during recent years in Poland. The litter bed surmounting the tank is filled with lignite or brown coal, on top of which is placed a layer of peat. Alternatively, the two substances can be mixed together in generally equal proportions. Where a preliminary layer of lignite is placed on the mesh base of the tray, it can be about 5 centimetres deep, with a covering of up to 5 centimetres of peat moss. Normally, a total depth of 10 centimetres in a litter bed should be quite adequate for most plants, although root crops such as potatoes, carrots, or beets will require considerably more litter to provide satisfactory coverage. It has also been found at the University of Wroclaw that a regular supply of fresh air circulating in the space between the bottom of the litter bed and the surface of the nutrient solution is vital for good growth. Holes or apertures of about one to two centimetres diameter should be cut at intervals in the sides of the tank just above the top level of the solution. These can be fitted with plugs which will be kept fixed in position when the solution level is at its highest, just after sowing or planting has taken place. When the solution level drops, as the roots of the developing plants descend into the nutritive liquid, the plugs can be removed and thus currents of air will circulate through the space under the litter bed. Additionally, vertical circular passages can be left at suitable intervals in the litter to permit air to move freely. This aeration of the substrate in water culture has been found in Poland to overcome any difficulties that may have been experienced in Gericke's original method.

Sand culture

In its most elementary form, sand culture is perhaps the simplest kind of hydroponic system to instal. Beds can often be laid down directly upon hard or stony ground, with very little waterproofing, while retention of moisture, even in hot weather, is generally good. The main drawbacks of the system are a liability to waterlogging in rainy periods, and a tendency to be wasteful of nutrient salts.

SURFACE WATERING METHOD.   Often called the slop method, this technique involves the growing of plants in improvised beds or pots containing sand, the requisite nutrients and water being supplied in solution from a hosepipe or garden can to the surface of the medium. Free drainage is permitted, and watertight troughs are unnecessary. Considerable wastage of fertilizers, however, is bound to occur with the surface watering method. Heavy rainfall in out-of-door units might lead to waterlogging of the troughs. In addition, labour could well become an expensive item as at least three or four applications of the nutrient solution may be required weekly. Despite these snags, the technique is very easy to operate.

NEW JERSEY METHODS.   These are essentially a development of the surface watering technique. In the original New Jersey method the required nutrients were supplied by mixing the necessary chemicals in an elevated tank of water from which the solution flowed by gravity to impregnate the bench of sand in which crops were grown. Later this was abandoned in favour of waterproof troughs into which the liquid nutrient was forced several times a day by electrically driven centrifugal pumps.

Window boxes filled with sand can be fitted with rubber squeeze bulbs and oppo-

FIG. 7.
Original New Jersey sand culture trial. The solution is allowed to flow slowly by gravity into the sand in which the plants are growing.

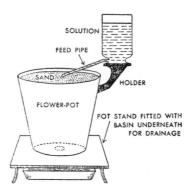

sitely placed check valves so as to allow periodic manual irrigation of the growing medium to be carried out. Another way is to spray the solution over the surface of the sand from time to time.

In order to operate the New Jersey, or Withrow methods, as they are known in the Middle West, with some degree of success, culture under glass is axiomatic, because rain falling on a hydroponicum of this nature would destroy the regulated balance of the entire system. On the other hand, virtually automatic working is ensured, and labour charges are reduced to a minimum.

AUTOMATIC DILUTION SURFACE WATERING METHOD.   In order to reduce the amount of labour and space required for the storage of liquid nutrient, Jealott's Hill Research Station introduced a method of automatically diluting a concentrated solution, and of applying it by means of a system of sprays to the sand bed. A low pressure main water supply is needed, in addition to an Autominor injection pump and a 45-litre reservoir. Improved drainage is obtained by a layer of small-sized gravel on the bottom of the troughs underneath the sand.

WICK METHOD.   A double pot arrangement is used. The upper receptacle consists of an ordinary flower pot filled with coarse sand and fitted with a glass-wool wick which passes through the bottom aperture into the lower container. This second vessel is watertight, and holds the nutrient solution. The wick, which is divided at the top, and branches out to facilitate adequate distribution of the solution in the root zone, draws up water and chemicals from the lower to the upper pot.

DRIP METHOD.   By means of a feed line, diluted nutrient solution contained in an upper tank is allowed to drip continuously on to a bed of sand in which plants are grown. The solution percolates through the medium, is collected in a sump, and pumped back to the reservoir at intervals. Waterproof troughs are necessary, and constant checks on solution concentration and pH are essential. The method has been employed on a large scale by Ohio State Agricultural Experiment Station.

CONTINUOUS-FLOW METHOD.   The cultural vessel is placed upon a stand under which is kept a basin to receive any drainage. From an adjacent reservoir, a siphon and feed pipe maintain a continuous flow of solution onto the surface of the sand in the pot. The method is very handy for household use.

MODIFIED SLOP METHOD.   This technique was developed by Dr F. M. Eaton of the United States Department of Agriculture. The solution is pumped through headers which flood the surface of the sand beds, at regular intervals. It then percolates down through the growing medium and eventually drains back into an underground storage tank. Certain crops, such as lettuce, are, however, unable to tolerate excessive amounts of free liquid around their root crowns.

DRY APPLICATION METHOD.   Dry mixed nutrient salts are sprinkled periodically over the beds and immediately watered in. This is a very simple and economical technique, and it has given good results in practical work. There are, nevertheless, two points that need careful attention. Considerable wastage of fertilizers may occur owing to leaching during heavy rains, and a risk exists of temporary over-concentration of salts soon after they go into solution in local areas of the growing medium, unless especial care is taken to ensure even distribution of the chemicals while spreading is proceeding.

Aggregate culture

Of the numerous different media that can be used in aggregate culture one of the most popular is gravel, and for this reason the system is frequently known as gravel culture. There are, however, numerous other aggregates which have given excellent results, such as cinders, broken bricks, clinkers, plastics, and vermiculite. In many cases, one or the other of them, or even a mixture of two or more, may produce better growth under certain conditions than gravel by itself would.

Aggregate culture has proved very advantageous in commercial units, and it has been the technique most commonly employed in the nutriculture installations of the United States Armed Forces.

SUB-IRRIGATION METHOD.   A watertight trough is filled with gravel or some other hard aggregate coarser than sand. The bed is periodically flooded with dilute nutrient solution, and then allowed to drain. Generally speaking, two types of irrigatory apparatus are available: direct-feed, and gravity-feed. Cascade tanks or troughs are often built, so that the solution flows from one to the next before discharging into the sump. Each bed may be built of precast concrete, jointed with asphalt or of boards lined with polyethylene sheeting; other necessary equipment consisting of a reservoir, or a reservoir and a sump, as well as a centrifugal pump. The entire method is automatic and, by virtue of the ebb and flow of the liquid nutrients, the roots of the plants are well aerated. Periodic renewal of the solution is essential. Sub-irrigation is one of the most economical ways of supplying water and fertilizer chemicals to crops. There is no loss through leaching, and control over the plants in the culture is practically one hundred per cent effective.

On the other hand, sub-irrigation may be costly to instal, and the units perhaps more complicated to build, although the expenses of maintenance are relatively low, while once in position troughs last indefinitely without any repairs.

THE FLUME.   This is a device for use with gravel beds consisting of a long curved artificial channel down which the liquid nutrients are directed, so that each trough may receive a correct proportion of the solution as the flush sweeps by. Flumes have been employed with great success by growers in Florida.

BUCKET AND GRAVITY-FEED METHOD.   Usually a small trough is constructed at a height of about one metre off ground level, with a taller post secured to the rear for hooking the bucket on to, or if a larger unit is contemplated then with an overhead rail to which a series of buckets may be attached. A hose is joined at one end to the bottom of the bucket and at the other to the base of the side-wall of the trough containing the growing medium. When the bucket has been filled with the nutrient solution and raised to the elevated position, the liquid flows down into the bed, irrigating the roots. By dropping the bucket to the ground level, drainage of the medium is accomplished by the outward and backward flow of the solution. This method is very convenient for the householder.

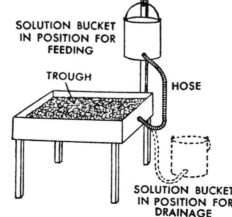

FIG. 8.
Bucket and gravity feed method in hydroponics.

COMPRESSED AIR DESIGN.   The solution is contained in large glass carboys or steel drums, placed at ground level, from which it is driven up into the beds by small portable air compressors. Drainage is by the usual gravity flow. This technique has been used by the Ohio State University Floriculture Department at Columbus, and in Israel and the West Indies.

WICK DEVICES.   This method may also be utilised in small aggregate cultures, and it has a certain value for seedling propagation. Basins containing the nutrient solution are located underneath greenhouse flats filled with inert growing medium, which is moistened by the capillary action of the wicks. These are fitted so as to draw up a constant supply of solution from the basins to the aggregate in the trough above.

BENGAL METHOD.   This technique was developed at the Government of West Bengal's Experimental Farm, at Kalimpong, in the Darjeeling district of India, during 1946–47, and it has subsequently been extended, with various modifications and adaptations, to many other parts of the world. The plants are grown in troughs constructed from any suitable material and filled with a fairly coarse inert aggregate, consisting of five parts of rock chippings or gravel, and two or three parts of sand or attritus. The nutrient salts are applied, usually in the dry state, at regular intervals, by sprinkling them evenly between the rows of crops. They are then immediately watered-in either manually or by means of certain specialised machinery. Normal irrigation facilities are provided through a system of pipes. Recently, the use of improved slow-release nutrients, such as frits, diatomaceous carriers for the fertilizing elements, and synthetic ion-exchange materials, has been developed extensively with the Bengal method, which is particularly suited to such techniques, due to the good moisture retention of the farraginous aggregate.

The method is simple to maintain, easy to operate, and inexpensive to instal, while considerable use can often be made of indigenous materials when employing this technique, if improvisation should be called for.

THE VERMICULITE METHOD.   Sometimes termed vermiculaponics, culture in vermiculite has become popular in hot countries. In temperate climates, care has to be taken to ensure that its water-retaining properties – so desirable in arid regions – do not give rise to an excess of moisture in the beds, which could encourage the spread of mildews or other fungus diseases. Vermiculite may hold supplies of available water for plant growth for up to ten times as long as some other aggregates do. It is very light, and easy to transport.

Vermiculite may be used alone as a growing medium in hydroponics, or else mixed with sand. It is not always recommended for sub-irrigation, though it has been occasionally used with that technique, but when employed in various types of modified slop culture, it gives excellent results. Local atmospheric humidity is normally the deciding factor.

Miscellaneous cultural techniques

THE GERMINATION NET.   For starting seeds, or for forcing bean sprouts for culinary purposes, the germination net method is ideal. A piece of ordinary mosquito netting, first dipped in hot paraffin wax, which is then allowed to harden after stretching it tightly over the top of a basin full of nutrient solution, forms the anchorage for the roots. The seeds are always in contact with the solution below the net, yet at the same time they are freely exposed to the atmosphere.

THE HANGING BASKET METHOD.   Shallow trays or 'baskets', filled with litter or some kind of aggregate are suspended over troughs of nutrient solution. At regular intervals, the trays are dipped into the solution by means of a simple mechanical arrangement, after the style of the pulleys used in raising and lowering clothes racks. Hanging baskets are also quite effective in sludge tanks.

THE FLOATING RAFT METHOD.   Flat rafts, constructed of wood, or kept afloat with inflated rubber tubes, may also be used in hydroponics. These devices are really modern counterparts of the Mexican *chinampas*, or the floating gardens of the Kashmir lakes. A layer of some suitable growing medium is spread over the floor of the raft, which is perforated with holes for the roots of the plants to descend through into the water

FIG. 9.
A *chinampa,* the ancient floating raft or water garden used by the Aztecs in Mexico.

below. Nutrient salts are applied to the aggregate to nourish the crops from time to time.

BOTULIFORM DEVICES.   These are often used for the culture of algae as a source of food and raw material. They may be made of plastics or polyethythene, and are transparent. Nutrient solution circulates inside the apparatus.

SPROUTING CABINETS.   Tiers of shallow trays, about 3 to 5 centimetres deep, lined with two or three thicknesses of matting, newspapers, sacking or a layer of underfelt, which is kept moist with nutrient solution, are ideal for sprouting forage to feed to racehorses, poultry, and dairy cattle. Vermiculite may also be used to retain the solution in sprouting cabinets, but should be covered by paper or hessian to prevent the fine particles from adhering to the roots of the young forage.

FODDER GROWING MACHINERY (GRASS INCUBATORS).   The main object of grass production in hydroponics is to obtain regular supplies of fresh forage throughout the year in the shortest possible space of time. Basically, soilless culture incubators or units consist of series of trays or benches arranged under some protective covering, and irrigated by nutrient solutions continually. The methods date back to the 1930s, but it is only recently that expansion of the technique has occured on farms or in stables and studs. The process takes normally about seven to ten days from sowing of the seed in the hydroponic unit to the harvesting of the crops when they attain a height of about 20 to 22 centimetres. By proper management it is possible to provide a constant series of harvests with no breaks in production. Hydroponic forage is nutritious and palatable and has been found to increase milk yields in dairy cows appreciably, as well as improving the vigour and performance of racehorses and brood mares. In arid areas, where there is little or no grazing at certain seasons for livestock, the technique has much to commend it for farmers and ranchers.

To secure optimum growth and quick harvests it is necessary to maintain the temperature inside hydroponic grass units at from 22° to 25°C, with good lighting.

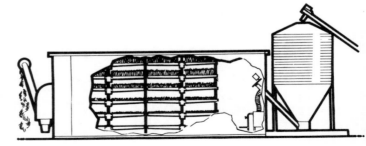

FIG. 10.
Design for a hydroponic grass growing unit. This can produce fresh fodder or sprouted grain all the year round.

Heating and illumination must be provided artificially in cold areas, but in the tropics this is not generally required because the natural climatic conditions are favourable. In fact, shading from sun scorch and excessive warmth may be needed.

Various designs for grass and green forage soilless units are available. A number of manufacturers have commenced to market machinery and equipment which may be purchased by farmers and set up without difficulty.

RING CULTURE.   This is really a modified form of aggregate culture and has been found to be most efficient in damp areas or during periods of heavy rain. Plants are grown in pots or containers, filled with soilless media or composts – usually peat, sawdust and sand – sometimes fortified with nutrient mixtures of fertilizers compounded to standard hydroponic formulae. The receptacles are then placed on beds of moderately coarse sand or of fine aggregate, made up of small cinders, broken bricks or uncrushed gravel or pebbles. Any number of containers may be grouped together. As necessary, solution is supplied to this sub-stratum and will ascend by capillary attraction into the pots or containers above. The roots of the plants also pass out through the holes in the bottoms of the receptacles and may enter the aggregate in the beds. Various other modifications or adaptations are often used.

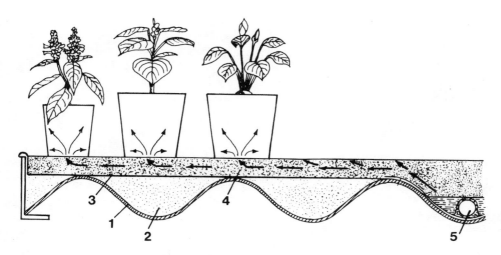

FIG. 11.
Form of ring culture used in Sicily. 1: Asbestos panel; 2: Concrete or filler; 3: Plastic film; 4: Bed of sand or aggregate; 5: Perforated irrigation tube carrying solution. The arrows show the movement of the liquid nutrient.

2. Soilless grown cucumbers in the Persian Gulf area at Abu Dhabi.
(Government of Abu Dhabi and Manley Inc.).

BAGS.   These devices are plastic envelopes or bags which have been filled with soilless compost, sand, straw charcoal, foam plastics, or other materials. Hydroponic formulae are added to the growing medium. The plants are inserted through holes made in the side of the bag which is uppermost when it has been laid on the ground. The growing medium must be kept moist constantly by adding water at appropriate intervals.

PLASTIC LAYFLATS.   Sometimes called nutrient film layflats, these devices are made from polyethylene sheeting, or synthetic rubber known by the name of butylite. The material is cut into strips about 35 to 40 centimetres wide and of any convenient length, after which it is folded to provide a central passage or tube, through which nutrient solution can move, and additional side enclosures for surface feeding roots to develop in. The solution is pumped, using a small submersible pump, continuously from an adjacent tank so that it enters the higher end of the layflat, which is laid on slightly sloping ground, and it then trickles very slowly through the device, leaving the lower end and returning to the reservoir or tank. The method is based on the recycling principle and there is no wastage or loss of nutrients. No aggregates or troughs and tanks are required as in the cases of sub-irrigation, water culture and similar systems. One small reservoir can supply large areas of hydroponic layflats. Plants are inserted into the devices through slits cut in the top of the folded plastic material.

AEROPONICS.   In this method crops are raised in vertical or horizontal tubes or containers through which suspensions or sprays of air and nutrient solution are passed continuously. The technique has been devised in Italy. Plants must be inserted in the apparatus by means of small holes cut into the sides or tops of the tubes and containers. The roots are kept moistened and nourished by the mixture of air and solution present inside the aeroponic system, while the stems and foliage protrude in a normal manner. Semi-spray cultures are of somewhat similar style and are well liked in Japan (see page 239 and Figure 41.)

YAG.   Working in the West Indies, on the island of St. Croix, E. Yaryan has introduced a method called the Yag. The container consists of two sections – an upper portion filled with aggregate and a lower portion left for solution to stand in. Nutrients and moisture ascend through the growing medium and feed the plants. A flow of solution, controlled by a ball-and-cock arrangement, from an adjacent tank replenishes the liquid in the container as necessary.

NOTE: These lists of hydroponic systems and methods are not exhaustive. A number of adaptations and refinements of the various techniques have been developed in different localities. Research and practical trials are in progress throughout the world and investigators and growers are constantly evolving new or modified procedures to suit special circumstances. We may expect to see other designs for hydroponic units announced from time to time. Consequently, it is not possible here to expect to include every device that may have been produced or to anticipate all the possible further advances. For this reason, several blank pages have been left below for readers to enter their own notes about any new techniques that they may encounter in the future.

Detailed descriptions of important techniques will be found in the section of Unit Design and Construction (Chapters 6 to 10).

ADDITIONAL SYSTEMS AND METHODS
(Enter name, type, and brief account of operation and purpose)

ADDITIONAL SYSTEMS AND METHODS

ADDITIONAL SYSTEMS AND METHODS

CHAPTER 3

Practical crop physiology

Hydroponicists are deeply concerned with high output and the responses of various plants to soilless culture formulae. To judge effectively, however, the value of different nutrients, it is vital to be well informed about the roles of the individual elements in crop feeding. The functions of the fertilizers which are the vehicles for delivery of nutrient ions to green plants are also highly significant. A good knowledge of how the essential elements are utilised by vegetation is an important part of successful commercial hydroponics.

Basic laws and the first four elements
Intensive soilless crop culture, as we know it today, represents nothing more or less than the practical application of the theories of the inorganic nutrition of plants to hydroponic growing. Under proper conditions of light and temperature, combined with a satisfactory supply of water, green vegetation is capable of manufacturing all the numerous organic substances that enter into its composition from the simple inorganic compounds, containing certain essential elements, which it secures from the air or absorbs as solutes through the root hairs.

The number of elements utilised by plants fluctuates according to the physical and chemical nature of the environment, the species in question, and the particular stage of growth. Plants are supposed to exercise selective absorption, rejecting or accepting nutrients according to their needs at the time. This inherent 'feeding power' on the part of crops is thought by some investigators to be due to the regulatory action of the absorbing cells of the roots, while others consider that the differences in the amounts of the elements used may be traced to the specificity of the protoplasm, which requires variable proportions of materials for its development in individual plants.

Between 50 and 60 different elements have been detected during analyses of plant material. The presence of the majority of these elements is, however, probably purely incidental, and due only to their occurrence in the solution surrounding the roots. Of the remainder, whose essentiality has been definitely proved, the following are the most important: carbon (C), hydrogen (H), oxygen (O), nitrogen (N), calcium (Ca), magnesium (Mg), phosphorus (P), potassium (K), sulphur (S), boron (B), copper (Cu), iron (Fe), manganese (Mn), molybdenum (Mo), and zinc (Zn). Very strong evidence also exists regarding the significant parts played by aluminium (Al), chlorine (Cl), gallium (Ga), and silicon (Si), in the growth of some crops. Certain other elements, such as iodine (I), selenium (Se), and sodium (Na), may, in addition to those already mentioned, perform useful functions from time to time.

The main bulk of a plant is composed of a relatively small number of elements. Carbon and oxygen together may account for as much as 95 per cent of the total dry weight. Hydrogen is normally present to the extent of between 6 and 7 per cent while nitrogen constitutes up to 2 per cent. The other elements are present in varying quantities, not usually exceeding, in each individual case, a figure of 1.5 per cent of the total dry weight, and in some instances very much less. All the essential elements are, however, vital to good growth and development, irrespective of the fact that some are only needed in very small quantities.

Green crops obtain most of their carbon and a substantial part of their oxygen from the atmosphere, but in the case of the fungi there is extensive utilisation of organic carbon. The hydrogen and the balance of the oxygen comes from the water absorbed by the plants. All the other nutrients, comprising nitrogen and the mineral elements, that enter plants must be generally available to them in the form of soluble compounds. The intake of water and dissolved substances by plants, and their translocation within the organism, depends upon the behaviour and relationships of membranes and solutions, especially the rate of osmosis and the concentration of nutrient ions in the root zone.

The effective utilisation by plants of the various essential elements which constitute their source of food is conditioned to a great extent by the influence of certain physical factors, such as light intensity, temperature range and water supply. The inter-relation of these different factors with each other and with the available amounts of the vital nutrients, has led to the conception of the multi-conditioned physiological processes. This was first expressed by Liebig's *law of the minimum*, which states that the yield of any crop is always dependent upon that nutritive constituent which is present in minimum amount, and subsequently elaborated by Blackman's *law of limiting factors*. The law of limiting factors lays down that when a process is conditioned as to its rapidity by a number of separate factors, the rate of the process is limited by the pace of the 'slowest' factor. It will therefore be apparent that the growth and development of crops are governed by the quantity of the particular factor or element in least supply, and that a deficiency of even one minor nutrient may have serious effects upon plant metabolism.

The physiological roles performed by the various elements are factors of the utmost significance in intensive cultivation. It is consequently only appropriate to consider them in further detail.

CARBON (C). Green plants obtain practically all their carbon from the air in the form of carbon dioxide. This gas (CO_2), which is present in the atmosphere to the extent of approximately 0.03 per cent by volume, diffuses through the stomata into the leaves. This entrance of carbon dioxide into the leaf is the first stage of the photosynthetic process. Photosynthesis, or carbon assimilation, is an endothermal reaction, the outstanding fact of which is the building up, from carbon dioxide and water, of compounds of higher energy content, the energy being provided by the radiance of the sunlight. No known analagous reactions exist in which there is a comparable storing of energy. It is through this process that the energy of the sun becomes available for use on earth. Photosynthesis is commonly defined as the manufacture of a simple carbohydrate from carbon dioxide and water by the chloroplasts in the presence of light. It is the basis of support for all life, which in itself is proof enough of the essentiality of the element carbon in plant nutrition.

Carbon constitutes up to 45 per cent of the dry weight of plants. It has already been mentioned that the bulk of this is obtained from the air. There is evidence that carbon dioxide arising within a growing medium may also be of some significance. Water can absorb between 0.04 and 0.02 per cent of its own volume of CO_2 and this, of course, would be available through the roots in solution. It is a well-known fact that the content of the gas in the atmosphere at or below surface level is appreciably higher than it is at, say, one yard above the ground. Numerous experiments have been carried out in supplying plants with increased quantities of carbon dioxide, usually by liberating the gas from containers placed alongside the crops. The latest results indicate that concentrations of up to 15 per cent in a given atmosphere may prove beneficial and result in extra yields. At over 15 per cent growth is inhibited.

Plants are also capable of utilising in their metabolism certain organic compounds as sources of carbon. Formaldehyde has been presented to crops in nutrient mixtures by its introduction into the water in which aquatics are growing, and as vapour in the atmosphere surrounding the aerial parts. A number of sugars, including glucose, galactose, lactose, laevulose, maltose, and sucrose, have often been absorbed. Much depends, however, upon the particular species of plant and there is considerable variation as to the sugar they are able to use most efficiently. So much for the green plants. As far as the fungi are concerned they do, of course, absorb appreciable amounts of organic carbon during the normal processes of nutrition.

The carbon dioxide of the air that is combined by plants is constantly being replaced by the decay of organic matter, the combustion of different products, the escape of vulcanological gases and the respiration of all living things and creatures. By such means, the amount of atmospheric carbon remains practically constant.

HYDROGEN (H). This element constitutes about 6 per cent of the total dry weight of plants. It is necessary for the photosynthetic process, as well as being important in

3. Arid Lands Research Centre, Sadiyat, in Abu Dhabi. Hydroponic Power-Water-Food facility for vegetable and flower growing in the sandy wastes.
(Government of Abu Dhabi and Manley Inc.).

many other ways. Fats and carbohydrates are composed of hydrogen together with carbon and oxygen.

Plants obtain their supplies of hydrogen from the water (H_2O) which they absorb through their roots, and also to a certain extent through their stems and leaves from the atmosphere, which usually contains an appreciable, but variable, amount of water vapour. In the case of epiphytes, they do, of course, secure all their water from the air.

The quantity of free hydrogen ions in a fertilizing solution, commonly called the hydrogen-ion concentration, is a factor of considerable significance in practical soilless crop culture.

OXYGEN (O).   Nearly half of the total dry weight of most plants is made up by oxygen. In the absence of this essential element disintegration of tissue soon occurs. Observations have shown that the basic need for oxygen is not fixed at any particular minimum level, but that it varies according to changes in external temperature conditions. Generally speaking, in hot climates more oxygen is necessary for good growth of crops than may be the case in cooler regions.

Plants obtain their supplies of oxygen from various sources. Some is secured in the elemental state from the atmosphere. This enters through the stomata, and together with what is absorbed by the roots dissolved in water, may be termed 'external oxygen'. Oxygen is also liberated during the process of photosynthesis, and this additional supply arising within the plant, has been described as 'internal oxygen'. A considerable amount of this internal oxygen is emitted in sunlight as part of a gas which also consists of a proportion of nitrogen and a small amount of carbon dioxide.

The significance of oxygen as an essential element in plant growth and development lies in the vital part that it plays in the process of respiration, which provides the energy necessary for the performance of the important functions by a living organism. The potential energy stored up in the cells of plants by means of photosynthesis in the form of carbohydrates, fats and proteins, is released into the kinetic form primarily by chemical decompositions in which the stored foods and the cell protoplasm are involved. Respiration is the most important process occurring during energesis. Any failure of respiration would mean loss of energy and cessation of the functions of life.

Without an adequate supply of oxygen it is, of course, impossible for the oxidation of organic substances in respiration to take place. Under normal conditions, the atmosphere contains an average of nearly 21 per cent by volume of oxygen, but the air in growing media is usually slightly different in composition due to the proximity of the roots. In such cases the oxygen content may be only 20 per cent by volume. A fall of five per cent in the supply will have inhibiting effects upon plants. The importance of ensuring that the roots of plants obtain adequate aeration will therefore be appreciated. Exclusion of oxygen interferes with the respiration of the protoplasm of the root cells, causing its death and the consequent failure of the absorbing mechanism. Progressive decreasing turgor of the shoot and leaves ensues, followed by wilting and necrosis. Waterlogging is the chief cause of a curtailment of the oxygen supply.

NITROGEN (N).   The amount of nitrogen in the various parts of plants varies according to the age, the type of tissue, and the species in question. It occurs mainly in organic combination entering into the structure of chlorophyll, the amino-acids, the amides and the alkaloids, as well as being an essential constituent of the protoplasmic and storage proteins. On the average, this element accounts for up to two per cent of the total dry weight of the green plant. It encourages a rank growth of foliage, and contributes to good stem length. In its absence, leaves become stunted and yellow, and the whole plant soon assumes a starved appearance. Crops are, in fact, basically dependent upon nitrogen, together with carbon, hydrogen, and oxygen for their survival.

The concentration of nitrogen in fertilizer mixtures may be as high as 1000 ppm or as low as 150 ppm according to local circumstances. In hot, sunny areas plants generally have a greater requirement of this essential element than they have in cold and cloudy regions. For most work, a figure of 300 ppm is usually quite adequate. Some seasonal variation also occurs in the utilisation of nitrogen in plants.

The functions of nitrogen are numerous. It plays a vital part in the formation of protein, of which it constitutes approximately 17 per cent. It is also essential for the production of chlorophyll, protoplasm and the nucleic acids. Proteins are organic nitrogen compounds which are derived from the chemical combination of carbohydrates and inorganic nitrogen. Oxidation of the carbohydrates to organic acids, which then combine with ammonium ions to form amino-acids, is the first stage of protein synthesis. Some proportion of carbohydrates is deposited as reserve depending upon the carbohydrates/nitrogen ratio. If a deficiency of nitrogen is apparent, an unusually high reserve of starch or sugar will be accumulated in the plant tissues. Following upon this state of affairs comes a deposition of abnormal amounts of cellulose and lignin in the cell walls, with the result that the plant becomes 'hard', in horticultural parlance.

Hard and woody vegetables are useless for culinary purposes. Again, if insufficient carbohydrates are formed, but excess nitrogen is absorbed, the plants will become too soft and succulent, and in such a condition they will be susceptible not only to mechanical injury, but also to the attacks of various diseases. In this state, flowers often fail to set fruit. It is therefore most important to ensure that the carbohydrate/nitrogen relationship is properly balanced at all times.

Plants obtain their supplies of nitrogen both from the various nitrogenous compounds present in the hydroponic solution and from the combined and elemental nitrogen of the atmosphere. Some crops utilise either nitrates or ammonium salts, and the relative value of these sources depends upon a number of factors, including the reaction of the solution, the age and kind of plant, the amount of light available, and the presence or absence of other ions. In certain cases, nitrites may also prove beneficial to a range of crops. Nitrates, nitrites, and ammonium salts all come within the category of inorganic nitrogen, from which source the green plant derives its main supply of this essential nutrient. In addition, observations have shown that a varying amount of organic nitrogen can be directly assimilated by higher plants, and a long list of such compounds has been prepared by investigators. The stimulatory effects of small quantities of certain organic nitrogenous matter, often termed auximones, phytamins, or nutrilites, upon the rate of growth has also attracted some interest. The other important source of nitrogen is, however, the free or uncombined form present in the air, of which it constitutes nearly 80 per cent. The atmosphere, in addition, contains traces of ammonia, nitrates, and nitrites. In the case of legumes, certain micro-organisms enter into symbiotic relationships with the plants so enabling them to make use of this free nitrogen, or as it is commonly called, to 'fix' it. As regards the non-leguminous plants, much conflicting evidence is available. It has been claimed that not only the algae, but other higher species as well, are capable of absorbing free nitrogen.

Macro- and micro-elements

Extensive investigations carried out over a period of many years have revealed that no fewer than fifty different mineral elements may be utilised by plants during the processes of growth and nutrition. The essentiality of most of these is either extremely unlikely, or it has been proved not to exist, and in the majority of cases the presence of a particular element has been shown to be merely incidental, due to some peculiarity of the local environment or growing conditions. This does not mean that the significance of the non-essential mineral elements should be ignored, especially when the presence of any one or more of them is detected by analysis of plant ash. On the contrary, special attention will need to be given to such questions as toxicity, or the arising of inhibiting factors.

Mineral elements occur as constituents of compounds present in, or derived from, the minerals of natural rocks, and are therefore generally known as mineral nutrients. In practical hydroponic work, they can be supplied to the plants in the form of chemical fertilisers of various kinds. Not more than a dozen are of great nutritive importance, and the actual quantities required for healthy growth and development of crops vary considerably in each case. They may be divided for convenience into two classes – the major or macro-elements, also called the macronutrients, and the minor, micro- or trace elements, called the micronutrients. The former are needed in comparatively large amounts, while the latter are required in relatively small concentrations.

In addition to these mineral salts, other elements giving rise to varying effects may be absorbed by plants depending upon the species and the conditions of growth.

CALCIUM (Ca).   All green plants with the exception of some of the lower algae require a supply of calcium. The element is not, however, essential for the growth of fungi. The amount of calcium present in the plant varies considerably according to the species and the environmental conditions. For good growth, crops need a concentration of between 300 ppm and 500 ppm in the nutrient solution. One of the most important functions of calcium is to reduce the toxic effects of certain other salts.

The behaviour of calcium as an antidoting agent is apparent in two main ways. It neutralises the toxic action of magnesium within the limits of the calcium/magnesium ratio, which varies with the type of plants. It also assists in the neutralisation of organic acids in plant tissues, and in this connection the theory of a calcium/nitrogen ratio has been advanced by some investigators.

Calcium is one of the components of the middle lamella of the cell wall, and it also influences protein synthesis. A deficiency of the element results in a cessation of meristematic activity, which affects the tips and margins of leaves, as well as the size of the roots.

MAGNESIUM (Mg).   The main function of magnesium in the plant is the part that it plays in the formation of chlorophyll, of which it is a necessary component. It also acts as a carrier of phosphorus by forming a labile complex with that element.

Magnesium is relatively most abundant in seeds and leaves. Excessive amounts of magnesium are extremely injurious to plants, causing a rolling and curling of the leaves, with eventual necrosis of the tips. Symptoms of toxicity also occur in the roots. The provision of an additional supply of calcium frequently alleviates the condition.

From 50 ppm to 100 ppm of magnesium are usually adequate for the nutrition of most crops.

PHOSPHORUS (P).   The total dry substance of plants contains an average of 0.5 per cent of phosphorus. The element is most abundant in seeds, fruits, and in the meristematic tissues. A considerable part of the phosphorus found in plants is soluble in water. It is also relatively mobile.

Although most phosphorus is absorbed in the form of phosphates, plants can to some extent make use of organic phosphorus, especially nucleic acid. The usual concentration of phosphorous present in hydroponic solutions ranges from 50 ppm to over 100 ppm.

The functions of phosphorus in the metabolism of the plant are diverse. It is a constituent of certain protoplasmic proteins, and it influences the hydrolysis of starch to simple sugars, as well as the synthesis of starch from sugars. Phosphorus enters into the composition of phytin, as well as assisting in the nitrate-nitrogen reduction process, and exerting a buffering effect upon the acidity of the cell sap. The beneficial influence of this essential element in promoting the maximum development of root crops is well known. A deficiency of phosphorus seriously inhibits good fruiting and results in a spindling appearance, with dark or purplish discolouration of the leaves. An adequate supply of phosphorus, on the other hand, will encourage early ripening.

A relationship between phosphorus and nitrogen exists which often proves of considerable significance in using fertilizers. The presence of excess nitrogen tends to inhibit the plant's intake of phosphorus. Another factor of considerable importance is the iron/phosphate relationship. In some cases there is a likelihood that mutual precipitation of iron and phosphates may occur. Where the phosphate level is high, an iron deficiency may arise, and if unusually large amounts of iron are added to a mixture already low in phosphate a shortage of that element may develop. It is therefore advisable to maintain a correct iron/phosphorus ratio in all fertilizer mixtures.

During recent years, the study of problems in plant nutrition has been greatly simplified by the use of radio-active phosphorus tracers.

POTASSIUM (K).   This element is absolutely essential to the good growth of plants. All the meristematic tissues contain considerable amounts of potassium, and it is also well distributed in the mesophyll cells of the leaves, in the cells of the medullary rays, and in the phloem. It is highly mobile within the plant. The actual quantities of potassium needed by crops for growth and development vary widely. In nutrient solutions, the concentrations can range from about 100 ppm to as much as 400 ppm.

The role of potassium in the metabolism of the green plant is still in many respects obscure. It is thought to function as a catalytic agent. In the absence of an adequate supply of this vital element, normal formation of carbohydrates is checked. Potassium may also take part in the neutralisation of organic acids in protein synthesis. It is apparently essential either directly or indirectly for the initial stages in nitrate-nitrogen assimilation.

The characteristic symptom of potash deficiency in plants is the appearance of leaf scorch.

In many regions, where the light intensity is good, the plant's need for potassium is about 50% less than it is in dull cloudy areas with short days. This fact is generally considered to originate from the assumption that protein can be formed in the presence of brilliant sunshine, provided that a sufficient supply of carbohydrate and other material is available, in the virtual absence of potassium. Whereas when light conditions are poor or bad, protein will not be manufactured unless the potash concentration is reasonably high. In practical hydroponic work, it is usual to provide crops with more potassium salts in winter and less in the summer months. At the same time, the concentration of nitrogen in the fertilizer mixtures is raised in the summer and lowered in the winter. This arrangement, which can result in a substantial reduction of operating costs, is frequently known as the technique of the nitrogen/potassium balance.

Potassium is believed to improve the keeping quality of fruits. It may even have a frost protecting effect if additional amounts are given to plants late in the autumn.

SULPHUR (S). Plants contain appreciable amounts of sulphur. It is fairly well distributed throughout the various tissues, but the greatest concentrations are generally to be found in the leaves. The element functions as building material for the formation of protein and other constituents of the plant. As much as 7.2 per cent of sulphur has been observed in plant proteins in the form of cystine.

The presence of adequate quantities of sulphur produces certain formative effects such as a better root system, improved chlorophyll supply, and an increase in the number of nodules on the roots of legumes. A deficiency of sulphur lowers the rate of nitrate reduction and inhibits the oxidation of sugars within the plant.

The well known disease of the tea bush, called 'yellows', is caused by a deficiency of sulphur.

The amount of sulphur present in nutrient solutions may range from a concentration of 200 ppm to up to 1000 ppm. It is normally supplied through the sulphates of the main salts.

CHLORINE (Cl). The present state of knowledge concerning the influence of this element upon the metabolism of the green plant is incomplete in many respects. Several factors have to be taken into account before any conclusion is possible, notably the nature of the crop under consideration, the type of growing media in question, and the local climatic conditions. Chlorine diminishes to some extent the retarding effect produced by an unbalanced nutrient solution and it also has a morphological influence upon cereals, giving a waxy bloom to the leaf surface and causing a thickening of the cuticle.

Chlorine may, in addition, improve the water content of plant tissue, as well as affect the metabolism of carbohydrates, and produce an increase of chlorophyll. Most beneficial results have been obtained in the field by the proper application of chlorides to tobacco for protection of the leaves against 'drought spot'. Plants which have received this treatment can resist the injurious desiccation of a dry season. The salting of asparagus beds is an old garden practice, which has been found by experience to raise yields appreciably.

A concentration of 5 ppm of chlorine produces better growth and development of buckwheat and peas, while rice responds favourably to appropriate quantities of this element. Chlorine is present in practically all plants, except the conifers, but ferns, mosses, and epiphytes contain hardly any. Of its functions within the plants nothing definite is known, but the theory has been advanced that chlorine increases the cell acidity, so accelerating enzymatic action, which has a natural stimulatory effect upon growth and development.

COPPER (Cu). This element is very widely distributed in the higher plants, and concentrations of as much as 46 ppm of dry material have been found in certain crops. The greatest abundance occurs in the meristematic cells. Numerous instances of the marked effects of copper upon plant growth have been recorded. In one instance, where the amount in a laboratory solution was only 0.06 ppm the dry weight of tomato vines grown in the culture exceeded that of control plants raised from a copper-free solution by a figure of no less than 700%. Onions, lettuce, maize, and fruit trees respond well to applications of copper salts.

Despite its beneficial effects, copper in other than very great dilution is a deadly plant poison. Its uses as a fungicide are, of course, well known. The concentration of copper in nutrient mixtures becomes excessive at 1 ppm and the symptoms of inhibition steadily increase thereafter, with rapid necrosis at 5 ppm. For healthy growth, the optimum is 0.5 ppm.

In the absence of this element, plants exhibit lack of vigour, as well as exaggerated physiological disturbances characterised by the emergence of frenching. Chlorosis, spotting, and xanthema may become prevalent. Copper enters into the composition of the oxidising enzyme called catechol oxidase or polyphenol oxidase, which appears to be a copper-protein compound. The element functions as a catalyst in vital oxidations and the opinion has been expressed that it forms with zinc a pair of mutually co-ordinating catalysts for oxidation-reduction reactions in plants.

IODINE (I). Both the organic and the inorganic forms of iodine are present in plants. The element is absorbed more or less proportionately to the amount occurring in any particular solution or fertilizer. Such crops as peas, spinach, lettuce, beets, turnip and beans, are known to increase their iodine content when conditions are favourable.

One of the effects of iodine is to intensify the green colour of the leaf, which would appear to indicate some close association between it and chlorophyll. The greatest concentration of the iodine-absorbing materials is to be found in rapidly growing portions of plants. At maturity, some decrease is observable, while drying and storage further reduce the total amount.

Investigations have shown that a concentration of even 1 ppm of iodine in the nutrient solution has a depressing effect upon plant growth, indicated by a progressive dropping of the lower leaves, as well as slight chlorosis. The average iodine content of potatoes, assessed on a dry matter basis, is no more than 0.075 ppm so it is probable that a concentration of 0.01 ppm would prove ample for most growth purposes.

Enlargement of the thyroid gland, known as the disease of goitre, occurs in mammals in the absence of an adequate supply of iodine in the foodstuffs consumed. This gland contains the protein thyroglobulin, a constituent amino-acid of which, namely thyroxine, utilises iodine in its molecule.

ALUMINIUM (Al).   Small amounts of aluminium have been found in the ash of all types of plants which have had access to supplies of it during growth. It is certainly an essential element for the nutrition of a number of species, including peas, maize, sunflowers, the common cereals, and various hydrophytes and grasses. The addition of 1 ppm of aluminium to test plots in which maize plants were growing has produced an increase in dry weight of the vegetative parts of up to 20%; and in that of the cobs, of 150%. In concentrations of much over 10 ppm aluminium will prove toxic to plants, but the optimum figure permissible depends upon the species in question.

It has been suggested that aluminium may act as a catalyst performing a function in the assimilation of carbon by increasing the rate of photosynthesis. The influence of the element upon the colouring of the flowers of *Hydrangea hortensis* has long been known.

BORON (B).   The functions of boron in the growth and development of plants have received much attention. It is considered to exert a favourable influence on the absorption of cations, but to have a retarding effect upon anion intake. Boron may assist in the plant's utilisation of calcium, as well as play a part in the formation of pectic substances in the cell wall. It can affect the water relations of the protoplasm. The element also fulfills an essential part in carbohydrates and nitrogen metabolism.

Small amounts of boron are present in all types of plants, but the limit of tolerance varies widely according to the species and the local conditions of growth. Cotton will thrive on as much as 10 ppm of boron in the nutrient solution, whereas for tomatoes the optimum is 1.1 ppm. The presence of boron in irrigation water in excess of 0.5 ppm may prove detrimental in citrus trees.

Evidence exists regarding the relationship between boron and calcium which shows that in the absence of an adequate level of the former element in solution, plants are unable to absorb sufficient calcium to prevent poisoning by other nutrient salts. A proper supply of boron, however, facilitates the rapid intake of calcium so that the toxic effects of other elements are antagonised. While this effect may not be true for all crops, it is particularly apparent in certain kinds of beans. An increase in potassium concentration often has the result of checking the plant's utilisation of boron, and bringing about a lowering of the calcium/boron ratio.

A deficiency of boron is thought to cause a decrease in the oxidation rate of sugars, and of amination of carbohydrate derivatives so that protein substances necessary for maintenance of protoplasm are not formed.

IRON (Fe).   If the green plant is deprived of iron its growth and development will be completely inhibited. The characteristic symptom of iron deficiency is acute chlorosis. Chlorophyll formation ceases, followed eventually by necrosis of the cell protoplasm.

Plants vary considerably in the amount of iron that they contain. In cucumbers and watermelons the amount present averages under 0.0004 per cent, while tomatoes, celery, carrots, and onions contain between 0.0004 and 0.00079 per cent. Asparagus and beetroot usually have from 0.0008 to 0.00159 per cent of iron, and in parsley, spinach and watercress, there may be as much as 0.0020 per cent. Iron is comparatively immobile within the plant, and cannot readily be withdrawn from a place of occurrence to newer organs.

Iron functions as a catalytic agent in the formation of chlorophyll, but it does not enter into its composition. It is also considered to behave as an oxygen carrier in the oxidation-reduction process. An antagonism exists between iron and manganese in the growth of higher plants. It is known that the active functional iron in the tissues is in the ferrous state, and this may be oxidised by manganese to ferric iron. The significance of this process is dealt with briefly under the section relating to manganese. The utilisation of iron salts by plants is largely dependent upon the pH value of the nutrient solution.

The concentration of iron in a fertilizer mixture should not generally exceed 5 ppm, but lesser amounts have proved effective. The only sure guide is to make the general appearance of the plants serve as an index of iron supply. Changes in the environment often have pronounced influence upon the iron requirements of plants.

MANGANESE (Mn).   All plants contain a certain amount of manganese, but the actual quantity present varies considerably and is dependent upon a number of factors, such as climate, cultural conditions and the species in question. There is also a tendency for this element to accumulate in the foliage rather than in the stalk. Pineapple leaves frequently contain up to ten times as much manganese as do the other parts of the plant. Observations on maize have revealed concentrations of 0.043 per cent in the dry matter of the leaf, against only 0.017 per cent in the stem. Generally speaking, hydrophytes make greater use of manganese than dry-land plants, while the evergreens contain more than the deciduous trees.

Plants vary appreciably in regard to their need for manganese. For example, a concentration of 1/50,000,000 in the complete nutrient mixture is adequate for the healthy growth of rye, whereas certain varieties of oats require at least 0.5 ppm. *Lemna minor* flourishes on only 0.0003 ppm in water cultures, but if the concentration is raised to over 1 ppm toxicity symptoms develop. The reaction of plants to manganese depends mainly, however, upon the nature of the media in which they are growing. In the laboratory, the permissible concentration of manganese is usually between 1 to 2 ppm depending upon the amount of iron present. In the soilless unit, when crops are growing in standard troughs as much as 5 ppm may be utilised effectively. Under these latter conditions, the limit of tolerance can be very high, even up to 80 ppm, but to apply such large amounts in practical work would serve no useful purpose, as well as being uneconomic and a mere waste of fertilizer.

The absence or scarcity of manganese in the nutrient solution causes disturbance of the carbohydrate metabolism, retarded growth, chlorosis, a decrease in ash content, and failure of the plants to reproduce. The element is essential for the action of the oxidising enzymes, and there is also evidence that it is concerned in respiration. In addition, manganese directly catalyses nitrate assimilation.

A further significant factor is the relationship which has been found to exist between manganese and iron in the higher plants. It would appear that the former functions as a counter-reactant, oxidising excess ferrous iron to ferric form. If manganese is deficient in the plant, an increase of active ferrous iron occurs, which includes chlorosis to iron toxicity. On the other hand, when the manganese concentration is too high, active ferrous iron content is correspondingly low, resulting in a shortage and consequent detriment. It is, therefore, essential that the proportion of manganese to iron should lie within certain limits, otherwise healthy growth will not take place.

There is also an antagonism between manganese and calcium in their absorption by the plant.

MOLYBDENUM (MO).   The essentiality of molybdenum for the nutrition of higher plants has now been fully established. In the absence of an adequate supply of this trace element various pathological symptoms soon develop.

Mottling of the lower leaves occurs first, followed by marginal necrosis, and abscission of flowers. In the *Brassica* varieties, a condition often termed 'whiptail' may arise. The leaves die back almost completely, only the midrib remaining.

For practical purposes, a concentration of 0.001 ppm of molybdenum will supply the needs of the green plant.

SELENIUM (Se).   The quantity of selenium absorbed by plants depends upon a number of factors, such as the concentration of this element present in the nutrient solution, the species in question, its stage of development, and the amount of sulphur available.

Experiments have shown that certain plants utilise very substantial amounts of selenium. The most highly seleniferous species include *Astragalus bisculatus, A. pectinatus, A. flaviflorus, A. racemosus, Stanleya pinnata, Applopappus fremonti,* and *Xylorrhiza parry,* among others. Then come a group consisting of the asters, the sunflower (*Helianthus annuus*), and the common cereals: rye barley, wheat, and maize. These plants are capable of absorbing selenium in considerable quantity without injurious effects. Finally, selenium salts can be supplied to various ornamental plants, such as roses, carnations, and similar greenhouse flowers, in order to make them toxic to red spider mites.

Excessive concentrations of selenium in a solution will prove toxic to many crops after a few weeks, but the limit of tolerance is greatly raised if an adequate supply of sulphur is provided. Wheat seedlings grown in a test with only 0.1 ppm of selenium may exhibit distinct injury within a relatively short space of time when there is no sulphate present. If, however, an addition of about 200 ppm of sulphur is made, a concentration of 18 ppm selenium can be permitted safely. The selenium/sulphur ratio depends upon the relative amounts of the two elements available to plants. When the figure remains relatively constant, any increase in the quantity of selenium in the solution brings about a corresponding rise in the amount absorbed, but this intake is immediately checked if additional sulphur should be provided. For practical purposes, the selenium/sulphur ratio should be kept at 1/12, though this may be appropriately varied for different species.

It is, of course, hardly necessary to emphasise the fact that selenium in plants at a concentration of even 1 ppm is poisonous to animals, and no doubt to human beings also. Consequently, its inclusion in nutrient mixtures for food crops would be highly inadvisable, since a worthwhile stimulatory effect upon development would not be achieved unless about 5 ppm were used. For the protection of ornamental plants against the attacks of certain pests, however, selenium can prove a most valuable ally.

SILICON (Si).   This element occurs in greatest abundance in grasses, in the bark of trees, and in the common cereals. It is present in varying amounts in practically all plants, and is considered to be essential for the growth of many. More silica can be found in tropical plants than in those of the temperate zones, due to the effect of higher temperatures upon the dissolution of silicic acid.

Experiments have shown that silicon improves the growth of various crops. It is also believed to protect plants against the attacks of certain parasites, such as rusts, plant lice, and the mildew *Erysiphe graminis*. The resistance to fungi is correlated to silicon deposition in the epidermis, which makes that layer more impervious to their enzymic penetration. The suggestion has been made that silica may act within the plant by stimulating phosphate movement from relatively quiescent regions to places where assimilation and growth are active.

SODIUM (Na).   Under certain conditions the presence of sodium in solutions may have a marked effect upon the yields of some crops. Although it is not generally considered to rank as one of the essential elements, investigations have shown that it can, to a limited extent, replace potassium as a plant nutrient. When an adequate supply of sodium is available, plants tend to absorb less potash, thus conserving the latter element. Sodium may also act, in specific cases, as an antidoting agent against various toxic salts.

The substitution of potassium chloride by sylvanite, which contains a high percentage of sodium chloride, in beet cultivation, has resulted in bigger yields. Sodium usually accumulates in the leaves of hydroponic plants.

ZINC (zn).   Although the green plant utilises only very small amounts of zinc, it is nevertheless one of the elements essential for healthy growth and development. Excess concentrations are, however, extremely toxic, and cause rapid necrosis.

The concentration of zinc in fertilizer mixtures must not on any account exceed 1 ppm. Satisfactory results have been obtained with as little as 0.1 or 0.2 ppm. Beans, buckwheat, sweetcorn and peas respond especially to the stimulating effects of zinc, which often produces marked improvement in both flower and seed formation.

A shortage of zinc results in stunting, the arising of various deficiencies, and frequently death of the plants. The view has been put forward that the element is concerned with the functioning of sulphydryl compounds in their regulation of the oxidation-reduction potential within the cells, in consequence of which its absence or deficiency adversely affects the sulphur metabolism. Coacervation follows this disturbance of equilibrium. It has also been pointed out that a certain level of zinc in the plant is necessary for the maintenance of a normal auxin content. The connection between it and this growth-promoting substance is underlined by the fact that the terminal buds and stems of zinc-deficient plants contain little or no auxin, without which natural development is drastically retarded or completely stopped.

Apart from its functions as a catalyst, zinc is thought to be concerned in the removal of carbon dioxide.

Other elements

Various other elements are believed to exert some influence upon plant growth and development. In no case, however, has the existing state of knowledge been advanced sufficiently for any comprehensive pronouncements concerning their individual effects or functions to be made yet. Whatever information has been compiled is still extremely fragmentary. Further research is continually proceeding, and no doubt eventually enough evidence will be accumulated to fill in the remaining gaps. It is, of course, important to remember that although the addition of a particular element to the nutrient solution or medium in which plants are growing may bring some stimulatory effect, it does not necessarily follow that the element in question is an essential one.

ANTIMONY (sb).   This rare element is reported to improve the growth of certain grasses.

ARSENIC (As).   A low concentration of arsenic may have a beneficial influence upon wheat, beans, peas, and particularly radishes, resulting in appreciably greater vigour of the plants. Such crops as oats, cotton and various grasses are, however, very sensitive to any excess of arsenic salts.

BARIUM (Ba).   Increased yields and some acceleration of root growth, have been secured by the use of small amounts of barium compounds, but only in the presence of an adequate supply of calcium. In the absence of calcium, barium is toxic to plants.

BERYLLIUM (Be).   In small amounts, beryllium is said to stimulate growth.

BISMUTH (Bi).   Possibly of some advantage in minute quantities only.

BROMINE (Br).   Here again, very little is known of the effects of this element in plant nutrition, but quite possibly it may have beneficial effects in very low concentrations.

CADMIUM (Cd).   A virtually unknown factor, though it has been used in some fertilizer mixtures.

CERIUM (Ce).   Another element about which no certain knowledge exists at present, as far as its effects upon plant growth are concerned.

CESIUM (Cs).   Small applications of cesium are reported to improve the straw of rice plants.

CHROMIUM (Cr).   Although it is frequently used in tests, the value of chromium as a plant nutrient is not yet fully understood. Small amounts may improve the growth of cereals.

COBALT (Co).   While direct proof is still lacking that cobalt is essential for the growth of any plant, there is very definite evidence that it is vital to the health of sheep and cattle. In the absence of an adequate supply of cobalt, these animals develop pining disease. It is therefore important to ensure that the cobalt content of herbage is adequate to supply these needs. The actual amount of cobalt present in plants varies according to the nature of the medium or solution in which they are growing. At a concentration of 0.1 ppm in the solution, slight toxic effects may be apparent.

COLUMBIUM (Nb).   Certain evidence would appear to indicate that columbium may well be an essential element for plant growth, but there is no conclusive proof yet available. Its addition to growth mixtures has been found to stimulate healthy development.

FLUORINE (F).   The opinion has been put forward that fluorine is necessary for the growth of maize. In the case of tobacco, however, it may have toxic effects. This element is generally present in traces in most nutrient solutions, and in such minute amounts is unlikely to prove an inhibiting factor.

GALLIUM (Ga).   This element is certainly essential for the growth of a number of plants, including *Lemna,* and the fungus *Aspergillus niger.*

LANTHANUM (La).   Very little is known about the functions of lanthanum in plant nutrition, though it has been added to some mixtures, with beneficial effect.

LEAD (Pb).   Except in extremely low concentrations, lead is toxic to plants.

LITHIUM (Li).   Investigations have shown that lithium may exert a stimulatory effect upon some plants.

MERCURY (Hg).   It has been used in fertilizer experiments, but no definite information about its functions in plant nutrition is at hand.

NICKEL (Ni).   Small amounts of nickel may result in some increase in the growth rate of crops, but at a concentration exceeding 1.5 ppm toxicity symptoms, in the form of spotting and chlorosis of leaves, soon appear.

PALLADIUM (Pa).   Even low concentrations of palladium are injurious, but the limit of tolerance varies with the species of plant.

RUBIDIUM (Rb).   There is no evidence that rubidium has any adverse or stimulatory effect upon plants, but it has been suggested that where potassium is in short supply, its assimilation may be checked by the presence of appreciable quantities of rubidium salts.

SCANDIUM (Sc).   Suggestions have been made by some investigators that this element may be essential in certain nutritive functions.

SILVER (Ag).   The inhibiting action of silver upon plants becomes noticeable when the concentration of this element in a solution exceeds 0.2 ppm.

STRONTIUM (Sr).   This is not an important element in plant nutrition, but a considerable amount of attention has been drawn towards it in recent years, owing to the publicity given to the possible effects of the radio-active isotope Strontium 90 upon the future of the human species. A small amount of strontium may result in increased yields, if absorbed by the plant in the presence of calcium. In the absence of calcium, strontium is toxic to crops.

THALLIUM (Tl).   At a concentration of 1 ppm in a nutrient solution thallium is toxic to some plants. The growth rate decreases, with some yellowing of the sides of the veins in the upper leaves. Chlorosis then spreads to the newly developing shoots, followed by distortion, and a proliferation of the lateral buds ('witches'-broom' effect.) Often the young leaves consist of only a midrib. In smaller amounts, not exceeding 0.1 ppm thallium may result in some increased growth.

THORIUM (Th).   No definite knowledge of the uses of thorium in plant culture is available, though it has been added to solutions from time to time.

TIN (Sn).   Also an unknown factor, but often present in very low concentrations.

TITANIUM (Ti).   The beneficial effects of titanium in increasing crop yields have been known for some time. Various plants respond favourably to concentrations of as much as 5 ppm, including peas and pineapples. It is probable that titanium can to some extent replace iron in chlorophyll synthesis.

TUNGSTEN (W).   This element has been used for fertilizing trials, but little definite is known of its effects, although certain evidence has been put forward suggesting that it may have some essential function in plant growth.

URANIUM (U).   Nothing conclusive has yet been discovered regarding the role of uranium in crop nutrition.

VANADIUM (V).   Extremely small amounts of vanadium are reported to have exercised a stimulating effect upon the growth of plants. In any appreciable concentration, it has an inhibiting and detrimental influence.

YTTRIUM (Y).   Another unknown factor, but possibly beneficial in small amounts.

ZIRCONIUM (Zr).   No definite information is available concerning the influence of zirconium upon plants, though small quantities have been added to some solutions for test work.

This list is not fully exhaustive, and it is to be expected that analysis of plant ash will result in the detection of yet further elements, present in infinitesimal amounts, from time to time.

PART TWO

Unit Design and Construction

4. Carnations in hydroponics. View of flower-growing unit at University of Sassari, Sicily.

CHAPTER 4

The site

The choice of suitable sites for the erection of large scale commercial hydroponic installations is a matter which calls for careful study of the various factors involved. While it is difficult to lay down a set of rules that would be binding under all circumstances, owing to the considerable variations of climate and topography in different regions, experience has shown that the following points are usually of paramount significance:

(a) The site should be reasonably level with only relatively slight slopes, unless it is intended to go in for terrace or layflat cultivation.

(b) Provided that the basic desideratum of an adequate supply of water is satisfied, the area chosen should be as barren as possible.

(c) There should be a suitable supply of natural aggregates close at hand, except in the case of water or plastic-based cultures; but in any event care must be taken to ensure that material for trough construction is readily available nearby, or at economic prices if it has to be ordered from any distance.

(d) The locality selected should lie within reasonable reach of the markets in which the produce will be sold, or otherwise disposed of. If shipping or air-freighting of fruits and vegetables is envisaged the costs should be examined carefully.

(e) Satisfactory communications are essential for the delivery of fertilizers and other equipment, as well as for the shipment or air transport of vegetables and flowers.

(f) The grower should assure himself that a good demand exists for the crops that he will grow before embarking upon a venture in any given locality.

(g) Proper apparatus and equipment must be installed to meet the needs of any particular area. For example, in cold districts, glasshouses or cloches will be required, while in hot zones shading is often necessary.

Climatic considerations

If possible, hydroponica should be positioned to the leeward side of any source of dust. This is often a serious contaminant, since it may carry disease organisms, such as nematodes or eelworms, and it also covers the leaves and fruits of growing crops, thus choking the stomata and affecting plant metabolism. Roads, runways, and wide sandy spaces like deserts or dunes may give rise to a considerable volume of dust. In arenose districts, some system of screens or windbreaks is usually arranged for the purpose of protecting soilless culture units from excessive dust. Shelter from sea-spray is also important, particularly on small islands or near the shores of continental areas. Wind is another factor that may influence the choice of a site. If velocities of over twenty kilometres per hour are prevalent, efforts should be made to locate units behind a hill or other natural feature, by taking advantage where possible of the topography of the ground. Strong winds are capable of severely damaging many crops, such as tomatoes and cucumbers, unless they are grown in greenhouses or surrounded by shelter screens.

Rainfall plays an important role in the management of open air hydroponic installations, so that it is essential that the monthly precipitation in any particular district should be known beforehand. Provided that suitable precautions are taken, rain will not adversely affect the operation of a hydroponicum, though in monsoon climates some extra equipment may be needed to guard against waterlogging of the beds, and excessive dilution of the nutrient solution. Other meteorological factors that must be taken into account include very high or very low temperature conditions, the incidence of snowstorms, light intensity, and the relative humidity of the atmosphere. Each type of plant possesses a specific temperature range most suitable for its development. In greenhouses, temperatures can be regulated all through the year to provide crops with optimal growth conditions, but in out-of-door cultures the position is rather different, for although it is quite possible to provide some degree of protection against the elements by means of shade or windbreaks, this will inevitably be of little use where wide extremes of heat or cold exist. Temperature is always a limiting factor to plant growth and development, and it has to be borne in mind when considering a site for hydroponic use, mainly from the point of view that the erection of special protective structures like glasshouses implies an extra financial outlay. Poor light conditions, which often occur in towns and industrial regions, act as a check to the healthy growth of crops. Here again, an assessment should be made of the cost of installing additional illumination, in the form of electric lamps, before embarking upon any project in such places. The general vegetative responses of plants and their susceptibility to diseases are largely dependent upon the relative humidity of the local atmosphere. Water losses are much higher when this is low, since the transpiration rate is obviously controlled to a great extent by the amount of water vapour present in the air at any given time. On the other hand, during periods of high relative humidity, the incidence of certain disease organisms increases; hence the introduction of official systems of warning farmers of the likelihood of disease outbreaks, such as potato blight, based upon the occurrence of a 'Beaumont period'.

Ground conditions

Flat sites, with a slope not exceeding thirty centimetres in every twenty-five metres, are excellent for hydroponics. In such cases, the natural configuration of the ground lends itself readily to the construction of troughs or beds, without the need of extensive grading or levelling. Hillsides may be terraced, each trough following a contour line, after the fashion of Oriental ricefields, except where layflats or aeroponics are used. In towns, or urban areas, units can be built in backyards, on flat rooftops, along the edges of pavements or sidewalks, or at any spot where sufficient light and air are available. It is, however, important to choose places away from factory chimneys, especially those emitting noxious fumes or toxic gases, and out of reach of poisonous effluents. Amateur gardeners will find window boxes or portable kitchen units very satisfactory.

Water needs

The water requirement of a hydroponicum is appreciably lower than that of an equivalent area of soil garden, but it is nevertheless absolutely vital that soilless cultured plants should receive a minimum amount of moisture at all times. A dry period, even of short duration, may prove fatal. Consequently, all hydroponic sites must be assured of a regular source of water. This may be obtained in various ways, such as mains supply, wells, rivers, boreholes, stored rainfall, melted snow in arctic regions, or distilled sea-water. Before finally deciding on a site for a commercial installation, tests should be made both of the quantity and the quality of the proposed water supply. In most arid regions in the tropics ample underground sources of water may exist, which can be tapped by means of boreholes, after an initial survey has been carried out using a resistivity meter. It is therefore inadvisable to reject an otherwise suitable site on the grounds of apparent non-availability of surface water until such trials have in fact been properly undertaken by a qualified person.

Growing media and trough materials

Not only can a wide range of aggregates be employed for the growth of crops without soil, but it is also possible to utilise a number of different materials for bed and trough construction in hydroponics. The cultural containers may be made from suitably treated or very hard woods, concrete, shaped and dressed stones, bricks, plastics, non-erodible mud plaster, and various other substances, such as alkali-puddled clay, and properly painted metal, all of which are commonly available or are easy to instal at the site. Examination of a proposed hydroponic situation should include an investigation into the practicability of using some indigenous materials for trough building, so saving the expense of importing more costly substitutes. In the same way, native aggregates should be pressed into service whenever possible. The majority of barren places contain an abundance of arenaceous and lapideous media, while in volcanic regions pumice and scoriae are plentiful. In the south Pacific, coral rock, suitable for crushing, is often to be had merely for the taking. In towns, there is generally a good stock of cinders. Other areas are well supplied with vermiculite, river gravel, charcoal, or similar substances, which make good substrates.

Markets and supplies

The question of markets is an important one. It is obviously useless to grow large crops of flowers and vegetables in an isolated place where no substantial local demand exists, unless there is a good service available to transport the produce to distant potential consumers. For this reason, care may have to be taken to locate hydroponica in the vicinity of centres of population, except, of course, in the case of military units, or those intended to meet specific needs like the provision of fresh greenstuff to industrial sites, oilfield personnel, or arctic explorers by air or other means. When a favourable site is selected in a desert area of equable climate, isolated in itself, but provided with fast air or ground communications, however, the grower can market his high grade crops with a minimum of delay. Vital as the efficient delivery of produce to the consumers is, it is equally important to ensure that a site is accessible for the import of regular supplies of nutrients and other requisites. Finally, the prospective hydroponicist should make certain, before embarking upon any scheme of development, that all essential apparatus and equipment will be obtainable at reasonable prices, which should include transportation to the place of operations.

Judging sites

Each site has to be judged individually. Many problems may arise, depending upon the topography, climatic conditions, materials available, and other factors. These call for thorough evaluation before any engineering or constructional work is actually commenced.

Many unusual, but satisfactory, sites have been suggested for hydroponic farms and gardens. J. S. Newman, of Rissington, near Napier, in New Zealand has spoken of the merits of the pumice areas in that country. Commenting upon their possibilities, he says: 'Pumice is a warm porous material, rich in potash. Pumice and sulphur are responsible in New Zealand for making a tree which normally takes seventy years to attain full growth, mature in twenty-five years. This is *Pinus radiata*, the new-found wealth of New Zealand. Underneath the pumice land is thermal steam, making a natural hot house. Hydroponics on this land combined with sunlight are all that are needed to grow anything anywhere at any time.' Another grower, living in Guildford, Surrey, England, who started some small experiments in soilless cultivation in 1956, has described his early beginnings as follows: 'I commenced growing in a disused aquarium, 60 centimetres by 30 centimetres by 30 centimetres deep, having drilled five holes, each 0.75 centimetre in diameter, for drainage in the base. It is proving very satisfactory for plants, and I had excellent results with tomatoes and a melon.' Later on, this amateur built troughs on the staging around his greenhouse, at a height of 0.75 metre from the ground. The Ahmedabad Municipal Corporation, in India, completed in 1955, a new museum building, designed by the well known architect, Le Corbusier, with a large top terrace specially constructed for hydroponics. This public terrace is intended for the instruction and entertainment of visitors. It is waterproofed and the beds are made of concrete.

At Gurutalawa, Uva Province, Sri Lanka, the soil is rather acid and has very little humus. The headmaster of St Thomas's College, Gurutalawa, which maintains a farm in that area, has recorded this description of the site: 'It might be a suitable place for trying to see if a better yield could be obtained by using hydroponic beds. The elevation is 1300 metres above sea level, and the area is in the up-country dry zone. The annual rainfall is less than 1500 millimetres, and it falls mainly in November–January, with some heavy thunder showers in April. Much of the year is very dry, and all water for cultivation has to be drawn from wells . . . river sand and broken road metal may be obtained for filling the beds.' Garden Produce Ltd., of Dar-Es-Salaam, Tanzania, sited their first units in a coconut plantation, which provided partial shade for salad crops, like lettuce.

An enterprising Rhodesian farmer, of Bulawayo, adopted a very ingenious way of siting his hydroponicum. He says: 'I built my house in difficult soil and to get good foundations I went down nearly 3 metres. I converted this into a basement with a suspended floor, so that I now have an area of over 150 square metres with a clearance of 2 metres and no pillars to worry me. This basement is wired for both power and light and ventilation is provided by slots in the walls above ground level. The outside walls of the house are cavity ones, and weep holes allow the basement air to go up through the cavaties to the roof. I have a big home-made ventilator in this and as the roof is made of iron sheets it acts as a gigantic pump. The result of all this is that the basement is always sweet and fresh, and has an annual temperature range of from 20° to 22°C. I had the idea that I might put a 4.5 metre apron around the house, and convert both it and the basement area into a hydroponicum. The basement would be frost free, and enable me to grow out-of-season crops. I would need some form of artificial light . . . I am most interested in early potatoes, lettuce, tomatoes, water cress, various bulb flowers like hyacinths, chrysanthemums, and possibly roses.'

General preparation

Out-of-door sites should be thoroughly cleaned before any constructional work is started. All undergrowth shrubs, tall herbaceous plants, and rubbish of every description should be cleared away. Trees must be thinned out, except where they can constitute wind breaks, as they tend to cause etiolation of some crops. Native vegetation is always undesirable when located too close to the site of any soilless culture installation. It often serves as a source of disease infection, and it may harbour destructive insects or vermin. The immediate vicinity of hydroponica is best cleared of all undergrowth for a distance of at least fifteen metres. The site may be levelled by means of a grader. Where the ground is dusty, a layer of gravel about 2.5 centimetres thick can be spread over the area. This will prevent the occurrence of spiral dust columns caused by wind erosion or whirlwinds in hot areas. Alternatively, it may be planted with some type of low, creeping grass, such as *Cynodon dactylon*. The direction of the prevailing winds should also be studied, with a view to the erection or planting of shelter barriers or belts, if necessary.

When converting greenhouses to soilless culture, it is absolutely essential to thoroughly cleanse and fumigate all parts of the structure prior to installing the hydroponic troughs. Any woodwork should be freshly painted, and any debris or rubbish removed and burnt. Hydroponic sites should be kept spotless and free from dirt.

CHAPTER 5

Layout

A convenient and well designed layout is essential, if any group of hydroponic units is to work efficiently and economically. It must always be borne in mind that labour charges can be the single biggest item in any commercial grower's budget. Although labour requirements in soilless culture projects are far lower than they are in conventional agriculture or horticulture, they may still account for as much as 50 to 60 per cent of the annual production costs. It is therefore imperative that installations should be planned to permit a very wide spreadover of the wage factor. This is particularly significant in the case of highly paid technical personnel, employed in supervisory capacities. The larger the area and the greater the number of units that can be brought under the management of one trained individual, the lower will be the expense per tonnage of the fruits and flowers grown. Consequently, every effort should be made to incorporate in the original design of any installation all the latest labour-saving devices, dependent, of course, upon the finance available.* The engineering of hydroponica presents many problems, the details of which have to be solved in terms of the site in question. A wide variety of plans has been proposed, following from the results of careful studies carried out on existing field installations, which may serve as a general basis for the preparation of designs for new layouts. In all cases, however, allowance must be made for local conditions, which will often necessitate a number of modifications or adaptions, depending upon the topography of the site selected, the materials available for constructional work, and several other factors. Work study methods may be applied with advantage.

The basic parts of a hydroponic installation consist of:

    (a)   the propagation section,
    (b)   the main bed section, and
    (c)   the service buildings.

---

*This would not, of course, apply in regions where the object of hydroponic development may be primarily a social one and where the need is to utilise plentiful manual labour, rather than machinery.

Propagation section

The purpose of this section is to produce small plants for eventual transfer to the main bed or trough area, where they will mature as the finished crop. Although some kinds of seeds may be sown directly in the main troughs or containers, by far the greater number do better when germinated separately in propagation boxes, from which the young seedlings are transplanted to permanent positions at the age of about four to ten weeks in the case of most vegetables or flowers, and longer for cuttings and

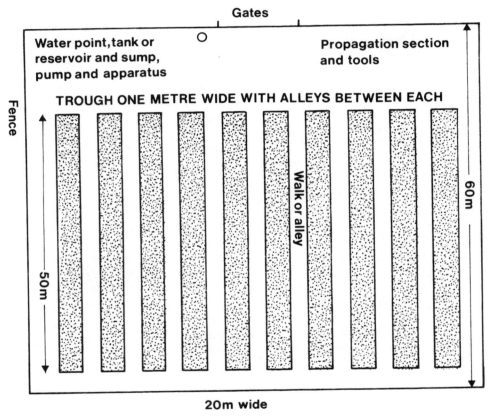

FIG. 12.
Typical layout for open-air hydroponic unit.

shrubs. Tomatoes, in particular, develop a better root system as the result of transplanting. It is also possible to cull more easily if germination has taken place in propagation boxes, and thus ensure that only the best seedlings form the eventual cropping stand in the main beds.

As a general rule, the total bed space of the propagation section should be 3 to 4 per cent of that of the main troughs. This proportion provides an adequate area for keeping the installation continuously supplied with young plants. Shade is essential in the tropics for shielding the surface of the growing media from excessive or scorching sunlight. In dull, cloudy regions, artificial protection from cold, and artificial illumination may be practised with advantage.

The propagation section of any large installation should constitute a self-contained unit, situated adjacent to the main troughs, in a convenient and sheltered spot. In greenhouses, it can be easily located upon one or other of the benches. Propagation beds should whenever possible be raised above ground level. This saves much time and trouble, since it avoids any need for kneeling or stooping during the routine operations of watering, transplanting, and seeding.

Main bed section

The main troughs should be grouped into a series of conveniently laid out units. Several plans have been successfully proposed for the economic operation of soilless culture installations. The United States Army uses as its standard growing unit a set of ten troughs, each about 100 metres long by 1 metre wide. Individual beds are divided into three sections on three separate elevations, the first of which is about 40 metres long, the second 33 metres, and third 27 metres. A ten bed unit occupies approximately one quarter hectare of ground. Any number of units may go to make up one installation. In glasshouse commercial work, troughs may be erected upon existing benches. Often five to ten beds, each 33 metres long by 1 metre wide are operated as one unit. The usual walks are provided between the rows of troughs. The Lago Oil and Transport Company's experimental unit at Aruba consisted of nine beds, each 33 metres long by 0.75 metre wide with a depth of 17 centimetres. The Klotzbach* flume, upon the original design of which are based many of the Miami hydroponic gardens, envisaged a section of up to one hundred troughs, each some 33 metres long by 1 metre wide and having a depth of 18 centimetres, served by an open conduit with a depth of 26 to 30 centimetres and a width of 26 to 35 centimetres.

Growers using the Gericke method of water culture often favour narrow troughs or basins. Widths of as little as 26 centimetres have been used successfully, with lengths

---

*Named after the inventor, Carroll Klotzbach, of Kendall, Florida, U.S.A.

of from 8 to 33 metres. The depth of these tanks should be not less than 15 centimetres nor greater than 20 centimetres. The advantage of having narrower beds lies in the fact that it may be easier to attend to the plants, but against this facility it may be quite rightly argued that there is inevitably much wastage of room, as well as the need for more construction materials to set up a given area of trough space.

For the experimental cultivation of azaleas in a vermiculite aggregate, S. F. Cort-vriendt and R. de Groote, at the Station de Recherches de l'Etat pour l'Amélioration des Plantes Ornamentales, at Ghent, Belgium, have employed a very interesting layout, consisting of a series of separated troughs, irrigated by means of a subterranean piping system. The principal advantage of this design are listed as follows:

(a) Uniform irrigation of the plants' root systems. In effect, the level of the nutrient solution remains the same throughout all the troughs (on the principle of communicating vessels);

(b) The system of application and drainage is simple;

(c) The rhythm of nutrient utilisation and aeration can be controlled easily;

(d) The substrate or aggregate is kept at a high level of oxygen content;

(e) It is not difficult to exclude any single bed from the operation of the system as a whole, which is particularly useful when special distinctive crops have to be grown with different requirements in nutrition.

During the winter of 1946, the Horticultural Station of the University of Reading converted the whole of one glasshouse, measuring 33 metres by 7 metres, to soilless culture. In the middle of the house, six sub-irrigation tanks were constructed, 8 metres long by 1 metre wide with a mean depth of 16.5 centimetres in each case. On the western side of the house, which falls 68 centimetres in its length, three pairs of sub-irrigation troughs were installed, arranged to operate in cascade, while on the eastern side two sand culture beds each 30 metres long by 1 metre wide and 20 centimetres deep were positioned. A rather similar conversion was made at the Kent County Council's Glasshouse Demonstration Station at Swanley, England. There, four beds for sand culture and four for sub-irrigation, arranged in two series of four beds (two sand and two sub-irrigation alternately in each series) were built in 1945 in a greenhouse 33 metres by 8.5 metres. Each trough measured 13 metres by 1 metre. They were constructed *in situ*, with centre channels for drainage. At Winkfield, England a large-scale experiment was carried out using sand beds, 50 metres long by 1 metre wide by 14 centimetres deep, using the surface watering method. Yields of good quality carnations and tomatoes were obtained.

On the Tanzanian coast, troughs of 90 metres long by 1.5 metre wide have met with favour. These are sunk in shallow trenches below ground level so as to check evaporation during very hot periods. In South Africa, a scheme has been designed for arranging the beds individually, each trough constituting a separate unit, of 16 metres in length by 1 metre in width, with a basal slope of 5 centimetres in 16 metres. At the higher end, a drum is placed fitted with a tap to open directly onto the bed. This container holds the nutrient solution. Sunk into the ground at the lower end is another drum, which acts as a sump for seepage. The solution drains through the growing medium and is periodically returned to the feeder drum by manual handling. A variety of troughs were built during the first trials conducted at Umtali in Rhodesia, including three of 16 metres by 1 metre, one of 13 metres by 1 metre, and one of 8 metres by 1 metre. All proved satisfactory.

In Bengal, especially in the mountainous Himalayan foothills of the Darjeeling district, terraced troughs built along the contour lines of the steeper slopes have given excellent service. Such beds are eminently suited to undulating districts. It is always advisable in hot, tropical areas, to site units upon a North-South axis. This alignment greatly facilitates the effective shading of plants from the scorching rays of the noon-day sun. In temperate zones, care must be taken to position troughs in places where good light is readily available, unless, of course, artificial illumination is to be provided. Where strong air currents exist, it is best to arrange for the beds or tanks to run parallel to the direction of the prevailing wind.

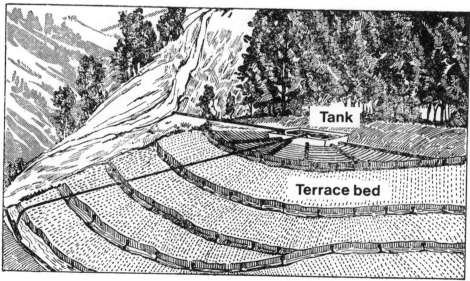

FIG. 13.
Hydroponic terrace cultivation in hilly area.

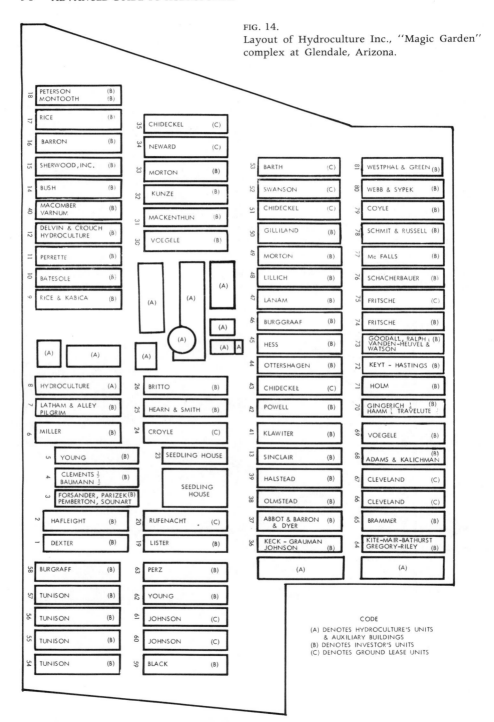

FIG. 14.
Layout of Hydroculture Inc., "Magic Garden" complex at Glendale, Arizona.

CODE
(A) DENOTES HYDROCULTURE'S UNITS
    & AUXILIARY BUILDINGS
(B) DENOTES INVESTOR'S UNITS
(C) DENOTES GROUND LEASE UNITS

Perhaps the largest single hydroponic trough to exist was that installed at the farm of Flager Hydroponics Inc., Miami. This covered an area of 1000 square metres, and regularly yielded $10,000 (in the 1950s) worth of tomatoes every $3\frac{1}{2}$ months. Vita-King Farms at Hypoflux in the same State averaged one tonne of tomatoes per crop from each of their 50 metre beds. Plants in these units came to maturity in 70 days, as against 160 days for ordinary soil cultures. The fruit was definitely tastier, and fetched higher prices at the local grocery stores.

As economy of space is usually an important factor in hydroponic installations, the walks between individual beds should not normally exceed 0.75 to 1 metre in width. These are probably the most convenient dimensions for passageways: 0.50 metre may be too narrow for the movement of barrows and other appliances.

Whatever shape or style of layout is eventually chosen for the main bed section, it should be tailored to fit existing circumstances. On rocky ground, terraced beds will no doubt be the most suitable, while on flatter land square or rectangular designs are the best. In many cases, however, the grower may find that it is necessary to compress his units into the most awkwardly shaped places, which calls for the exercise of considerable ingenuity and engineering skill. In particular, the layout of roof units and gardens often demands much care and attention, and it is frequently advisable in such circumstances to ask the advice and aid of an architect, to ascertain with certainty that the building in question will bear the extra weight of the hydroponicum. For home units, no such elaborate precautions or layouts are needed. Any amateur can, with the exercise of a little imagination, design for him- or herself, very satisfactory and attractive troughs.

Service buildings

A big commercial installation requires service facilities for the storage of tools and equipment, the washing, packing, and despatch of produce, a laboratory, and an office. Where certain types of mechanisation are employed there should also be a garage for the tractor and implements.

The storage room should contain sets of shelves, and racks, for the reception of hand tools, buckets, watering cans, hosepipes, and other equipment. Additionally, dry bins will be needed for keeping fertilizers in, as well as a table for the weighing scales. This room must be well constructed to prevent rain from spoiling the nutrient salts and the apparatus. The washing and despatch shed should be fitted with proper workbenches, and a large sink, consisting of two or more tubs having separate water connections and drains. Provision should also exist in this department for the writing of labels, and the grading of fruits and flowers. The laboratory should be well lighted and ventilated, with an average floor area of about 33 to 36 square metres, though this will vary with the size of the installation. Bench space, shelves, and cabinets are essential, together with the usual acid-resisting sink and a draining rack for drying glassware. In the tropics, it is desirable to instal a small refrigerator for the storage of seeds and chemical reagents. Further details of the equipment and apparatus used for hydroponic laboratories will be found in Chapter 22 of this book. Office space of about 30 square metres is generally adequate for most installations. A desk, typewriter, shelves for reference books, filing cabinets, and a table will be needed, together with the normal amount of stationery. Any garage for transport or service machinery should be equipped with a stock of fuel, and a set of servicing tools.

Construction materials

A very wide range of materials has been used for the building of hydroponics. In practice, nearly all the fittings and essential apparatus may be purchased as ready-made articles, but it is generally agreed that the construction of beds, sumps, solution tanks and reservoirs, windbreaks, and other major works, as well as the installation of pumps, pipes, and similar equipment may be best and most economically undertaken by growers themselves. Normally the choice of a particular material will be governed by its availability and price. Local supplies should always be utilised, whenever practicable, since they are likely to be far less costly.

CONCRETE.   This is one of the most satisfactory and durable materials for the construction of troughs, flumes, tanks, or sumps. Dense, smooth surfaced concrete can be moulded readily to any desired contour. It is permanent, and does not deteriorate if properly treated with asphalt. Because concrete is calcareous, it reacts with the acidic components of the nutrient solutions, making it difficult to control pH and phosphate level in the beds. Thus all interior concrete surfaces should be well coated with asphalt.

Three types of asphalts are commonly available, often under various trade names. These are: hot asphalt, cut-back asphalts, and asphalt emulsions. Hot asphalt should only be applied to completely dry concrete, at a temperature of about 204°C after the surface has first been primed with a cut-back asphalt. Waterproofing can also be carried out by the use of cut-back asphalt alone. Here, the mixture consists of a petroleum asphalt dissolved in petrol (gasoline) which does not contain any toxic substances like tetra-ethyl lead. As for hot asphalt, cut-back asphalt must be used on dry concrete. It will not adhere to moist surfaces. Asphalt emulsions, made up of petroleum asphalts dispersed in water by means of a non-toxic emulsifying agent, are available as concentrated pastes. Before use, they should be mixed with two parts of water to each part of paste. They adhere well to damp concrete surfaces.

Concrete troughs will require two coats of asphalt, the first, or prime coat being applied very thinly, so that it may penetrate the pores thoroughly. The second painting should be heavier. Normally from $4\frac{1}{2}$ to 9 litres of asphalt mixture will cover 11 square metres of concrete, depending upon whether the surface is rough or smooth.

ASPHALT MACADAM.   Beds can be made quite cheaply from a macadam prepared by mixing hot asphalt with sand or some other fine aggregate. While still hot, the mixture should be cast into beds in much the same manner as concrete is poured. Dry aggregate is essential for the preparation of macadam. The best proportions are three parts of aggregate to one part of asphalt, heated to a temperature of 176°C.

PREFABRICATED BITUMINOUS SURFACING.   Commonly known as PBS, this material is made of burlap, or some similar fibrous substance, saturated with asphalts. It is tough, flexible, and waterproof, and is supplied in rolls about one metre wide. The best technique for using PBS is to first form the sides and ends of the beds by setting-up frames of 18 to 20 centimetres wide boards on the selected site. These are secured in position by stakes driven into the ground along their length, at intervals of 0.75 to 1 metre. The surfacing is then nailed to the top edges of the boards, and shaped to the required contour of the inside of the troughs. Where the strips meet in the middle of the beds, the overlap may be sealed by mopping with hot asphalt, asphalt paint, or petrol. It is also advantageous to give all surfaces a protective coating of asphalt after the beds have been completed.

METAL.   Both aluminium and sheet (galvanised) iron are quite suitable for trough building, provided they are given a thorough coating of asphalt paint before use. Galvanised buckets or baths also require this treatment. Water culture trays are usually made of one centimetre diameter wire mesh.

WOOD.   Although comparatively cheap, and easy to work, wood is liable to rot unless properly treated when employed in bed construction. Good woods are cypress, oak and California redwood (*Sequoia gigantea*). For small household units, however, which may be regarded as expendable, and are in any case easily replaceable, wood is ideal. Two coats of asphalt paint will preserve such installations indefinitely. For preventing deterioration of wooden posts and stakes in tropical areas, creosote is excellent, but it must not be applied to the inside of beds.

ASBESTOS.   This substance, and its derivatives, like asbestos-cement materials, have excellent trough building properties. The sheets can be cut in the same manner as for wood, provided that care is exercised. It is also possible to purchase prefabricated asbestos-cement troughs or basins.

STONES.   Practically all types of shaped and dressed stone are suitable for bed construction. Stones should be placed end-to-end and firmly joined with mortar or a good plaster.

BRICKS.   Many kinds of bricks are obtainable, including soil-cement and sand-cement blocks. Both these last named are easy to make in a brick-making machine, which will turn out from 3000 to 6000 blocks per diem. Such blocks are best made at the site of operations. No burning is required, and the machines work entirely by top and bottom pressures.

GLASS.   Glass jars are used in laboratory water cultures, and they are also very satisfactory for home units.

ROOFING FELT.   Provided this material is handled with circumspection, owing to its fragility, and is supported by wooden battens, or shaped to fit beds sunk below ground level, it can be successfully employed for hydroponic work. Linoleum is also satisfactory.

PAPER.   Stout paper, or old paper sacks, if well coated with asphalt, and supported by a solid surface, will make serviceable temporary beds.

PLASTICS.   Many forms are available, and all may be used in soilless culture. For the growth of algae, polyethylene bags or other containers are often employed. Plastic and butyl rubber sheeting make excellent trough liners for general hydroponics or for making nutrient film layflats.

EARTHENWARE.   A number of forms of earthenware, including pottery, china and porcelain (old sinks), and tiles, are suitable for bed making. Ordinary plant pots come within this category of materials. Native earthenware is often very porous and may lose water fairly rapidly.

ENAMELWARE.   Enamel basins make ideal tanks for small solution cultures.

PLASTERS.   Several mixtures of plasters can be prepared. One of the cheapest is that recommended in the Punjab for irrigation works. It can be easily made by unskilled persons.

METHOD OF MAKING NON-ERODIBLE MUD PLASTER
The following quantities of material will be required to cover an area of 28 square metres with a plaster 10 centimetres thick:

> 3 cubic metres of earth,
> 1 cubic metre of sand,
> 54 kilos of cement,
> 240 kilos of straw or dried fibres,
> 10 kilos of sodium carbonate.

Dissolve the sodium carbonate in sufficient water to soak 240 kilos of straw, add the earth and work the whole up until it resembles dough. Leave this mixture for a week, working it up every day, and adding enough water to replace any loss due to evaporation. After seven days, the soil will have dispersed completely, and the straw will be well rotted. Then thoroughly mix the cement with the sand, and add the mixture to the other ingredients, working up the pultaceous mass to a suitable consistency, with more water if necessary. Use as soon as possible. Keeping the relative proportions constant, the quantity of the mud plaster can be varied to suit individual needs, such as the area to be plastered and the thickness of the walls. The plaster can be moistened with a gentle spray of water during very hot, dry periods. This improves its keeping qualities. This non-erodible mud plaster will last indefinitely.

ALKALI-PUDDLED CLAY.   Clay, treated with alkali and puddled to render it impervious to water, forms an inexpensive method of building troughs. Such beds must, of course, be either sunk into the ground, or if above the surface the sides will require some reinforcement. To the ordinary mixture of sand and clay used for puddling, a little soda ash should be added.

COMPOUNDED MORTAR.   This is prepared in the following way:
Mix 4 cubic metres of unscreened coal cinders with 1 cubic metre of slaked lime. To these ingredients add 180 litres of unrefined brown sugar solution (specific gravity 1050), and 90 litres of silicate of soda solution (specific gravity 1050). Mix the whole lot well, using a further quantity of plain water, if necessary, to produce the right consistency for plastering or brick-making. The specific gravity is determined by a Baumé hydrometer. $\frac{1}{2}$ kilo avoirdupois of unrefined brown sugar in 18 litres of water usually gives the required specific gravity. The more lime and molasses are used, the greater will be the eventual hardness of the cement or blocks. Blocks of this material make good hydroponic beds.

MISCELLANEOUS.   Other materials that have been used in, or have possibilities for hydroponic construction work, include many kinds of metal, especially those which can be easily shaped, like tinplate; breccia; impregnated matting; parchment; oilcloth and oilskin; rubber sheeting; waterproofed ground sheeting or mackintosh; tarpaulin; lavas; coral rock; and similar substances. Various proprietary compounds are also available.

Care should always be taken to ascertain that any material proposed for the building of hydroponica does not contain toxic substances. In case of doubt, a thorough coating with asphalt paint is advisable before the beds are brought into use.

CHAPTER 6

Water culture

Installations for water or solution culture fall into three classes; first, those intended for laboratory research work; second, units designed to be operated by amateurs in home, garden, or suburban backyard; and third, large-scale commercial hydroponica built for competitive production. Although certain differences in constructional details, planning, and size, naturally exist between the various types of water cultures, depending upon the purpose for which they are required, the basic principles remain the same throughout, whatever the method employed. In most cases, the distinctions are merely those of size and amount of apparatus used, but in one or two instances the method in question may not be suitable for adoption on a large scale. It would, for example, be obviously impracticable to attempt to use standard jars in the market garden. Again, there is no need for the elaborate precautions of the laboratory to be copied exactly by householders.

Standard jars

Almost any kind of container is suitable for growing plants in water culture under household conditions. Glass jars, earthenware vessels, flower vases and pots, old sinks, metal buckets painted inside with asphalt emulsion, and similar types of receptacles can be used, provided they are watertight and do not leak. For laboratory trials, it is generally agreed that pyrex glass containers are the best.

Care should be taken to select cultural vessels of sizes in some manner relative to those of the plants it is intended to grow. If made of translucent material, jars must be painted a dark colour to exclude light from the roots. The top of the container is closed with a flat cork about 2 centimetres in thickness, which has been thoroughly impregnated and lightly coated with paraffin wax, applied when hot and allowed to cool, thus forming a water resistant surface. In the case of larger vessels, litter trays or covers of wood, asbestos, porcelain or similar materials can be used. One or more holes of sufficient size, depending upon the number of plants it is intended to culture in each vessel, should be bored in the cover, which can be made in two separate halves fitting tightly together, so as to facilitate easy placement or removal of seedlings. Experience has shown that holes of about 3 centimetres in diameter are the most convenient size

FIG. 15.
Conversion of an old sink for hydroponic cultivation. The wire mesh grid may be one centimetre gauge, and an air space of 5 to 7.5 centimetres should be allowed for between the base of the litter tray and the surface of the nutrient solution.

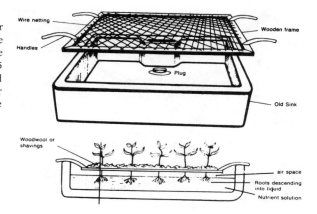

for general use. These are packed with pieces of ordinary cotton, which remains dry and becomes compressed as the stem enlarges during growth.

Various techniques have been devised for the aeration of static water cultures. The normal way is to replace or agitate the solution at regular intervals, but it is also quite practicable to insert a glass tube through a perforation in the cover, so that one end nearly touches the bottom of the inside of the jar, while the other protrudes about 5 centimetres into the open air. Using a bicycle pump, with a rubber connection affixed to the free end of the glass tube, or an aquarium aerator, air can be forced into the root zone of the culture whenever necessary.

Continuous-flow method

The essential parts of this apparatus consist of:

(a) The cultural vessel, holding the plant's roots, and ranging in size from about 2 litres to 9 litres. It must be watertight.
(b) The constant level reservoir, consisting of an inverted $\frac{1}{4}$ or $\frac{1}{2}$ litre glass jar, resting on a flat dish, and containing the nutrient solution.
(c) The siphon tube. This is made to an appropriate length, and has a bore of 0.5 mm.

The siphon tube is bent to fit over the edge of the flat dish, so that the short arm extends about 2 centimetres under the opening of the solution reservoir, when this has been placed in position. A notch should be filed in the edge of the reservoir to admit the tube. Tilting of the inverted jar will allow a certain amount of air to enter, so that the solution will flow into the dish until the opening is sealed. When the siphon is in operation, the level of the liquid in the dish falls gradually until this seal is broken,

5. Hydroponic floriculture. Anthuriums thriving in gravel troughs in the Netherlands.

whereupon more air enters the reservoir causing a fresh efflux of solution, thus re-sealing the opening. The fluctuation of the solution level in the dish is not sufficient, however, to cause any appreciable change in the rate of flow through the siphon; consequently the solution may be regarded as draining from an approximately constant level. A more rapid solution flow can be secured by using a larger bore siphon tube. These capillary tubes do not block or clog easily, but an occasional cleaning is necessary to remove sediment. The inlet tube, which is fitted with a small funnel at the top should be long enough to extend below the surface of the solution in the culture vessel, while the outlet siphon tube is bent in three places. The long arm of this last mentioned tube extends nearly to the bottom of the culture vessel, and it is possible by raising or lowering it to control the level of the nutrient solution in the container. The aerating tube is used for pumping air into the culture. Its bottom end should be ground to make a sharp angle with the direction of the bore. The apparatus needs a suitable support to hold the reservoir and dish at a height of about 10 centimetres above the culture vessel.

Drip method

This installation is virtually identical to the continuous-flow method, except that the inlet tube outside the culture vessel must be made about four or five times as long. In addition, a gap of some 10 centimetres is left between the bottom end of the siphon tube and the top of the funnel, for the purposes of aeration.

Plantanova

These outfits are marketed as complete sets, accompanied by the instructions for use. Essentially, they consist of a culture jar, with a specially designed cover, and an interior support for the roots.

Wicks

A container of any convenient size and type should be obtained, and fitted with a small tray having a perforated base. The wick, which can be either an ordinary cylindrical one, or else made from glass wool, must be of approximately the same length as the combined height of the container and tray together. It should be carefully shredded at the top after passing it through a hole punched in the bottom of the tray, so that it comes into contact with as many of the roots of the plant as possible. The body of the wick is allowed to dangle in the nutrient solution contained in the cultural jar. It is advisable to make the sides of the tray about 5 to 10 centimetres high, and if desired it may be completely covered in. Periodic renewal of the solution, and regular manual

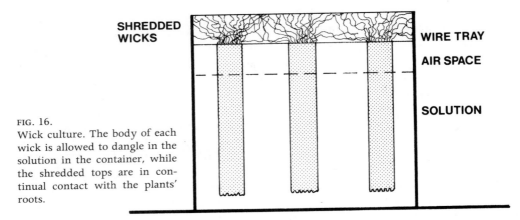

SHREDDED WICKS

WIRE TRAY

AIR SPACE

SOLUTION

FIG. 16.
Wick culture. The body of each wick is allowed to dangle in the solution in the container, while the shredded tops are in continual contact with the plants' roots.

aeration, are essential to encourage healthy growth. Wick devices can be purchased ready made.

Gericke tanks

The construction of a Gericke tank for hydroponics may be conveniently divided into three stages: (a) the basin, (b) the tray, and (c) the litter bed.

THE BASIN. Basins must be watertight and large enough to make frequent additions of solution unnecessary. The best depth is probably between 16 and 24 centimetres, while any desired length may be used. The question of width depends upon the personal preferences of the operator, and it may vary from as little as 30 centimetres to as much as 2 metres. In dry climates, where the relative humidity of the atmosphere is low, a greater depth of basin will be needed than would be the case in a damp area. A number of materials have proved suitable for basin constructional work, including concrete, sheet metal painted with asphalt enamel, plastics and hardwoods. For small home units, glass, glazed earthenware (china and pottery), and enamel bowls, have given good results.

THE TRAY. The framework of the tray must be strong and rigid, and if necessary, should be braced at the corners. Concrete, metal strips, wood, or wire mesh alone, are the materials most commonly employed for building trays. They may rest on the top of the tanks, or else be fitted into a recess previously provided. Where wood is used, 2.5 centimetre thick boards are the most satisfactory. The best depth for trays is not over 10 centimetres, while their length and breadth should correspond with the dimensions of the basins upon which they will be placed. The wire mesh on the bottom of the framework needs to be tightly stretched and well supported by cross pieces at distances of at least 50 centimetres apart to avoid sagging. It is often a good plan to make trays intended to cover very long beds of 30 metres or more in sections; this facilitates removal for cleaning. Nineteen or twenty gauge wire with one centimetre mesh is very good for general purposes, but for all-wire trays where the sides are also made of this material, 'hardware cloth' of 0.50 to 1.25 centimetre mesh is suitable. All galvanised surfaces should be painted with asphalt enamel.

THE LITTER.　A layer of straw, lignite or brown coal, dried grass, or excelsior, previously dampened, must be laid to a depth of 2.5 to 5 centimetres on top of the wire netting inside the trays. This should not be tightly packed, or else the roots of the plants will be unable to penetrate through it into the solution in the tank below. On the other hand, it has to be firm enough to prevent dislodgement of any loose material from the upper part of the litter bed. On top of the coarse bottom layer, a variety of substances may be used to form a further depth of up to 5 centimetres, materials such as wood shavings, chaff, short straw, dried leaves, fine hay, wood wool, peat moss, rice hulls, and coarse sawdust are suitable. The litter serves as the anchorage and cover for the plant roots, which are supported upon the wire base of the tray. It is kept moist at all times, and well softened with water before sowing or transplanting is attempted. It is always advisable to test new litters for possible toxicity before use by germinating a few seeds in the material in question, and growing them on for a couple of weeks. If healthy development ensues, the litter may be regarded as quite safe.

The litter in the tray should be level with the top edges of the framework, or about 0.50 of a centimetre below it. Exposed or untidy litter will tend to be carried away by wind. The packing of a litter bed is a skilled task, calling for the greatest attention to detail.

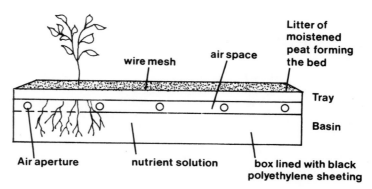

FIG. 17.
Construction of a Gericke-style water or solution culture tank, showing main features. Inexpensive units can be made by lining boxes with polyethylene sheeting. The cutaway portion shows root growth inside the basin.

Tanks need to be provided with sets of three regulating holes, 2.5 centimetres in diameter, at either end. These are fitted with plugs, preferably with screw heads. The lowest should be flush with the bottom of the basin, for drainage purposes, the second may be halfway up, while the third or highest should be 2.5 centimetres below the wire floor of the litter tray. These holes are used not only for controlling the level of the nutrient liquid in the basins, but also for adding extra solution from time to time, by means of a removable inlet pipe. In the Wroclaw technique, an adaptation of the Gericke method, extra aerating holes are placed around the sides of the tank. Apertures are also cut vertically through the litter bed to allow additional air to penetrate to the solution.

CHAPTER 7

Sand culture

The construction of units for sand culture may be divided into three phases:

(i) the preparation of the bed, trough, or container,

(ii) the provision of the growing medium, and

(iii) the positioning of the solution dispensator, if such contrivance is required.

BEDS. This term may be taken to include all the various types of receptacles and containers that can be utilised for small scale home installations, such as wooden boxes, flower pots, bowls, cut-down barrels and cans, drums, or other miscellaneous vessels. Numerous different materials have proved suitable for making sand culture beds or troughs. In big commercial units, wooden boards, asbestos, concrete, and plasters, have given excellent results. Galvanised metal must, of course, be painted with asphalt before use. Except with certain methods the containers or troughs need not be absolutely watertight, and in any case, a proper system of regular drainage has to be provided under all circumstances. The size of beds will, generally speaking, be conditioned by local requirements. In commercial installations, a width of one metre is the most practicable, accompanied by a depth of from 15 to 25 centimetres. If built upon greenhouse benches, troughs should be at least 75 centimetres above ground level, unless the grower prefers to have them on the floor.

GROWING MEDIUM. A sieve size-range of from 14 to 100 mesh is usually recommended for the sands employed in hydroponics. Beds filled with too fine media are liable to become waterlogged, with consequent lack of satisfactory aeration of the root system of plants growing in them. Sands with a uniform particle diameter of under 30 mesh should not be used alone, but should be mixed with a proportion of coarser materials. The mechanical analysis of the sand used during the most successful trials at Jealott's Hill Research Station (1938–1946) read as follows:

GARSIDE'S GRADE 2L	Sieve Size	%
	Mesh 10	1.51
	Mesh 10–20	20.45
	Mesh 20–30	24.24
	Mesh 30–40	34.09
	Mesh 40–50	9.85
	Mesh 50–80	8.35
	Mesh 80–100	1.51
		100.00

At Habbaniya, in Iraq, the sand available on the shores of the local lake contains approximately twenty-five per cent of material which grades out between 10 and 60 mesh, with a satisfactory percolation rate. In Aruba coarser sands have been employed with reasonable success, even those having a particle diameter of 1.5 to 3 millimetres. In such cases, however, more frequent irrigations are essential during hot weather. For practical purposes, it may be said that under most conditions, the growing medium used in sand culture should contain about 50 per cent of material under 30 mesh sieve size, with the balance made up of larger grains. Naturally, in cold, damp, climates, coarser sands of uniformly greater mesh give better aeration, since the evaporation factor is lower than it is in warmer regions. When used alone in tropical countries, coarse sands are liable to 'dry out' too rapidly.

It is important to ensure that sand growing media are of the same physical texture throughout. This is particularly significant when several types of sand are mixed together. Should an accumulation of very fine material be allowed to settle at the bottom of the bed, especially where this is not solid enough, a dry area will develop in the central root zone.

EXAMPLE OF BADLY MIXED
SAND MEDIUM USED WITH
THE SURFACE WATERING
METHOD

SAND SURFACE
_____

Wet Area 1.75 cm
— — — — — — — — — — — — —

Dry Area
— — — — — — — — — — — — —

Wet Area at bottom of trough due to an accumulation of very fine sand, with capillary attraction only back to dry area.
_____

GROUND SURFACE
(Base of Bed)

Improved drainage in sand cultures may be secured by placing a layer of 3 to 9-millimetre type gravel at the bottom of the bed underneath the sand. If any surface caking occurs, it can be checked quite easily by spreading a light covering of one centimetre grade gravel over the top of the growing medium. The addition of between 25 and 50 per cent by volume of peat moss to coarse sand improves moisture retention. Peat will also 'loosen-up' a very fine sand, and improve aeration in such materials.

Sand for use in hydroponics must not contain an excess of any toxic substances. For the special cultures designed to meet the needs of scientific investigators, silica or white quartz sand is the best. In ordinary soilless growth of crops, a wide variety of sands may be employed with success. It is, however, desirable, that the calcareous content should not exceed 20 per cent. If this is as great as 50 per cent, treatment with a concentrated calcium phosphate solution may be needed. The technique is as follows:

Dissolve 8 kilos of triple superphosphate $(CaH_4(PO_4)_2.H_2O)$ containing 45–50 per cent P_2O_5 in 4500 litres of water, and soak the sand with this solution by flooding the beds until the liquid stands on the surface of the growing medium. Wait until a rapid decrease in the phosphate content of the solution ensues. If all the phosphate is removed, add an additional amount of superphosphate, repeating if necessary, until a stable solution content of not less than 10 ppm is achieved. The liquid may then be drained off, and the sand used for normal cultivation purposes. In the event of the final concentration of the phosphate solution exceeding 125 ppm of phosphorus before it is discharged from the trough, the medium should be flushed through with plain water prior to planting up.

Sands with calcareous contents of very much over 50 per cent are rare in most areas. Their use in hydroponics can present some problems, but if no alternative media are available, a series of treatments with calcium phosphate solution may do a lot towards adapting them for soilless culture. However, nutrient solution variation for such cases has been evolved and is given in Chapter 13.

For general work, a quick test of the suitability of a sand may be undertaken by germinating a few seeds in a small sample of it moistened with water. If these develop into healthy seedlings, all should be well. The admixture of some peat moss helps to control any slight alkalinity. Certain fine media can be substituted for sand, notably pumice, scoriae, and rock dust. Coral sands improve with repeated croppings.

The detailed chemical analysis of a good sand used for hydroponic trials by Jealott's Hill Research Station is reproduced below:

GARSIDE'S GRADE 2L (LEIGHTON BUZZARD, ENGLAND)		%
	Water	0.14
	Silica	98.43
	Alumina	0.48
	Iron oxide	0.70
	Magnesia	0.14
	Alkalis	0.11
		100.00

SOLUTION DISPENSATORS.   In small household units, the solution is usually applied manually, with the aid of a garden watering-can fitted with a rose, and watering is done by means of a sprinkler attachment on the end of a hosepipe. Where dry salts are employed, a solution tank is of course unnecessary. Other methods, however, call for the installation of some type of dispensator, such as elevated tanks in which the water and salts are mixed prior to flowing by gravity or being pumped through headers onto the surface of the sand in the beds. Machinery has also been developed for the purpose of efficiently distributing the liquid nutrients. Storage tanks may be made of concrete or metal, painted with asphalt enamel, or glass carboys, enamel buckets; or large fuel oil drums can be utilised.

Surface watering (slop) method

Pots and small containers of various types are suitable for growing individual plants, using the surface watering method. In all cases, good drainage is vital, and care must be taken to ensure that the vessels are provided with one hole each, about 1.5 centimetres in diameter, in their bases. The aperture will need covering with a small piece of glass or broken crockery to prevent the sand from escaping. The seepage may be caught in a flat dish, which is periodically emptied. For larger units, troughs made from one or other of the different materials listed in Chapter 6 (page 96) are suitable. They should be at least 15 centimetres deep, and up to one metre wide, with a length suitable to the circumstances. Free drainage is essential. Where this does not occur naturally, as for example through the cracks and between the boards in wooden troughs, the beds will require sets of holes at intervals of a metre along the base.

In filling the containers with sand, it is desirable to leave a small gap of about 1.5 centimetres between the top edges of the sides and the surface of the growing medium.

---

6. *(Plate opposite)* Hydroponic trial unit in Urbana, Illinois, where research workers of the Agricultural Department investigate the effects of nitrogen on nodule formation in the root system of soyabeans.   (USDA).

New Jersey methods

(a)   The sand bed should be prepared in the same manner as for ordinary surface watering, with free drainage, and provision for catching the seepage, if it becomes troublesome. A storage tank for the nutrient solution, the size of which will be dependent upon the dimensions of the troughs it is to serve, is placed on a stand elevated to a height of about 0.75 to 1 metre above the surface of the growing medium. The tank is provided with a cover, and an outlet pipe at the base. This pipe is then led down the entire length of each bed in turn. Smaller channels lead out from the main conduit at intervals of 0.75 metre, connecting it with the surface of the sand in the troughs. By opening a tap at the junction of the main piping system with the solution tank, the liquid nutrients are allowed to flow by gravity onto the beds, where they percolate through the arenaceous medium and nourish the plants.

(b)   R. B. Withrow and J. B. Biebel introduced a modified technique which involves the substitution of an electrically driven centrifugal pump designed to force the nutrient solution through the pipes into the sand, instead of relying upon a gravity flow. In this case, the troughs must be watertight. After percolation through the growing medium, the solution drains from the beds and is collected in a sump, whence it may be returned to the storage tank. Apertures (of about 1.5 centimetre in diameter) to permit the efflux of the seepage have to be made at the ends of the troughs, and connected by short pipes to a conveniently positioned second tank, which can be sunk below ground level, and is usually a quarter of the size of the main one.

FIG. 18.
Sand culture unit. The growing medium is kept moistened and the plants are nourished by gravity feed from the tank or reservoir.

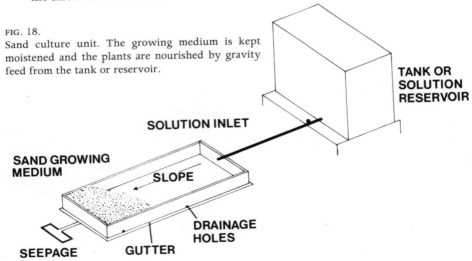

(c) Small units, especially window boxes, can be constructed from some watertight material, like treated wood or metal sheets painted with asphalt enamel. A reservoir for the nutrient solution is fitted at the top rearside of the unit, with a series of capillary tubes to deliver the water and chemicals to the growing medium. The bottom of the container is provided with four drainage slots, covered with wire gauze to permit the percolation of the solution into an enclosed sump affixed to the lower part of the box, after it has seeped down from the root zone. A rubber squeeze bulb, connected by tubes with both the reservoir and the sump, serves to circulate the solution twice daily. Oppositely placed check valves control the flow. Boxes of this type require reservoirs of a capacity of about 2.5 litres.

(d) Hand sprays, and similar appliances, can be employed to apply nutrient solutions to surface watered sand cultures. These may be purchased ready made.

Automatic dilution surface watering

Before the apparatus for the operation of this method is installed it should be ascertained whether a main water supply of relatively low pressure is available. Watertight beds are unnecessary, as the small amount of seepage is permitted to run to waste.

The essential parts of the installation are set up as follows. The main supply pipe is connected with a water meter, some of the water pressure being bypassed through a filter to the diaphragm of a small Autominor injection pump. This is attached to a 45-litre reservoir containing concentrated nutrient solution. The outlets from the meter and the pump are taken into a cylindrical mixing chamber fitted with a single opening valve leading to the spray line. This line consists of a pipe surrounding the bed where the plants are grown, and it is provided with spray nozzles at regular intervals. On opening the valve the pump is set in action automatically, and concentrated nutrient solution is forced into the mixing chamber in direct proportion to the flow of water through the meter. The stroke of the pump is variable. A suitable adjustment to give a dilution of 1 in 100 is satisfactory for most cases. Fourteen litres of diluted solution may then be sprayed onto a bed about 4.5 metres long by 1 metre wide by 20 centimetres deep in two minutes merely by opening and closing a single valve, the motive power being supplied by the pressure of the water main.

Under certain conditions where the water supply is deficient in calcium, it is desirable to have two injection pumps. These are needed because precipitation of calcium sulphate may occur if it is included in a concentrated solution made up for use in areas of soft water. Consequently, when two separate nutrient solutions have to be prepared in individual tanks, pumps are required to inject them simultaneously into the water in the mixing chamber at the correct dilution, so that the final liquid emerging from the sprays is of the same composition as it would normally be. The stroke of each automatic pump must be regulated to give a dilution ratio of 1 in 500 when two solutions are used.

Wicks

(a)   Two pots should be obtained, one of which is slightly smaller in size than the other. The larger vessel must be watertight, but the smaller one will need a hole about 2 centimetres in diameter making in the base. Fill the upper pot with coarse sand after inserting the wick through the aperture at the bottom. The nutrient solution is placed in the lower container, whence it is drawn up by the wick into the root zone of the plant growing in the sand.

(b)   Another way is to stand the pot of sand in which the plant is growing in a shallow bowl filled with glass wool moistened with nutrient solution. Part of the wool should be pushed up through the drainage hole in the bottom of the vessel containing the cultural medium.

(c)   For larger scale work, Geo. J. Ball Inc., have designed a method of watering greenhouse flats with wicks. These containers measure 40 centimetres by 60 centimetres and are constructed from wood. The wick descends from the sand bed through an aperture in the base into a bowl of liquid nutrients, placed under the raised trough. In bigger units, more than one wick may, of course, be used.

Drip method

The reservoir for the nutrient solution, which may be made from an old barrel, a metal tank, or some other watertight drum, should be slightly raised above the level of the bed. A feed line conveys the liquid from the reservoir to the surface of the growing medium. This pipe can be improvised from ordinary laboratory glass tubing, and it should have several outlets just above the surface of the sand. A sump must be provided to collect the solution as it percolates through the bed, and seeps out of the drainage holes. Watertight troughs are necessary, made from treated wood, asbestine materials, or concrete. At intervals, a pump can be connected to the sump and the reservoir for the purpose of returning the used solution from the former to the latter. Large scale drip method units are comparatively simple to instal. At Ohio State Agricultural Experiment Station, steel fuel oil drums properly asphalted inside have been employed as solution reservoirs. Attached to each large tank is a smaller secondary pressure regulating device, consisting of a 14-litre vessel fitted with a ball-cock (as used in water closets) and a valve. The header is made from 0.75 centimetre iron piping with 3-millimetre nipples attached every 0.50 to 0.75 metre. These outlets or jets deposit regular amounts of solution at the base of each plant stem. Drippers made of one-millimetre bore capillary glass tubing are affixed to every nipple by means of 5-millimetre rubber holders.

It is important to ensure that the delivery devices which exude the drips of solution are several centimetres below the level of the regulatory apparatus outlet pipe. Quite big units can be operated on the drip method, provided an efficient system of pipes is installed. The bases of the troughs can be slightly sloped to provide a fall of about 2.5 centimetres in 16 metres. This encourages the effective movement of the solution, after it has percolated through the sand, along the bottom of the beds until it seeps out from the drainage holes into the sump. To facilitate this flow, a line of half-round tiles may be laid under the growing medium to form a low drain.

Continuous flow method

A capillary siphon tube conveys the solution drop by drop from the reservoir to the surface of the sand in the culture vessel. Instead of glass piping, cord-siphons can be used. These consist of strips of surgical bandage or cheesecloth, twisted into loose cords, and coloured black with carbon ink. The rate of flow of the solution may be partially controlled by adjusting the width of the cord and the height of the reservoir above the culture vessel. Bandages about 2.5 centimetres in width are suitable for making cord-siphons. In case of clogging, the cloth should be sterilized with boiling water, and rinsed clean. The container for the growing medium has to be placed on a small stand, underneath of which is positioned a sump in the form of an enamel bowl to catch the seepage. Ordinary flower pots make good cultural vessels.

Modified slop method

Watertight troughs built of any suitable material are needed. The beds are fitted with headers through which the solution is pumped onto the surface of the sand from a reservoir sunk below ground level. After percolation through the growing medium,

FIG. 19.
Sand culture. Lines of half-tiles are laid under the growing medium on the bottom of the trough to facilitate the draining of the solution after irrigation.

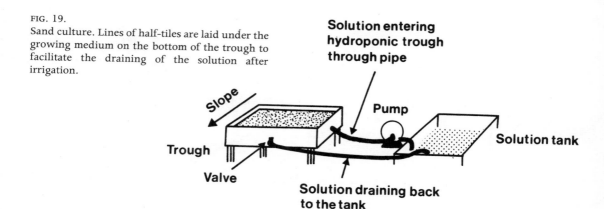

**Solution entering
hydroponic trough
through pipe**

Pump

Slope

Solution tank

Trough

Valve

**Solution draining back
to the tank**

the liquid flows from the beds back to the reservoir through an exit pipe connected with the drainage hole. The apertures for the seepage are placed at one side or end of the troughs, and lines of half-round tiles run down the slope of the bases of the beds to facilitate rapid outflow. Only one solution tank is needed, and a small pump. Each irrigation is thorough, and calls for the complete inundation of the surface of the sand. A fall of 2.5 to 7.5 centimetres in 16 metres is needed along the bottom of the troughs to ensure that the solution drains away fairly quickly.

Dry application

Watertight containers or beds are not necessary to the successful working of this technique. Natural drainage may be allowed through the cracks in the wood from which troughs are made, or by seepage from the plaster walls and base. Beds should be not more than one metre wide to permit easy spreading of the nutrient salts. Various manually operated and mechanical devices are available for speeding up the application of the chemicals, including hand sprinklers, hoppers, and travelling spreaders towed by a tractor. The dry application method has been used successfully at Ohio State University, in the Central Experimental Farm, Ottawa, and at the Royal Horticultural Society's Gardens, at Wisley, in England, as well as in many other places. Both small household units, employing pots and boxes, and large scale commercial type installations are easy to set up. Irrigation for keeping the sand constantly moist, and washing in the dry salts after spreading, is provided by hosepipes or stirrup pumps, in most instances.

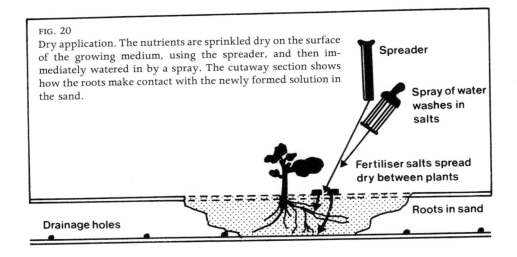

FIG. 20
Dry application. The nutrients are sprinkled dry on the surface of the growing medium, using the spreader, and then immediately watered in by a spray. The cutaway section shows how the roots make contact with the newly formed solution in the sand.

Spreader

Spray of water washes in salts

Fertiliser salts spread dry between plants

Roots in sand

Drainage holes

CHAPTER 8

Aggregate culture

The apparatus for aggregate culture is usually considered under ten main headings. These are:

(a) media;
(b) the trough or bed;
(c) the distribution tank for the nutrient solution;
(d) the sump;
(e) the irrigation conduits, piping, or flume;
(f) the drainage system, including the tiles;
(g) the pump;
(h) the motor;
(i) the time clock;
(j) the valves, compressors, or other special equipment.

Owing to the considerable variations that exist in the designs of the different methods of aggregate culture, certain of the items listed above are not used in some types of units. On the whole, the physical conditions obtaining in the growing medium are more exact under this system than they are in sand cultures. For that reason, care in the selection of aggregates is most desirable, and where necessary pre-treatment should be carried out methodically. To avoid any confusion, the constructional details of, and the essential apparatus for, each particular method are discussed separately under the heading of the technique in question, except in the case of media. An account of the building of installations for sub-irrigation will be found in the next chapter.

Media

Almost all of the naturally occurring, well-weathered aggregates may be used in hydroponics. Many suitable artificially prepared growing media are also readily available. In certain areas of low rainfall, local aggregates may contain soluble materials which are toxic to plants; consequently proper tests should be carried out on them before they are employed for soilless cultivation. The most direct and simple method is to germinate a few seeds in a sample of the aggregate that has been moistened with water. If the seedlings develop normally for two or three weeks without any signs of root injury, hard growth, or chlorosis, it can be assumed that the medium is relatively free from toxicity. Leaching of a suspicious aggregate with water may remove some of the undesirable substances. In doubtful cases, the preliminary trials should be extended to cover a period of at least one month. Porous aggregates are generally speaking superior to smooth ones for hydroponic beds. They have a higher surface volume ratio and therefore a better water holding capacity per unit volume. For sub-irrigation, aggregates should be well screened for particle size, hardness, and durability.

Alkaline media, like some kinds of cinders, calcareous gravels, coral, and similar substances should be treated as follows before use:

Add 225 litres of 5 per cent sulphuric acid to 4275 litres of water to make a five per cent solution by volume. Soak the aggregate in this liquid overnight. If the acid solution changes to an alkaline reaction, add more sulphuric acid, until it remains definitely acid for several hours. Then flush out the growing medium with plain water. To check the final result, take a few ounces of the aggregate, and place in a jar, adding enough distilled water to cover the media. Test the pH of the water after twenty-four hours with a Universal Indicator. If under 7.0 the aggregate will be suitable for use. In difficult cases, the treatment may be repeated several times.

Very acidic media may be improved by soaking them in a solution of lixivium for a day or two. 180 kilos of sodium hydroxide (lye) should be added to 4500 litres of water to form a 5 per cent solution for the treatment. The pH is best adjusted to about 6.5 or 7.0, and a final flushing with plain water must be given.

A large number of different kinds of aggregates have been utilised for soilless culture work. These include: crushed granite, broken rocks of various types, soft and hard coal cinders, volcanic cinders or lava, silica gravel, crushed limestone, crushed corals, broken bricks, charcoal, quartz gravel, plastics and substances such as polyurethane-foam, vermiculite of many sorts (proprietary preparations), burnt shale (haydite), leca, slate chippings, river gravels, and pebble phosphate rock, as well as other materials.

The particle size of aggregates, except in the case of farraginous media, usually ranges from 2 to 8 millimetres in diameter. Perhaps the best types have sizes of 3 to 5 millimetres. The relative percentages of the several sizes within a specific range is often important. In a 3 to 5 millimetres gravel, at least 50 per cent of the particles should fall in the 3 to 4 millimetres range, and the other half in the 4 to 5 millimetres size. The United States Army recommends 12 and 4 mesh screening of the aggregates used in its sub-irrigation units for propagation work, and in the case of main beds, the preference is for smooth relatively round aggregates up to 5 millimetres diameter, or irregular porous media of about 8 millimetres diameter. Nevertheless, the point is made that the ideal aggregate would be free of very fine particles below 2 millimetres in size or coarse chippings exceeding 4 millimetres grade.

Farraginous, or mixed, aggregates, such as have been extensively employed in

Bengal, East Africa, and other areas, consist of from three to five parts of coarse media (5 to 15 millimetres grades) blended with about one to three parts of sand or rock dust by weight. During trials conducted by the Royal Horticultural Society of England (1942–43) the following mixture of sand and gravel was found to be very satisfactory for carnation culture under southern British conditions.

SAMPLE OF SAND AND GRAVEL MIXTURE FOR SOILLESS CULTURE SCREENED WITH 30 AND 70 INSTITUTE OF MINING AND METALLURGY STANDARD SIEVES	Aggregate	Size in millimetres	%
	Coarse gravel	over 2	25
	Fine gravel	0.4–2	30
	Coarse sand	0.18–0.4	40
	Fine sand	under 0.007	5
			100

Another sample was made up of slightly different proportions, including 13 per cent of coarse gravels exceeding 2 millimetres in diameter, and 62 per cent of finer material less than 0.016 millimetre in diameter.

Although it is normally assumed that most growing media are inert, this is never strictly speaking the actual case. Some chemical effects of the aggregate upon the nutrient solution are often observable. It is therefore of more than academic interest to give some account of media that have been used successfully in different places.

CHEMICAL ANALYSIS OF GROWING MEDIUM EMPLOYED AT THE GOVERNMENT OF WEST BENGAL'S EXPERIMENTAL FARM, KALIMPONG			%
	Silica	SiO_2	60.65
	Alumina	Al_2O_3	15.98
	Oxide of Iron	Fe_2O_3	9.14
	Titanium Oxide	TiO_2	0.70
(Crushed rock ex-Himalaya Mountains)	Phosphoric Acid	P_2O_5	0.18
	Lime	CaO	1.50
Analysis on sample dried at 100°C	Magnesia	MgO	1.62
	Potash	K_2O	4.22
	Soda	Na_2O	1.65
	Loss of ignition		4.24
	Undetermined		0.12
			100.00
Soluble in 1% Citric Acid	Phosphoric Acid	P_2O_5	0.024
	Potash	K_2O	0.022
	Lime	CaO	0.045
	Magnesia	MgO	0.052

			%
WASTE ROCK FROM A LOCAL MINE, USED AT GEITA, TANZANIA	Silica	SiO_2	49.60
	Oxide of Iron	Fe_2O_3	33.70
TYPE: A ferruginous chert, with very small amounts of encased pyrite, siliceous and slightly felspatic. Crushed to 4 millimetre grade for hydroponic work.	Lime	CaO	2.80
	Also small amounts of Fe_2S, Sn, and I		

VERMICULITE (Latin, *vermis*, a worm)

This product is obtained from naturally occurring deposits in various parts of the world. It is classified as a hydrated magnesium aluminium silicate. The ore is laminated and is made up of two minerals, vermiculite and biotite. In the former, the scales are bonded together with water molecules, and in the latter with potassium. When the ore is heated to a temperature of about 1094°C., the water is converted into steam, which expands the material to from twelve to fifteen times its original volume. The resulting product is sterile, light in weight, highly absorbent, and retentive of water and air. These physical properties make vermiculite a useful growing medium for hydroponic cultivation. In addition, the available calcium, potassium, and magnesium are suffi-cient for seedling growth. The name is derived from the fact that when heated with a blow-pipe, the material curls into the shape of worms.

Various grades of vermiculite are available today. Fine mesh sizes are very suitable for seed germination and rooting of cuttings. pH is sometimes slightly acid, and occasionally on the alkaline side. There are some proprietary products with a guaran-teed pH, for example, Natkruit in the range 6.2 to 6.8 and Collite at 6.5. Others include Microfil, Exflor, and Vermicult.

FLORIDA PEBBLE PHOSPHATE ROCK AND DEFLUORINATED PHOSPHATE ROCK

Trials have been carried out in the experimental section of the United States Bureau of Plant Industry, Soils, and Agricultural Engineering, Beltsville, Maryland, with both these materials. It was found that six varieties of chrysanthemums were able to obtain sufficient phosphorus from the pebble medium to equal the growth of plants in gravel supplied with 15.5 ppm of phosphorus every two weeks. Development of plants in the defluorinated aggregate was inferior to that in the untreated phosphate rock. The phosphorus content of each solution was determined photometrically, using the amino-naphthol-sulphonic acid and ammonium molybdate method. The plants received no other phosphatic nutrients, apart from what they obtained from the rock aggregates.

The same two aggregates have also been employed successfully for the growth of antirrhinums and lilies.

EXPANDED PERLITE

This is a medium of low density (0.1) with excellent water holding properties, while at the same time it provides good aeration, if a coarse grade is utilised. Perlite is an acid volcanic glass with perlitic structure, showing little concentric spheroidal or spiral cracks between rectilineal ones.

EXPANDED PLASTICS

These materials possess light weight, have low transport costs, are free from virus or pathogenic agents, have insignificant microbial decomposition, and there is the possibility of expanding them on the site. On the other hand, they may not always provide enough support for plants, and offer poorer buffering capacity than natural rock aggregates in some cases, with flat pF curve and lack of adsorptive power, while they can be forced upwards during irrigation or become too waterlogged, depending on their behaviour when saturated. Consequently, it is necessary to employ such aggregates formed of expanded plastics with discretion, and only after careful observation of their performance. However, good results have been reported in hydroponics with these materials in many cases. Some types include:

> Baystrat expanded polyurethane flakes (made by Bayer);
> Hygropor, a mixture of expanded ureaformaldehyde and
> polystyrol with 70% open and 30% closed pores
> (manufactured by BASF);
> Styromull or polystyrol;
> These substances come in the category of foam-plastics.
> Similar materials are prepared by various firms.

LECA

Leca is a light expanded clay aggregate, produced by blending and bloating clay in rotary kilns. It was originated in Denmark in 1939. There are stated to be seventeen manufacturing plants producing this aggregate in various parts of the world. The material is spherical, tough and strong and will not compact. Coarse, medium and fine grades are available for plant growing.

MINERAL FIBRE FELTS, fibre-wool materials and several other artificial growing media have also been used in soilless cultivation.

QUANTITIES REQUIRED. The amount of media needed to fill hydroponic troughs depends mainly upon the types of aggregates employed. In the case of gravel cultures, approximately 38 to 40 cubic metres of 5 millimetres to 8 millimetres grade of growing medium will be adequate for a bed area of 210 square metres, allowing for a depth of from 15 to 20 centimetres. The weight of various aggregates differs greatly. For example, 70 cubic decimetres of vermiculite weigh only about $6\frac{3}{4}$ kilos, whereas an equal volume of sand turns the scale at about 113 kilos.

When setting up troughs, it is quite easy to estimate the total amount of any particular growing medium needed to fill them by first calculating the cubic capacity of the bed area, and then weighing one cubic decimetre or metre of the selected aggregate(s). The final figure, which will supply the required information, is arrived at after multiplying the weight of one cubic decimetre or metre of the medium or mixed aggregate by the number of cubic decimetres or metres in the unit.

Gravity feed methods

The bucket and gravity technique requires very little equipment for its successful operation. Small troughs of a convenient size, which must be waterproofed are set up in any suitable spot, preferably on legs raising them about one metre from ground level. They may also be placed on greenhouse benches, on window ledges, or on some other existing support. A drainage aperture of 1.25 centimetres diameter should be cut in the base of the trough, and a nipple inserted. The bucket, which if made of galvanised iron should be asphalted, is hung just above the trough on a hook. It is also supplied with a nipple and hole in the bottom. The two nipples are then connected by a length of hose or rubber tubing. When the bucket is filled with the nutrient solution

A. Gravity feed method.   FIG. 21.   B. Trickle feed method.

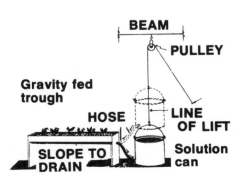

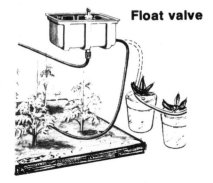

and secured to the hook, the liquid runs down into the aggregate in the bed. To drain the trough, the bucket is lowered to ground level, upon which the solution flows back into it from the outlet in the base of the cultural bed. The operation may be repeated several times a day. Units of this kind are especially suited to home conditions, and the operator can raise and lower the bucket without difficulty as he or she passes to and fro' during daily tasks. Small units, with beds measuring about 60 centimetres long, 46 centimetres wide, and 15 centimetres deep need a 13.5-litre bucket to hold enough solution for regular irrigations. Bigger troughs, with dimensions of 1.20 metres in length, 60 centimetres in width, and 18 centimetres in depth, will require a solution reservoir of about 54 litres capacity. Large reservoirs may be hoisted up and lowered by means of a rope and pulley arrangement.

Compressed air designs

These apparatuses are well suited to greenhouse culture and the carrying out of experimental trials with special plants. The equipment includes an air pump controlled by a time clock. A bleeder is made by placing a pinch clamp over a piece of 5-millimetre by 2-millimetre rubber tubing, almost closing the aperture. A small valve, similar to those used in laboratories on Bunsen burners, connected at the end of the main line, will serve as a further bleeder as pressure is released through the valve. There are air outlets for the various carboys, and as many as forty plots may be operated simultaneously. Each plot is 60 centimetres by 1 metre by 15 centimetres in size. The troughs contain half-tiles, a growing medium and a hose connection screwed into the front board. A 5-millimetre by 2-millimetre laboratory rubber tube, cut long enough to allow for complete removal of the rubber stopper and glass tubing from a carboy, is used for additions of water and nutrients. A 9-millimetre glass tube constitutes the main air line issuing from the pump. A 9-millimetre glass tee connected by a 5-millimetre by 2-millimetre rubber tube is joined to the main air line, also an 8-millimetre glass tube. The short piece does not extend into the solution, but the long piece extends to about 10 centimetres from the bottom of a 45-litre carboy. A No. 6 two-holed rubber stopper must fit tightly enough into the neck of the carboy to prevent any escape of air. A given level of nutrient solution is maintained in each 45-litre carboy. The solution level should be maintained at a point at least three quarters up the carboy, as some air space is necessary to keep the liquid from backing up into the main air line; furthermore, the volume of solution in the carboy at this point should be just sufficient to fill the size of trough mentioned to within 2 centimetres of the top. Pumping to this level inhibits the growth of algae on the surface of the aggregate. An inexpensive pump and motor, as used for paint spraying, is adaptable for providing a supply of compressed air. When the motor is in operation, compressed air is pumped through and pressure is built up in the air space above the solution level. This pressure forces the nutrient liquid into

7. Quartz gravel aggregate in hydroponics. Seedlings grown for experimental purposes by United States Department of Agriculture.
(USDA).

the long piece of glass tubing leading to the trough, thereby filling the bed. A time switch is a convenient device for regulating the period necessary to empty completely a carboy. Some pumps are so constructed that air will leak back through them, so dissipating the pressure. No bleeders are required in such cases, as the solution will drain back by gravity into the carboy.

As many as forty small troughs can be operated successfully with a paint sprayer motor and pump. About eight minutes are needed for pumping, and twenty minutes for complete drainage. If the pump is connected at the end of the series of forty plots, uniform pumping will not be obtained from all the carboys. Those nearest the pump will naturally empty first, releasing the pressure so that the remaining partially pumped beds will begin to drain immediately. In order to secure uniform pumping of all the plots simultaneously it is necessary to assemble the main air line from 9-millimetre glass tubing, 9-millimetre glass tees, and 5-millimetre by 2-millimetre rubber tubing. Bleeders are similar to those previously described. By diverting the air so that each series of ten plots receives approximately the same pressure, pumping is made uniform. As an alternative to this scheme of sub-headers connecting with a main header, the airline can be a larger pipe which contains as many 5-millimetre nipples as there are separate troughs. The area of the main air line must then be slightly greater than the total area of the sum of the air outlets. Air compressors operate at a maximum pressure of about 2.5 kilos per square centimetre. Cylinders of compressed air, which may be purchased, are generally filled at a pressure of about 130 kilos to the square centimetre, so if they are employed, regulating valves will be essential.

Troughs for use with 45-litre carboys or drums are built in the following manner. The bottom of the bed is constructed by placing two pieces of 2.5-centimetre by 30-centimetre by 1-metre timber side by side and nailing them to two other sections of 5-centimetre by 5-centimetre by 55-centimetre wood. These latter pieces prevent sagging of the bottom when the trough is filled with growing medium. The sides are then cut to fit on top of the base of the bed. A hole should be bored in the board that will form the front of the plot. This aperture must be flush with the bottom to permit complete drainage. The best diameter for the hole is about 5 millimetres, so that the hose coupling will fit securely into it. The sides must be nailed onto the base and to each other. Naturally the cross bracing pieces must be outside the trough on the bottom. Small 5-centimetre angle braces should be screwed inside at each corner about 10 centimetres up from the bottom to prevent the boards pulling apart when the trough is filled with aggregate. The bed is waterproofed on the inside only with asphalt emulsion. If the wood is warped or cracked, strips of muslin may be laid on top of the wet asphalt and thoroughly impregnated by the addition of more paint. Two coats are usually adequate. For greater safety, the cheesecloth may be placed behind the angle irons before they are screwed into place. Reinforced concrete can also be employed for trough construction.

Before the assembled trough is filled with aggregate, a half-tile is set in position on the inside bottom of the bed, in line with the hose connection. The purpose of the tile is to allow the solution to spread uniformly and rapidly throughout all parts of the trough, and prevent the entrance of the medium into the rubber tubing. Gauze can be placed at the open end of the tile. Perfect fitting of the tile to the base of the bed is undesirable – a slight space must be left to permit the solution to filter through. When all is completed, the trough is filled with aggregate, and the connection to the carboy made. Beds must be tilted very slightly forward to facilitate free drainage.

The successful operation of compressed air devices depends, first, upon balance of air pressure, and secondly, maintenance of proper water levels. Complete pumping of some plots while others are only partially full will result in a release of air pressure, and immediate drainage of all troughs.

Carboys made of glass must be covered with some dark material to exclude light. For larger units, 225-litre or similar sized fuel oil drums, made thoroughly airtight can be utilised. A pressure equalizer fitted to each solution container is a great help. As many as a hundred drums arranged in series can be operated from a big service air compressor. (See photograph No. 15).

Wicks

Wick devices for use in aggregate culture are similar in design to those employed in sand culture. Care must be taken to ensure that only fine grades of media are utilised for filling the receptacles in which the plants grow. Wicks are very suitable for home units.

The Flume

The construction of flumes demands a certain amount of attention to engineering detail, since they are laid out in most cases on open ground, and it is important to see that the flow of solution is smooth and regular. A flume is essentially a type of conduit or aqueduct which conveys liquid to the points where it is required from a central cistern or tank. Concrete is the best building material for use with these works.

The storage tank may be elevated or excavated or sited at ground level. No piping or valves are required, but a pump is essential, and in some cases a sump. The flume has an average depth of 30 centimetres and a width of up to 45 centimetres. Depending upon the length, a slope falling not more than 15 centimetres over the entire distance of the channel is built into the floor of the flume. The lower end should be adjacent to the sump or cistern, and the higher part at the limits of the conduit. Where the beds touch the flume, holes 10 to 15 centimetres in diameter are placed 5 centimetres above the base of the side wall. These admit the solution to the troughs as it flows along the flume.

Some conduits are covered to prevent foreign matter from entering the channels. Sluice gates or penstocks are installed at three points – at the junctions of the two flume sections, and in front of the solution reservoir or the sump. The middle gate controls the entrance of the liquid nutrients into the sump, or on their return after an irrigation, to the tank; the other two are responsible for regulating the solution flow into the respective flume sections. The opposite ends of the conduits should also have penstocks fitted so as to permit external draining when needed, in addition to periodical cleansing of the channels. Partial operation of any section may also be effected by fitting extra gates as desired at any point along the flume.

Any reasonable number of beds may be worked with one flume, depending upon the lay of the land where it is sited, and the size of the storage cistern. For practical purposes, about 100 beds are ample for one tank to handle. Smaller installations may, of course, be built. It is simplest to have the half-sections equal in size and layout to one another. A one hundred bed unit will require a flume of a total length of about 60 metres, allowing for approximately 27 metres in each half-section and some 3 metres for the outflow and drainage area in front of the tank. The individual beds should, in this case, each be 30 metres long by one metre wide by 20 centimetres deep. A lengthwise slope of about 7.5 centimetres is formed in the bottom, with the side walls on the level. This ensures that the troughs become progressively deeper towards the lower end by the flume. The centre of every trough is slightly lower than the edges to facilitate drainage. This forms a small channel, which is covered by a line of half-round tiles of 15-centimetre radius. This depression ends at the hole opening into the flume. Wooden plugs should be supplied to close these apertures when necessary. Between the beds, walks will be required. The whole apparatus of a one hundred trough flume unit will cover an area of nearly one hectare.

Where both a solution reservoir and a sump are used, the former should stand above ground level. If one tank or cistern both delivers and receives the nutrient solution, it should be of the subterranean type. In most cases the former scheme is to be preferred. For the sake of economy in building materials, the tank should be made to hold enough solution to fill a half-section of the beds at a time. Each section can be irrigated in turn. Either a self-priming centrifugal pump, or a sump pump, will be needed to operate the apparatus. Pumps delivering between 2250 and 5000 litres per minute are the best. The whole of the working of flumes can be quite easily automotivated.

Bengal method

The beds for use with this method may be made from any suitable and preferably inexpensive materials, provided they are not likely to prove toxic to the crops. The recommended width is one metre, while the height of the side-walls should be about 20 centimetres. They are filled with a growing medium, consisting of from three to

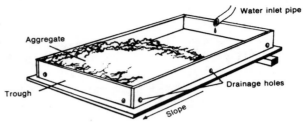

FIG. 22.
Bengal method. Standard type of trough, filled with mixed aggregate.

five parts of coarse aggregate, like gravel, broken bricks, crushed rock, or cinders, with which are mixed one to three parts of sand or other inert dust. These measurements are volumetric. Drainage holes 5 millimetres in diameter are built into the base of the sides of the troughs at intervals of one metre apart. The seepage from these apertures is caught in guttering fitted around the beds, and conveyed to a sump. Watertight troughs are not essential. Water is admitted to the beds by means of a system of inlet pipes spaced out at one metre intervals along the tops of the walls. Storage tanks for nutrients, pumps, and other apparatus, are unnecessary, since the formulae are normally applied dry, and in some cases are watered in with a hosepipe. Various machines have been designed to spread the dry nutrients on to the aggregate in the beds. The method lends itself to improvisation and adaptation to local conditions, and it may be used both in greenhouses, or in outdoor installations, depending on the climatic conditions, especially the temperature factor.

Vermiculaponics

This technique really means nothing more or less than the substitution of beds of vermiculite for the gravel or other aggregates which are generally employed. It is well suited to hot arid areas, owing to the good water-retentive properties of the growing medium. Three methods of operating vermiculite troughs have been suggested by M. Bentley of Glenhazel Research Station at Johannesburg. The first involves the use of a watertight container, fitted with a solution reservoir and a sump. The liquid nutrients flow through the bed, and are recovered for re-use. The second is similar to the surface watering method employed with sand culture; while the third technique calls for dry feeding of the fertilizer salts, with subsequent watering in.

The standard vermiculite tank for the flow through scheme is 15 metres long by 1.2 metres wide by 22 centimetres deep. The bottom of the bed is filled with a 2.5-centimetre layer of stone chips, followed by another 2.5 centimetres of river sand, and covered by 16 centimetres of vermiculite. Smaller troughs may of course be built, but all must be watertight. Beds can be constructed from steel sheets, precast concrete, cement blocks, hardboard, or ordinary brickwork. At either end of the trough, 20 or 22-litre drums are placed. One is elevated, but the other is sunk into the ground. The higher drum acts as the solution reservoir, while the lower is the sump. The solution flows by gravity onto the vermiculite aggregate, through the basal stone chips, and out from a drainage hole into the sump, whence it is manually returned to the reservoir. The whole of the inside surfaces of the apparatus are painted with two coats of asphalt emulsion or else lined with polyethylene sheeting. The base of a bed of this type should have a slope of 7.5-centimetres in 15-metres towards the sump end.

For the surface watering and dry feed techniques in vermiculaponics watertight troughs are not necessary. Surrounds must, however, be built to hold the aggregate in position, and to control the effects of wind and other hazards. The base of the bed should be as hard as possible, and may be supplied with a covering of roofing felt, plastic sheeting, asbestos, or some type of material that will check undue loss of solution. There is, of course, no recovery of nutrients with these techniques.

CHAPTER 9

Sub-irrigation

The sub-irrigation technique is, of course, basically nothing more than another type of aggregate culture. In its original form, the method was devised by R. B. Withrow of Purdue University as a means not only of securing greater technical control over the day-to-day nutrition of plants growing in soilless cultures, but also of substantially reducing the number of manual operations involved. As the name implies, sub-irrigation calls for the moistening of the root substrate from the bottom of the bed rather than from the surface. Uniform irrigation of all parts of the growing medium is secured, while the necessarily coarse aggregates that are used to fill the troughs ensure that adequate aeration is provided automatically, because the air in the voids is regularly replaced with the rising and falling of the solution level.

Although many styles of sub-irrigation installations can be built, there are only two general types of unit: *direct-feed*, and *gravity-feed*. The former is more suitable for small size units, while the latter is well fitted for large scale production. It also effects a saving in the dimensions of the pump employed and the energy required for its operation.

DIRECT-FEED TYPES. The nutrient solution is stored in a subterranean reservoir or sump, whence it is forced into the beds by a centrifugal pump, which is operated for a sufficient length of time to fill, or nearly fill, the troughs with the cultural liquid. At the appropriate moment, the pump is stopped, and the solution drains back by gravity through the pump into the reservoir. When air lift pumps are utilised the beds have to be emptied by opening a valve. The nutrients enter each trough through a drain in the bottom, which is loosely covered by a series of half-round tiles, or boards nailed together to form a V or U section. The same drain also permits the solution to flow back to the storage tank after the irrigation has been completed.

GRAVITY-FEED TYPES. Usually, each bed is divided into three sections on three elevations, each part being longer and a trifle higher than the one following. A small amount of the irrigating solution is retained by each section because of the removal of water by the plants and evaporation from the aggregate. The liquid enters the first part of the bed from an elevated tank. The flow is controlled by a valve between the reservoir and the upper bed section. As soon as the solution in that section has reached its proper level, the valve is closed, and a section drainage valve opened, permitting the efflux of the nutrients into the next part of the trough. In due time, it is once again transferred into the lowest section, and finally into an underground sump. A small pump is situated near to the drainage sump which should be capable of pumping the solution back to the main tank in about three hours. Sub-irrigation units of the gravity-feed type may be either open or closed in construction, and a number of different modifications have been used successfully, depending upon local conditions.

Ohio gravel design

This style of sub-irrigation was designed especially for the culture of ornamental greenhouse crops. Concrete troughs with a V bottom are considered the most suitable form of bed. The bench or trough should slope 2.5 centimetres in about 30 metres, although when an auxiliary pipe is used for inlets and outlets this is unnecessary, since the pipe can be slanted to provide good drainage. The sides of the trough should be between 15 and 20 centimetres in height. The bottom must be shaped so as to have a slope of 3 centimetres from the sides to the centre to form a V. If flat bottomed concrete beds are already in existence, they can be easily converted to sub-irrigation in the following way:

A form should first be made to fit within the bed. The insides of the trough should be well painted with asphalt emulsion to prevent the old concrete from binding with the new mixture. Drainage holes, if large, can be stuffed with muslin and asphalt. A dry concrete mix should be prepared from one part of cement with four parts of sand. After moistening, the wet concrete is placed in the bed and tamped roughly into the form of the modified V. To secure a smooth finish, the prepared form should then be pushed down into the concrete and moved backwards and forwards. A final smoothing with a metal trowel completes the job. To minimize the amount of water that may collect in the bottom of the V, a short length of 2.5-centimetre piping should be rolled to and fro in the V to make a notch or small depression. It is important to ensure that the thickness of concrete between the base of the V notch and the top surface of the old bench is at least 1.25 centimetres in depth, otherwise cracking may occur.

Wooden benches with bottom boards running across them can be converted for soilless culture by placing additional supports underneath to stop any sagging. The insides of the trough should be thoroughly clean, with level sideboards. For an all-wood bed, the joints must fit perfectly, and the staging be rigid. A lining of plastic sheeting will waterproof the bed satisfactorily. After construction, all kinds of troughs must be tested for leaks, before they are filled with aggregate. These can be effectually stopped by covering the cracks with muslin soaked in emulsified asphalt.

Tanks for sub-irrigation should be watertight, acid resistant, and of sufficient size to hold about forty per cent of the total volume of the troughs that they will fill. Concrete, hardwood, plastic sheeting or metal may be utilised as construction materials. Concrete reservoirs should be given an initial coating inside of sodium silicate, diluted one part to four of water, or of emulsified asphalt paint. Wooden and metal tanks will need asphalting. For troughs over 30 metres long, the tanks can be positioned in the middle of the greenhouse, so that the bench drains from each end to the centre. The beds can also be divided into sections for irrigation purposes, to avoid the expense of building very big cisterns. Black iron pipes should be used for the inlets. For a hundred-foot trough, one inlet of 2.5- or 3-centimetre pipe near the pump will be adequate, though better drainage may be secured by placing a separate outlet pipe under the bench or alongside. In the case of longer beds, more inlets may be required. The inlet into the trough should be flush with the bottom of the V and completely waterproofed. Valves for controlling the flow of the solution are fitted to the various sections of the inlet and outlet pipes, while a series of half round tiles, or inverted wooden V screens are used to cover the central drainage depression at the bottom of the bed. Small wedges should be placed between the tiles and the base of the trough, if needed, to facilitate seepage, any excessively large cracks or openings being covered with black iron gauze to prevent the medium from clogging the outlet channel.

A. Laurie and D. C. Kiplinger have recommended the undernoted pumps as suitable for small sub-irrigation units, operated on the Ohio technique. The aim is to ensure that the troughs can be filled in about thirty minutes, and drained out completely in one hour. The quicker the pumping and drainage are finished, the better will be the results.

Deming No. 4000–M–No. 1 Side Suction centrifugal pump. Capacity 14 litres per minute, 3 metre head. Grease cup lubrication on main bearing.

Deming No. 4602 Sump pump. Capacity 18 litres per minute, 3 metre head.

Gould 'Cid' Sump pump, No. 3151.

Myers No. 6101 Sump pump. Capacity 11 litres per minute, 3 metre head.

Many other manufacturers make pumps that are quite as suitable for the work. At least 15 centimetres should be allowed from the surface of the solution to the electrical box on all sump pumps for slopping of the solution when agitated.

Submersible electric pumps can be used for smaller units.

Automatic control of the number of pumpings per diem may be obtained by installing a time clock. Both the General Electric Company's Type T–27 time switch, single pole, single throw, 115V or 230V; or the Sangamo Electric Company's Type K–11 time switch (for a maximum of three pumpings daily), are quite satisfactory for use in hydroponics.

Purdue design

The constructional details of the Purdue University sub-irrigation units are not dissimilar to those of the Ohio installations. The solution reservoir is located at a level below that of the lowest section of the cultural troughs. In practice, this means a drop of about 22 centimetres from the bed to the cistern. Tanks may be situated at the ends of the troughs or underneath them. The pumping unit consists of a centrifugal sump pump, connected to the bed with piping, which screws into the nipple on the trough end, and so connects with the row of tiles lying loosely along the bottom of the inside of the bed. Troughs may be positioned above or below ground, according to local requirements. When several benches have to be pumped together, a manifold is constructed to equalize the pressure. In the large central type of manifold, the cross-sectional area should be slightly larger than the sum of the areas of the nipples. With step type manifolds, a 6-centimetre pipe forms the main tube, and is connected to the pump. The sub-manifolds are attached to the main line at suitable intervals. They are usually made from 3- or 4-centimetre piping. For the purposes of pressure adjustment, valves can be installed on the sub-header by the bed, as well as on the main manifold. There is, in addition, a by-pass line on the discharge side of the pump to allow the solution to flow back into the cistern or tank. This line can also be employed to regulate the force of the liquid entering the beds, and for mixing the nutrients in the reservoir. Discarded solution is run to waste along another pipe, fitted usually on the manifold near the beds. The normal valves are placed at convenient points on these pipes. The pump needs a large intake pipe to ensure efficiency of operation. With a 5-centimetre intake port, a 9-centimetre suction line should be fitted together with the proper reducers. An electric motor drives the pump through a direct flexible coupling, operated either by a time clock, or manually.

Mullard's design

Beds should be built of precast concrete sections jointed with hot asphalt, and with the interior surfaces coated with asphalt paint to ensure that the troughs are watertight. The solution tank is sunk below ground level, and pumping is effected by a centrifugal pump operated by means of a time switch. This can be started automatically. The nutrients are pushed up through the inlet pipes to the aggregate saturating it within 2.5 centimetres of the surface. At that point, a trip switch, working on about $\frac{1}{4}$ litre of overflow, cuts out the pump, and the solution then drains back into the reservoir by gravity through the pump system. No return pump is needed. The level of the bottom of the bed falls towards the pump end. At Jealott's Hill Research Station, a slope of as much as 5 centimetres in 4.5 metres was employed. Several troughs can be worked from a single solution tank. The automatic switch has to be re-set after each irrigation by emptying the overflow container.

S. R. Mullard has also designed a sub-irrigated window box, for use in small household installations. This consists of an expanded steel frame, lined with aluminium, and provided with a funnel for feeding of liquid nutrients, and a drainage channel.

Lago design

T. Eastwood, working in the West Indies, has recommended the open system of subirrigation under tropical conditions. The first experimental unit, built on Aruba, consisted of nine beds, served by a tank 13.5 metres long, 18 metres high, and 0.75 metre wide, holding about 225,000 litres of nutrient solution. The beds themselves were each 33 metres long by 0.75 metre wide by about 18 centimetres deep. The solution is permitted to irrigate the troughs by gravity flow after opening of the valves. Standpipes fitted inside the beds enable simultaneous flooding of the media in each to be carried out. After the filling of the troughs with solution, the 5-centimetre drain pipes are opened, causing the liquid to run into a concrete storage sump, whence it can be pumped back to the gravity feed tank.

C.P.I.M. design

This is a closed system, the original unit was built for the Shell Oil Company on the island of Curacao. The beds are fitted with automatic siphons, which discharge when the solution reaches a certain level in the growing medium. A centrifugal pump returns the nutrients from the reservoir-cum-sump to the inlet tubes and standpipes. The pump may be shut off automatically by means of a time clock, as soon as the beds are full. Drainage from one trough to another is accomplished by the siphon devices. Each siphon is made from 8-centimetre pipe, at the discharge side of which a small can is placed. The end of the siphon fits into this can, which remains full of solution during the siphoning period. It is the level in the can that determines the height at which the solution in the bed starts the siphon operating. This may be raised or lowered as desired by modifications in the can.

Side flumes

Instead of a series of tiles laid along the centre of a bed, a partition is placed between the aggregate and one side of the trough so as to maintain a 5-centimetre wide channel, along which the nutrient solution can flow. The partition wall should be fitted with apertures at 30- or 60-centimetre intervals to permit the liquid to penetrate to the growing medium. Alternatively, it may be made of fine wire gauze.

Cortvriendt's and de Groote's design for vermiculite culture

To avoid the dangers of insufficient aeration when using a vermiculite aggregate,

S. F. Cortvriendt and R. de Groote have designed a system of beds, supplied by reservoirs, and fitted with siphons and conduits, which is provided with an ingenious mechanism for ensuring that the plants get normal supplies of air.

This is constructed and operated in the following manner:

Troughs are painted with asphalt inside, to avoid any ion exchange taking place between the solution and the bed material. At about 5 centimetres from the base of each trough is placed a gauze or mesh, which is very important for aeration. On top of this is a layer of 3 centimetres of fine gravel. The rest of the trough is then filled with vermiculite of 8- to 10-millimetre grade. The solution tank or reservoir, which is connected by pipe to the beds, should be covered to inhibit the growth of algae. Branch pipes lead from the main solution pipe to each trough. Siphon mechanisms are employed to return the nutrient liquid to the tank after it has flowed down into the space below the gauze, and then risen up through the gravel and the vermiculite substrates to irrigate the crops, for the desired periods.

Filippo's method

This method, developed in the Netherlands by H. Filippo, permits the solution to enter the troughs by free fall, to secure optimum aeration. It then streams through the

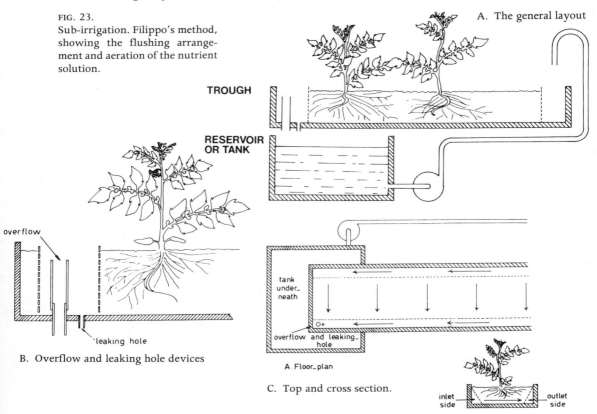

FIG. 23.
Sub-irrigation. Filippo's method, showing the flushing arrangement and aeration of the nutrient solution.

A. The general layout

TROUGH

RESERVOIR OR TANK

overflow

B. Overflow and leaking hole devices

leaking hole

tank under neath

overflow and leaking hole

A. Floor plan

C. Top and cross section.

inlet side   outlet side

Cross-section

gravel aggregate and flows to the opposite end of the bed, where part is returned to the reservoir through a leaking hole device.

The balance of the solution fills up the culture trough and then passes out through the overflow aperture. Various modifications exist, but the main advantage is that the nutrient liquid is well aerated by flushing through the growing medium.

United States Army designs

The maximum width of the troughs should not exceed one metre at the top, with the sides sloping to about 0.75 metre across the bottom. The contour of the base is slightly V-shaped, allowing for a drain in the middle. This is covered with a tile. The drain at the end of each bed section opens into a box of about 0.093 square metre, fitting loosely on the bottom of the trough, and made from wood or mesh. To guard against possible cracking of the beds in regions subject to earth tremors or great diurnal variations in air temperature, expansion strips of copper or asphalt-asbestos mastic are placed at intervals of from 3 to 9 metres in concrete troughs at the time of pouring. Copper strips must, of course, be well coated with asphalt before the beds are used. A lengthwise slope of about 2.5 centimetres in 30 metres towards the drainage end is recommended. Sumps are provided of a size commensurate with the area of the unit, the capacity in any given case being calculated upon the percentage of voids in the aggregate. In most coarse growing media, this amounts to some 40 per cent of the whole, so that a sump needs to be about half the size of the total bed space. In practice, it has been found that a capacity of 10 litres per 0.01 square metre of bed area is adequate. The sump is covered to exclude light and dirt.

For small propagation units, the Army employs air lift pumps. These are constructed simply from standard pipe and fittings. Air is injected near the bottom of the standpipe, and a mixture of air and water having a lower density than the water surrounding the pipe is produced. This mixture rises above the level of the sump water to a height which depends upon its density. If the pipe is submerged to a depth of a metre, and the density of the air-water mixture is one half that of the water, then water can be pumped to a height of a metre above the surface of the liquid in the sump. A tee connection and side arm at the top of the standpipe carry the air-water mixture over to the bed. The central air pipe may be made of 10-millimetre black iron or 1.25-centimetre aluminium tubing. From 56 to 85 cubic decimetres of air is required for each cubic decimetre of water pumped, but the pressure need not be greater than 0.75 to 1.25 kilos per 6.45 square centimetres. The bottom end of the air pipe should be capped, and raised several centimetres above the bottom of the standpipe. Two 2-millimetre holes are drilled through the tubing just above the cap. The air is injected at this point. The foot of the standpipe projects down into a tile to allow adequate submergence when the surface of the solution in the sump is at the lowest level. The submergence should be at least fifty per cent of the total height of the standpipe. The tile in the bottom of the sump adds sufficient depth. It must be 25 centimetres in diameter, with a 7.5-centimetre lip, and screened at the upper end. The beds are drained with a quick opening valve, beyond which is a tee connection and overflow.

Main beds in the Army installations are usually set on, or just below, ground level. They are each divided into three sections, arranged on three elevations, with a 2.5-centimetre drop from the upper end of one section to the lower end of the same section, and a 30-centimetre drop between sections. The solution is transferred from one division to another by means of quick opening valves, usually of 5-centimetre size. A small conduit (or flume) conveys the solution from the lower sections of the troughs to the sump. It also acts as a collector and discharger of surplus rain water. A 25-centimetre pipe is installed to carry excess water from the conduit to a waste drain. The sump is also the main storage reservoir or tank for the nutrient solution. For a ten-bed unit (each bed about 100 metres long by one metre wide at the top) a tank with a capacity of some 350,000 litres will be needed. The feed tank at the head of the beds should also be of the same capacity. This container is connected to the beds by short lengths of piping fitted with valves.

In most cases, electrically driven motor pumps are used, but petrol, diesel, or paraffin types can also be employed. One pump of about 250 litres per minute will serve two ten-bed units, if appropriately handled. For a single ten-bed unit, one 135 litres per minute pump is adequate. All intake pipes should be screened with gauze. The drain valves, four of which are used in each trough, are of the quick opening kind.

General

The average-sized gravel bed holds about one half of its volume of nutrient solution. The cost of construction of tanks or cisterns to contain such a large amount of solution would be extremely expensive, so it is most economical to irrigate units section by section. For general purposes, a tank capacity of up to fifty per cent of the bed space is satisfactory. The first step in ascertaining the minimum size of reservoir needed for any particular installation is to work out the volume of the troughs in cubic decimetres or metres. This figure should then be divided by two in order to arrive at the capacity of the tank.

The type of pump employed in sub-irrigation units depends upon the quantity of solution that has to be moved within a period of time. It is desirable that beds should be completely irrigated as quickly as possible, if possible within 15–30 minutes, and drained out in under one hour. If a total volume of 114,000 litres of solution had to be pumped into a unit within half an hour, the pump would need to have a capacity of about 3800 litres per minute. In practice, however, the beds are usually filled sectionally, thus enabling smaller pumps to be used. Where electricity is available, electric motors are normally employed for hydroponica. Small units for irrigating up to 90 square metres of trough space will be of $\frac{1}{4}$ h.p. In bigger installations, larger motors will be required, of over 10 h.p., with 675 litres per minute pumps.

For sub-irrigation, it is desirable to have a good grade of gravel, with a particle size of between 3 and 5 millimetres, although up to 12-millimetre grade has been used with success. The aggregate should not be so sharp as to cause injury to the roots, nor should it be friable and disintegrate easily after it has been in the beds for a short space of time.

8. Eternal Spring green fodder production unit, manufactured by Hydroponics Inc., of Indianapolis.

CHAPTER 10

Miscellaneous techniques

Apart from the three main systems of soilless culture, there are a number of methods of greater or lesser importance in existence which may be conveniently considered as a group in this chapter.

The germination net

Germination nets are useful for starting seeds for water culture purposes. The method of construction consists of taking a piece of common cotton mosquito netting, and dipping it into melted paraffin wax. While still as hot as possible the impregnated netting is tightly stretched over the top of an enamelware pan of convenient size, and bound firmly beneath the marginal rim of the basin with a heavy cord. The nutrient solution is poured into the pan until the surface of the liquid comes into contact with the bottom of the net. The seeds, which have been previously soaked between pieces of damp blotting paper to make them swell, soon develop on the net, where they are in constant contact with the solution, yet freely exposed to the air. After they have attained several centimetres in height they may be transferred to the water culture vessels.

Floating rafts

Near the old Mogul pleasance of Nishat in Kashmir may be observed a number of floating gardens built on rafts made from light wood and weeds. These are anchored on the surface of the lake. The roots of the plants descend through the rotting vegetation to obtain their water supply from the ample quantity of pure liquid below. Similarly, in Mexico, the ancient inhabitants of that country developed a type of floating raft, called a *chinampa*, upon which they built productive gardens. The practice still exists today. These apparatuses were the forerunners of the hydroponic raft. Instead of using water weeds or soil, the platform is covered with a 15- or 20-centimetre layer of light aggregate, which is kept moist by a number of wicks descending from it into the water below. The crops are anchored in this growing medium, and periodical aeration is secured by moving the raft or platform to a new site. Such devices are well suited to cities like Venice, Bangkok, and Stockholm.

Hanging baskets

The hanging basket consists of a tray or trough of the usual small dimensions (about 6 metres long by 1 metre wide) stoutly constructed from rustless metal, which is slung from a system of overhead pulleys above a shallow basin full of nutrient solution. At regular intervals the basket, which has a wire-mesh base, or else a set of inlet apertures, to enable the solution to penetrate to the root zone, is dipped into the liquid, thus irrigating the plants. At Sandford, in North Carolina, a large 'flower factory', growing mainly chrysanthemums, was operated on this principle.

Sprouting cabinets

The sprouting cabinet is especially valuable for farmers and racehorse owners or trainers. It consists essentially of a series of shallow trays, placed in tiers, and kept at a suitable temperature. Each tray should be of some convenient length and width, and of a depth of about 5 or 7.5 centimetres. Inside this trough is placed a thick piece of underfelting, such as is used beneath carpets, or else a layer of 2.5 centimetres of some growing medium. The medium is kept moist with a nutrient solution, and the grain to be sprouted is then spread fairly thickly in the tray. The apparatus should be kept in a semi-darkened room or a warm stable for a few days, until the grain germinates, after which additional light will be needed to encourage a good, green sprout to develop. Devices such as these, using hydroponic nutrient solutions, are extensively employed by the Chinese community of New York, for forcing bean sprouts, which are so important in the Chinese diet. It is said that beans sprouted in soilless cultures have better taste and flavour than those forced in the ordinary manner.

Botuliform devices

These apparatuses have been utilised for the artificial culture of algae in pilot plant experiments. They consist of thin-walled transparent plastic tubes, made from polyethylene, which provides a suitable combination of light transmission, chemical and physical stability under exposed conditions, freedom from toxicity, and strength. In trials at the Cambridge, Massachusetts, establishment of Arthur D. Little Inc., in 1951–52, tubing measuring when laid flat 1.2 metres across, and with a thickness of four millimetres was used. It was obtained in rolls of 150 metres. The construction of the unit was carried out as follows:

Two parallel tables each 21 metres long by 1.2 metres wide and 1.2 metres apart, were set up to support the tubing. The initial tube installation was in the form of a U, receiving culture by means of a pump from a polyethylene lined box at the end of one table, and discharging through a flat funnel of polyethylene to the tubing on the other table. Later, a second suction box, of plywood with sealed joints, coated on the outside with plastic emulsion, was substituted. 5-centimetre suction and discharge pipes were inserted into the top of the tube through slits in the film near the table ends. These slits were sealed, and the film was fastened to the pipes above the liquid level to prevent leakage. Horizontal cross pipes below the culture surface with slots on the lower side were used to distribute the intake and discharge flow across the width of the culture tubes. Finally, full turns were made at both ends of the tube, and the suction and discharge pipes were installed, as described, but close together near the middle of one of the straight runs. It was found that 1.25 centimetres of water in the tube as it was unrolled made manipulation easier, but care had to be taken to prevent misalignment. The eventual size of the tubes in the installation gave a total culture area of about 112 square metres. A 180° turn at each end was made by sealing a large number of narrow triangular pleats into a continuous tube, using an electrically heated clamp sealer. Inside the tube a liquid depth of between 5 and 7.5 centimetres was found to be the most suitable. A centrifugal pump was used to circulate the culture. This unit had a capacity of 495 kpm, giving a velocity of approximately 10 centimetres per second in the 1.2-metre wide tube when the culture was 6.25 centimetres deep. An indirect cooling system was provided to prevent the temperature rising unduly, owing to the check on the free evaporation of water by the closed tube. This consisted initially of spraying water on the polyethylene, then by using wet muslin, and eventually by installing a heat exchanger. Harvesting was carried out with the aid of a super centrifuge, having a bowl about 8 centimetres in diameter, and driven by a 2 h.p. motor at 13,000 rpm. Carbon dioxide was supplied through a surge tank system.

Botuliform (or sausage-shaped) devices of plastic material give quite good results in algae culture.

Grass and green forage growing

Sometimes known as grass incubators, forage production units fall into two classes: those made by farmers to their own specifications, following certain general principles; and those turned out by manufacturers of agricultural and hydroponic apparatus. A grass and green forage growing unit must provide optimum conditions for the rapid development of seed material into edible herbage within the space of a week or ten days. This means that not only the nutrition and environmental conditions within the installation should be excellent, but that the technical design, mechanics of operation and management must be first class.

Basically, the incubator or machine consists of a series of production trays or benches to which solution is supplied by irrigation or sprays continuously. In most areas, protective coverings are provided or the units are located inside existing buildings in order to ensure that average growing temperatures of from 22° to 25°C are

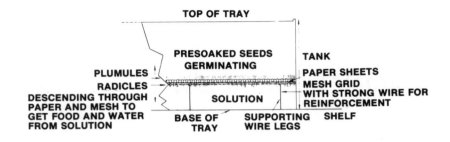

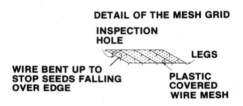

FIG. 24.
Grass production in hydroponics. Arrangement of culture tray.

maintained, with satisfactory humidity, ventilation, and aeration. Long shallow tanks, not over 10 centimetres deep, are arranged in tiers, with vertical gaps of not over one metre between each layer. Conveniently sized trays with one centimetre mesh bases, rather like those utilised for water or solution culture, should be placed over the tanks. The seed, normally that of cereal grasses, such as oats, barley, maize, rye, sorghum or wheat, is scattered thickly on newspaper spread inside each tray on top of the mesh bottom. About one kilo of seeds can be put into a tray of about 0.75 square metre. The yield from this quantity and area, after about a week's intensive culture, should be of the order of ten to twelve times its weight in fresh grass of up to some 20 centimetres

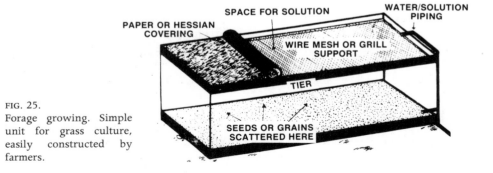

FIG. 25.
Forage growing. Simple unit for grass culture, easily constructed by farmers.

in height. The trays need to be regularly irrigated or sprayed with nutrient solution for the first four to five days and thereafter plain water should be given to secure the sweetest and most palatable forage.

The liquid plant food, consisting of standard hydroponic solutions of about half strength, is pumped through the tanks continually at a slow speed, not usually at a rate of more than one or two kilometres per hour, or sprayed from jets into the trays. The roots of the young seedlings absorb the solution and the high temperature forces them to grow very rapidly.

Alternatively, long benches fitted with bevelled or upwardly inclined edges may be employed. The seed should be scattered on these, and mist jets or gentle sprays of solution directed onto them. The liquid must be allowed to drain away and be returned to the solution reservoir.

Fluorescent 40 watt 'daylight type' electric tube lighting may be placed in the hydroponic grass growing unit to give continual illumination. Aluminium foil reflectors assist in distributing the light to best advantage. Heating and fan ventilators will also be required in cold or damp areas. In tropical districts, outside shaded units, with wind screens, may be constructed.

There is considerable scope for ingenuity and adaptation by farmers and other users of hydroponic grass and green forage. A little planning and improvisation will result in the building of serviceable machines at quite low cost.

Commercial machinery for green forage production has been marketed by several firms. Some of the units available are:

(A) ETERNAL SPRING SYSTEM.   This is essentially an insulated aluminium chamber, which has a thermostatically controlled heater, lighting around the sides, and an air circulating device. The method of irrigation is gravity feed from an upper holding tank through a series of automatic siphons.

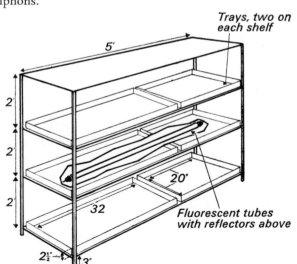

FIG. 26.
Hydroponic forage. Tier of shelving with lighting strips. (Note: in this drawing the measurements were entered in imperial feet and inches, shown as ' for foot, and " for inches. To convert to metric system: 1 foot equals 30.48 centimetres and 1 inch equals 2.54 centimetres.)

Trays, two on each shelf

Fluorescent tubes with reflectors above

The outer chamber is 60 metres long by 3.6 metres wide by 2.4 metres high. In this is a four-fold bank of six layered trays – one layer on top of the other, separated by about 30 centimetres. Each layer has a set of five aluminium trays 0.9 metre by 0.45 metre, giving a total area per layer of 2.0 square metres. Into each layer (5 trays) about 11.3 kilos of barley seed is placed daily. This is first soaked 16–18 hours in clean water, allowed to drain 24 hours and sometime on the third day it is placed on the trays at the rate just mentioned. A temperature of 22 to 25°C is maintained as well as a relative humidity of 65–70%. Lights are continuous and are of the ordinary fluorescent type.

The method of irrigation is simple. An 11-litre holding tank at the top of the series of layers is allowed to flow into a distributing canal which in turn flows into holding tanks on either side of it. These holding tanks contain the growing trays.

In the middle of each distribution canal is an automatic siphon which after filling, drains into the distributor below it. Complete drainage is achieved by arranging a bung on a float which closes a hole in the distributor when the nutrient first flows in it and opens it again after the liquid has siphoned from it. This allows drippings from the growing trays to drain away.

Under ideal conditions, and here viability of seed is the most vital factor, the 'eternal spring' unit can produce from 45 kilos of barley seed some 450 kilos of fresh green fodder. In practice, an average of no more than 275–300 kilos is produced.

This unit is American-made and operates basically by sub-irrigation. It is made by Hydroponics Inc., of Indianapolis, Indiana.

(B) VIVERBA.   This consists simply of a framework about 2 metres high, 2 metres long and 1 metre wide. On this framework provision is made for 5 layers of aluminium trays each separated by about 30 centimetres. Over each of the 5 layers is arranged three rotating type sprayers which are connected to the water mains through a valve. In the earlier models an ingenious water drip counter-weight device was used to open the valve at predetermined intervals. This allowed the sprayers to spray from overhead on to the germinated seed on the trays. A suitable nutrient mixture is placed in a capsule and the mains water slowly dissolves the nutrient as it passes through the capsule. Certain difficulties with blockage of nozzles due to too high a solids content and/or temporary hardness and/or silt caused abandonment of this method of irrigation. In its place a time clock and solenoid valve have been used. Although more expensive this system successfully overcomes the difficulties mentioned above. Each aluminium tray has an area of about 0.4 square metre so that 5 trays constituting one layer has an area of 2 square metres, and uses about 15 kilos of soaked seed. At a conversion ratio of 6 to 1 each layer will produce about 90 kilos of fresh green fodder daily.

The Viverba is a French manufactured machine and operates through overhead spray irrigators. These are arranged to come on every two and a half hours, giving some ten irrigations daily.

The buyer is expected to erect a structure over the unit or may have a suitable shed available. Provision for lights and heat (in winter) and ventilation has also to be made at extra cost.

The method of operation is briefly as follows. The 15 kilos of seed is placed in a plastic basket in the morning of the first day and left completely immersed in tap water for 10–12 hours in the case of maize or 8 hours in the case of barley. In the evening the basket is removed and the seeds allowed to drain overnight. They are then transferred on the morning of the second day into another plastic bucket to aerate and then soaked another 10 minutes in water, then drained and covered with paper. This process is repeated on the third day.

On the fourth day the seeds which have now started to germinate (radicles and plumules appear) are carefully placed on the top layer of trays. The cycle is continued and after the eighth day 90 kilos of fresh green fodder is removed and the production cycle is now continued. Ideal temperatures are for maize 25–30°C, barley 20–25°C, sorghum 30–35°C.

In many cases natural light is used through windows or plastic but where this is not possible artificial light must be arranged. A period of 15–18 hours per day is recommended.

It is claimed that approximately 90 litres of water per day per unit is necessary. The drainings are run to waste.

Sanitation is maintained by cleaning baskets and trays with calcium or sodium hypochlorite solutions. Irrigation lines, sprayers and valves however can only be cleaned during a break in the production cycle.

(c) GORDON.   The British designed 'Gordon' system consists of a suitably protected steel framework 7.3 metres long by 2.4 metres wide and 2.3 metres high. The framework has provision for five layers on which seed is placed. The layers are made of wood or masonite in two halves on each layer. The area has a slight slope of about 4 centimetres from centre to outside edge and each layer is separated by 33 centimetres.

A system of spray nozzles is arranged on the vertical sections of the framework directed on to the seed areas.

A pump is located on the side of the structure and draws from an 1840 litre nutrient reservoir placed on the floor beneath the lowest layer. The complete unit must be housed by the purchaser in a suitable building.

Continuous light is provided by vertically placed fluorescent tubes of 65–80 watts. This is reflected off the internally white painted walls. Temperature and humidity controls are to be provided by the purchaser. A console including a time-clock for controlling the two daily irrigations is provided by the manufacturer.

The total growing area is approximately 90 square metres. So for a growing cycle of 7 days, there is available 12.8 square metres per day.

Seed is placed in a hessian bag and soaked for 24 hours in water. The bag is then removed from the water and allowed to drain for 24 hours. A minimum temperature of 20°C is maintained during this process.

The drained seed is placed on the third day at the rate of about 5 kilos per square metre on the growing area of the first layer. Irrigation is twice daily by overhead spraying. The excess nutrient liquid runs down the slope into gutters which return it to the reservoir below the structure. The water level is topped up from time to time. Every week a new solution is prepared.

The conversion rate is normally 6 to 1.

(D) BAYLES.   This is an Australian unit. Basically the machine is made of two corrugated iron tanks. One is slightly smaller and is fitted inside the other.

The space between the two tanks has been filled with polyurethane foam for insulation and strength.

Inside the tank there is a central shaft and pivot, on which seven individual frames have been hung to form a complete circle. These frames each hold 14 fibreglass trays in which the pasture is grown. Each tray is about 28 centimetres wide and 60 centimetres long by 5 centimetres deep.

Also mounted on the centre pivot is a series of four high intensity wide spectrum lights which are switched on all of the time to provide light for growth.

On top of the tank, under a fibreglass cover, a refrigeration unit has been installed to maintain a constant temperature within the growing chamber. For oats this is 13°C.

There is also a pump on top of the unit which draws water containing the plant nutrients from the bottom of the tank and sprays it over the trays for 15 minutes every hour.

The trays have drain holes drilled in the bottom to allow the liquid to return back to the 20 litres reservoir in the bottom of the tank.

The water level in the tank is kept constant with a ball cock valve, but after each batch of pasture is taken out every day, a measured quantity of the highly soluble nutrient powder is tipped into the machine.

The grain is tipped onto the trays to a depth of 5 centimetres.

One of the seven sections is done each day to give a weekly cycle of growth. At the end of seven days the first crop is about 25 centimetres high and for every kilo of grain planted the total weight has increased eight times.

Various other manufacturers also produce green forage machinery and equipment for soilless grass growing. Hydroculture Inc., of Phoenix, Arizona, produce the well-known 'Magic Meadow' unit.

Layflats

Soilless culture units, prepared from synthetic membranes, plastics and similar materials, after adaptation commonly called layflats (old Norse, *leggia*, to lay, and *flatr*, flat or floor), have been in use in various parts of the world for some years.

The devices constitute a flat floor, upon which crops may be grown hydroponically. They can be made with black or non-translucent polyethylene tubing, butylite (butyl synthetic rubber) and substances of like properties. Butylite of 0.5 centimetre gauge has given good results, also heavy gauge polyethylene sheeting.

Layflats may be made by cutting the sheeting into strips of 20 to 30 metres long with a width of from 35 to 40 centimetres, according to the size of the plants to be grown. The cut edges of the strips are joined with plastic tape to form a tube. The material is folded over from the edges to the top centre, so that a gusset is effected at each side. The gussets are secured with plastic tape. This layflat is then rolled out or placed on smooth sloping ground, with the sealed cut edge at the bottom. Apertures at appropriate intervals are cut along the top in a straight line for inserting different species of seedlings, of about 1.25 centimetre diameter. The sealed edge at the base makes a slight V-form. A flume is not used, but a slight indentation may be made in the ground surface to secure firm siting of the layflat. A hose or plastic pipe, perforated with 1 or 2 millimetre holes is now run right through inside the butylite layflat tube. This provides the flow line for the nutrient solution.

The internal hose has a diameter of 2.5 centimetres. The higher end of the layflat is sealed up, leaving the internal hose or pipe projecting about 35 centimetres. The lower end is sealed except for one aperture to permit egress of nutrient solution. The lower end of the internal hose is also sealed.

The projecting pipe or hose at the upper end of the device is connected to a header pipe, with normal manifolds and valve arrangements for sub-irrigation. These ensure equalisation of pressure when several devices are connected in units to the tank or reservoir. It has been found preferable to site the solution tank at the lower end of the layflat installation, so that it can serve the dual purpose of reservoir and sump. The aperture at the lower end of the device discharges through a short pipe into the reservoir-cum-sump.

The system operates as follows: The tank-cum-reservoir is filled with the desired nutrient solution and a small diesel, petrol or submersible electric pump started. This pumps the solution up to the header pipe at the top end of the layflats, whence it enters each device through the internal perforated hose within the butylite deflated tubing. The solution is thrown out very gently through the 1 to 2 millimetre apertures and falls around the plants' roots. It then trickles down slowly along the layflat towards the discharge end, re-enters the reservoir-cum-sump and can be re-circulated

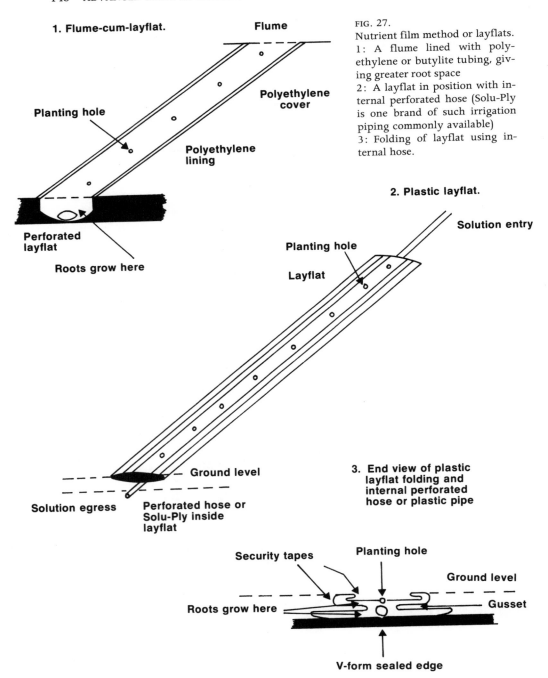

1. Flume-cum-layflat.

Flume

Planting hole

Polyethylene cover

Polyethylene lining

Perforated layflat

Roots grow here

FIG. 27.
Nutrient film method or layflats.
1: A flume lined with poly-ethylene or butylite tubing, giv-ing greater root space
2: A layflat in position with in-ternal perforated hose (Solu-Ply is one brand of such irrigation piping commonly available)
3: Folding of layflat using in-ternal hose.

2. Plastic layflat.

Solution entry

Planting hole

Layflat

Ground level

Solution egress

Perforated hose or Solu-Ply inside layflat

3. End view of plastic layflat folding and internal perforated hose or plastic pipe

Security tapes

Planting hole

Ground level

Roots grow here

Gusset

V-form sealed edge

indefinitely with regular recharging and usual testing. The devices or layflats can be laid out in series.

Root aeration is good, the plants receive a continuous supply of nutrients and it is thought that phytosanitary conditions will be better than in standard hydroponic beds or troughs.

Overhead shading may be necessary in very hot times, but so far the double irrigation devices, with the internal hose, reduce heating of solution in the layflats. For taller crops, wires with hanging twine are placed above the devices to support stems. For small and short crops, these are not required, as the method supports them adequately and the folded plastic is quite stiff.

The advantages of such systems are that the installation capital costs are low, only a matter of the cost of the plastic sheeting and the plastic hose, plus ancillary piping, small pump and very little labour. The method will operate almost automatically. In addition, all aggregates are obviated and no rigid troughs are needed. The units can be set out on bare ground in most areas, and will operate on gradients up to 65°.

Disadvantages may be extra crop support, need for the avoidance of rough handling by attendants and necessity for careful attention to detail. Because of the nature of the materials used, however, the roots do not entangle themselves within the devices and

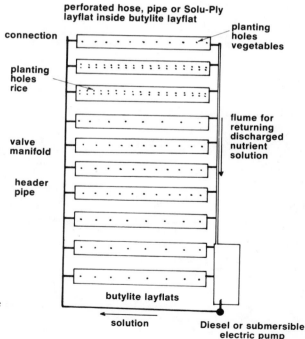

FIG. 28.
Typical layflat unit showing the layout.

FIG. 29.
Layflat unit.

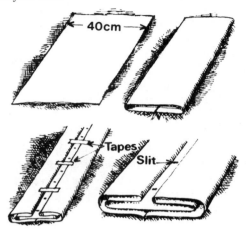

Submersible electric pump

1: Folding layflats, without using internal hose

2: Arrangement of the devices

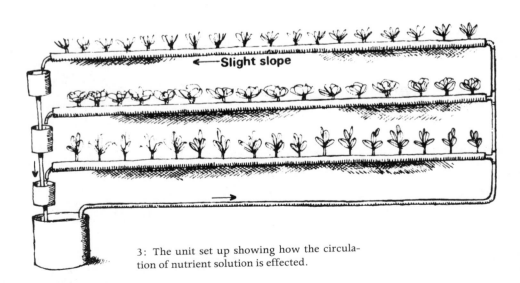

3: The unit set up showing how the circulation of nutrient solution is effected.

the whole plant can be pulled out easily at harvesting without disturbing or damaging the layflat or internal hose.

Alternatively, the internal hose in the layflats can be omitted and the plastic folded simply in the style shown in Figure 29(1). Here the nutrient solution runs down along the basal V-form produced by the join in the material and discharges through an open end into a small sump or bucket, whence it is returned by gravity flow to the reservoir for re-cycling.

Various other modifications exist, such as flumes lined with the plastic tubing or sheeting, or different ways of folding the material. For long rooted crops such as carrots or parsnips, the layflats should have wires inserted inside to raise the top portions enough to provide extra space for root development, while potatoes can be grown on tube surfaces above slightly larger apertures cut in the tubing to permit root access to the solution flow inside, and another long strip of black plastic put over the tubers to exclude light. Of course, small holes must be cut in this last noted covering to allow the stems to protrude and develop.

There is room for considerable ingenuity and numerous adaptations for different conditions and needs in layflat hydroponic culture. In some places this technique has been termed the nutrient film method.

Seeds are germinated in a small box of sand or some other sterile growing medium and go into the slits when they are about 5 centimetres high.

The system is so light that it could even be employed to make sloping rooftop gardens in overcrowded areas.

Domestic units of this type could help the food situation at very little cost, since salads and many other vegetables, including potatoes, can be grown by the method. Also, there is much less likelihood of disease with plants grown in this manner.

But there is a much wider aspect of the work, for the plastic strips can be rolled up, put in an aircraft and taken to disaster areas where they can start producing food the same day – especially in warm regions where there is no check to growth through cold.

Sixty or 70 metre strips set out over a hectare of ground and served by a 1000 litre tank of nutrient will produce quantities of fresh food within weeks of planting out. With a system like this, it is possible to load up with an electric generator to drive the pump and unroll the strips on the ground at the other end.

Mains electricity is not needed – a generator, even from a motor car, would do – and the amount of nutrient solution needed is very small, since it is recycled. The hotter the climate for this technique, the better – and butylite for instance should last up to 25 years, even in the harshest weather.

So in very warm climates there could well be three or four crops a year, which would be of enormous value to an area hit by earthquake, for example, which will take months and even years to put in order. This way, a hectare could produce up to 3000 tonnes of fresh food a year.

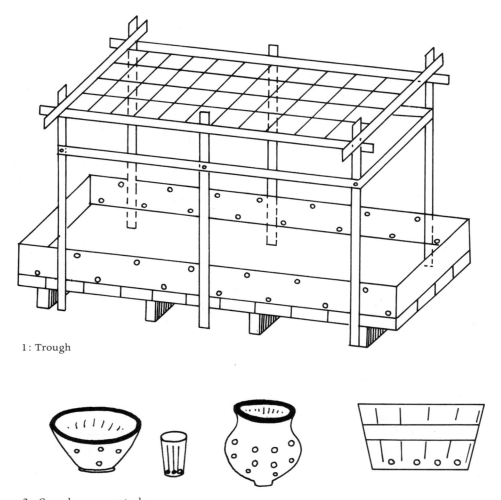

1: Trough

2: Capsules or receptacles.

FIG. 30.
Sharder process. Unit with overhead shading in Bengal. Capsules or receptacles of the types illustrated are placed at intervals in the troughs. When filled with nutrient formulae and sludge they will release plant food slowly over a long period.

Other designs

A number of other designs for the construction of soilless culture units have been proposed and developed from time to time, and more will undoubtably appear in the future. Indeed, there is considerable scope for the exercise of engineering skills in the field of hydroponics.

Mention has already been made in previous chapters of the method called aeroponics. Full details of this technique may be obtained from the Istituto di Agronomia Generale e Coltivazioni Erbacee, Pisa, Italy. The Sharder process is a simple method, developed in West Bengal at the Hydroponic Investigation Unit, Sibpur, Howrah, near Calcutta. The crops are grown in standard aggregate-filled troughs and nourished by means of a series of nutrient capsules or receptacles placed at appropriate intervals in the troughs, from which fertilizer mixtures are released into the growing medium over a period. Adaptations and modifications of these and other techniques are in use in many areas to suit local conditions.

CHAPTER 11

Special equipment

A certain amount of ancillary apparatus will be needed for the efficient operation of hydroponica. The usual tools, like hand forks, trowels, dibbers, wheelbarrows, and watering cans, together with such requisites as raffia, garden twine, and labels, are of course essential. In cold countries, greenhouses and cloches provide protection from inclement weather. All these items are, however, standard horticultural equipment, and as such, are common to both conventional and soilless cultures. Little need be said about them. A wide range of glasshouses and cloches of all shapes and styles is available from the various manufacturers, whose advertisements and specifications appear regularly in the agricultural press of the world.

The special equipment that may be required for the working of a commercial hydroponicum is, on the other hand, peculiar to soilless culture. It includes such items as wind barriers, shades, special sprayers, spreaders, lighting apparatus, and mechanised implements, in addition to tanks, troughs, and trays. Consideration must also be paid to dry fertilizer mixers, tablet-making machinery, and regeneration apparatus for ion exchangers, as well as equipment needed for algae culture.

Wind barriers

Winds of velocities of between 20 and 100 plus k.p.h. can cause damage to soilless crops, particularly tomatoes and cucumbers. Not only does mechanical injury result, but the excessive transpiration caused by the wind during dry weather encourages wilting and subsequent hardening of the plants. Additionally, 'wind rock' may occur, which damages the base of the stem. This is caused by bruising against the aggregate as the plants move to and fro' in the wind. Leaves are also broken and torn by gales, and the flowers and fruits may be irretrievably destroyed. Following the mechanical injury, tissues are often invaded by disease-producing organisms. Careful tying of tall plants reduces wind injury, but in severe cases, the erection of barriers is essential.

There are two types of wind barriers:

    (*a*)   Closed barriers; and

    (*b*)   Open barriers.

Closed barriers consist of solid screens of earth, wooden boards, canvas, or other obstructional materials, which divert the flow of air so producing a region of relative calm on the leeward side. The windward side of such a barrier should be sloping. This causes the wind to be diverted upwards, and consequently the effective height is greater than that of a vertical wall.

Open barriers allow some of the wind to pass through small apertures as in the case of a picket or snow fence. These barriers are subject to lower stresses during high winds than are closed ones. Open barriers can be built of lattice work, boards, netting, or strips of burlap. Not more than one-third of the total area should be open, and if possible less.

The range over which barriers are effective depends mainly upon the reduction in wind velocity required, the height of the screen, and the type of construction. These factors can only be assessed through a study of local conditions. Generally speaking, a barrier about 3 metres high can be considered effective over a distance of about 12 metres for reducing the initial wind velocity by one third. In cases where there is a prevailing wind, such as a trade wind, the beds may be orientated parallel to the wind, so that the air moves down the paths or aisles, rather than across the troughs. Wind velocities of from 72 to 135 k.p.h. are in the gale range. Hurricanes have velocities of over 135 k.p.h. There is really no practical way of safeguarding crops from these high wind velocities, and all that can be done is to protect the permanent installation. Fortunately, the aggregate in a hydroponicum is less likely to blow away than is the soil in a field, while it can be easily and quickly replaced. Hurricanes and typhoons, however, seldom visit the same area except at wide periods of time.

Shades

In tropical localities, it is desirable to shade beds, so as to reduce light intensity by about 40 per cent in bright weather. Shades should be readily removable. A system of

FIG. 31.
Three types of trough in open air hydroponic unit design, India. The shade over the last bed provides protection from sun scorch and heavy monsoon rains.

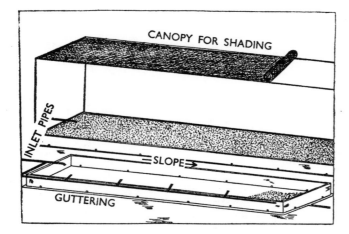

FIG. 32.

CANOPY FOR SHADING

INLET PIPES

SLOPE

GUTTERING

A. Matting shades in a hydroponic unit.

ROLLER

B. Roll shades for green-house.

posts and wires, which can be covered with thin cloth, grass or cane matting, or palm leaves, is perhaps the cheapest and most easily erected. Where small sized leaves are employed, it is necessary to put wire netting along the top of the supports. The posts must be set in the ground, in this case, in rows on one side of each row of beds, immediately adjacent to them. A single line of stakes is used for each trough, extending 2.75 metres in height. The posts are set about 9 metres apart, and a strong galvanised wire is strung parallel to the beds, one strand on each side of the post. Cloth can be sewed on the wire, in such a way so that it can be slipped backwards and forwards as need arises. To facilitate this operation, and to prevent tearing, the edges should be reinforced with a 5-centimetre strip of heavier material. It is often a good plan to have the shade cloth or mats slightly sloping to one side, so as to permit run off of excess rain. At the sides and ends of units, vertical shades or pieces of cloth fixed on screens can be positioned to ward off low angled sunlight.

Bamboos make good posts and supports for shade matting. They are light to handle and easy to cut and split.

Supports

Tall plants may be supported in aggregate culture by means of two wires about 50 centimetres apart running parallel to, and directly over, the beds. Tomatoes, for example, are tied when small with a twine at a point near the base of the stem, the other end of which is secured to the highest support wire. As the plant grows the stem is gently twisted around this vertical string, which holds it erect. Cucumbers need extra wires, at 0.30 metre intervals, so as to form a kind of lattice work. Peas are also rather similar. Carnations need nets of wires placed horizontally to the trough surface, fixed at staggered intervals as growth increases. These wires should be strung from posts along the entire length of the bed, 15 centimetres apart lengthwise, and also 15 centimetres apart crosswise. The first stage may be 22.5 centimetres from the top of the growing medium, and the following ones at similar intervals, up to about 1.25 metres. This results in a series of nets which provide the plants with firm support. Each is, in fact, treated as an individual within its own 'square' of the nets.

In large units, all support wires should be connected through turnbuckles to control tautness. Guy wires, anchored to 'deadmen', buried in the ground, will provide additional support for the end posts.

In Australia, tomatoes are often supported by a system of wires connected at each end of the bed to hinged posts. Initially, when the plants are small, the end supports are slackened, so that the wires hang loose. As growth proceeds, the posts are gradually drawn erect, so tightening the wires, which also tend to close in on the plants forcing them into a compact and upright position. The merit of this technique lies in the fact that whole beds can be conveniently handled as one unit when it comes to supporting the crop.

For ornamental plants, it is pleasanter to colour green the string or raffia used for tying, which makes it less conspicuous, and gives a more agreeable effect.

In small water cultures, uprights of light glass or wooden rods anchored to the cork may be used as supports for plants. In larger vessels, four sockets into which suitable sticks can be fitted should be placed equidistant around the top of the container, and held in position by means of wire tightly twisted along it. In the case of commercial solution systems, the usual posts with attached wires and twine, can be fixed at intervals beside the troughs.

Sprayers

The main problem in spraying in hydroponica is to ensure that excessive amounts of toxic materials do not accumulate in the growing medium. If any danger is thought likely the beds should be well flushed with plain water. The employment of proper spraying apparatus will, however, eliminate all such risks. Any type of paint spray gun suitable for high pressure operation is satisfactory for soilless cultural work. The fluid and the air adjustment valves should be set to provide a finely divided spray. This type of apparatus will use only about half the volume of spray at equal concentrations for comparable control that would be expended with conventional equipment. Practically no dripping occurs from the foliage onto the growing medium. Coverage is first class. The aerosol devices also give similar results.

Air under pressure can be supplied from an air compressor, or out of cylinders, fitted with regulating valves. The average operating pressures needed range from 40 to 50 kilos per 6.45 square centimetres.

Spreaders

Manual sprinklers for applying dry salts can be made by punching a number of holes in the bottom of a cocoa tin, and attaching it to a long stick. This is then filled with the fertiliser mixture, and gently passed along the rows of growing crops, which are supplied with the requisite quantities of nutrients by a light shaking of the tin. The salts fall through the holes in the bottom onto the surface of the aggregate. The device works after the manner of a pepper pot. The fertilizers can be washed into solution by means of a spray of water directed from a stirrup pump, a hosepipe, or a garden can.

For larger units it is desirable to use hoppers fitted with a special distributor mechanism. The standard rollers in these machines can be adjusted to deliver about 30 or 60 grams of salts to the square metre. For tall crops, the hoppers may either have big wheels fitted, or else they can be run on elevated rails over the beds. In very large commercial installations, run on the dry application method, specially designed

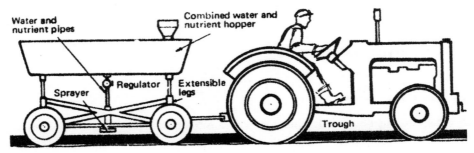

FIG. 33.
Travelling spreader for water and nutrients drawn by a tractor.

travelling spreaders may be employed. These deliver nutrients, followed by a jet of water to wash them down into the aggregate, to the beds. They may be self-propelling, or towed by a slow running tractor. The speed of working should not exceed 1 or 2 k.p.h.

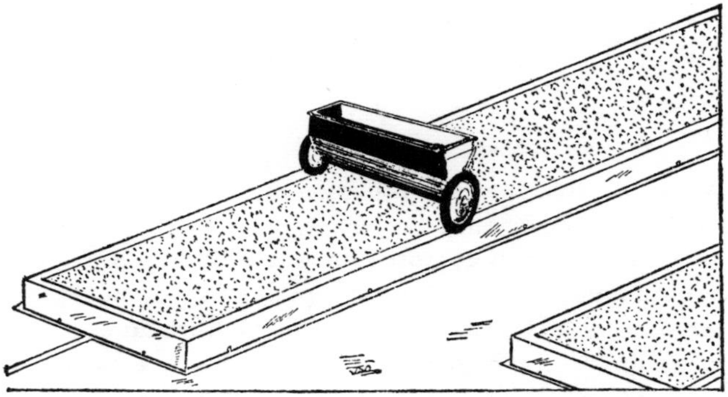

FIG. 34.
Spreading machine for use in soilless cultivation. The hopper may be self-powered if a second pair of wheels is fitted, or it can be tractor-towed in the form shown.

CHAPTER 12

Water supply

Water for hydroponic cultivation may be obtained from a wide number of sources, such as rivers, streams, boreholes, municipal supplies, rainfall, and distilled sea water or brine. In practice, most waters, the salinity of which does not exceed 2500 ppm, are suitable for the soilless growth of crops. Some waters do, however, contain small amounts of certain toxic elements, which would exert inhibiting or fatal effects upon plant life. It is, therefore, always desirable to test a particular water before using it in the hydroponicum. However, recent trials have shown that very saline waters, even sea water, can be used in soilless culture.

Waters containing salts of magnesium and calcium are termed 'hard' because the magnesium and calcium ions replace those of sodium or potassium in soaps, causing the formation of a curd. Both 'hard' and 'soft' waters are quite suitable for hydroponics. In the former, the magnesium and calcium are present as carbonates or sulphates. In low concentrations, the carbonate ion is not injurious to plants. Copper and zinc, as well as others of the heavy metals, are sometimes found in water supplies. To remove excessive concentrations of these elements, it is necessary to pass the water very slowly through a deep bed of fine calcareous media. Chlorine, in the uncombined state, is toxic to plants. It injures the roots, and if present in substantial amounts, will cause a hardening of the crops. High concentrations of chlorine are best dealt with by filtering the water through a quantity of organic matter, such as straw, dried leaves, or grass, and allowing it to stand in open tanks for a few hours.

Processed sea water is often distilled in thermocompression stills made of bronze and brass. In such cases, the copper and zinc concentrations may reach levels that are toxic for plants, although not detrimental to animals or humans. Where stills of this description are in use, it is essential to watch carefully for any indications of undue rise in the level of the minor elements. Solar distillers are recommended for work with hydroponics whenever the climatic conditions make their employment possible. Ion exchange methods are also now in use and various purifying membranes are available.

For small household units, simple trials of water can be made by placing a few cut flowers in a glassful over a period of a day or two. If no ill effects are observed, the water may be presumed satisfactory for use. In large commercial installations, it is always desirable to secure a proper analysis of the water supply before commencing operations. This is important both from the cultural and the economic angles. Analyses are usually available from the local municipality or township, or in country areas from the agricultural departments.

Rivers and streams

Watercourses rising in arid, or semi-arid, areas have higher salinities than those running through humid regions. The following table gives the salinity of some rivers, as well as that of a number of lakes in various parts of the world.

Name	Location	Salinity (ppm)
Persian Gulf	Bahrein Island	2220
River Thames	London	270
Mississippi River	Minneapolis	200
Mississippi River	New Orleans	166
Lake Superior	Michigan	58
Lake of Zurich	Switzerland	141
River Nile	Khartoum	174
River Rhine	Strasbourg	232
River Seine	Ile-de-France	252
River Hudson	New York	112
River Danube	Regensburg	204
Lake Huron	Michigan	105
Yellowstone Lake	Wyoming	118
Moorehead Lake	Maine	14
River Arkansas	Colorado	2134
River Arkansas	Arkansas	559
River Brazos	Texas	1066
River Colorado	Arizona	702
River Missouri	North Dakota	440
River Kansas	Topeka	766
Rann of Cutch	Saurashtra	1770
River Lee	Hertfordshire	335
River Hooghli	Calcutta	163
Lake Victoria	Tanzania	102
River Teesta	North Bengal	150
Umlaas and Umgeni Rivers	Natal	125
Vaal River	Orange Free State	179

Boreholes

Most waters from boreholes and artesian wells are satisfactory for hydroponics. Occasionally, rather saline waters from such sources may be met with, although the deeper the drilling or well the more likely is the water to be pure, especially where an underground stream has been tapped. Even in the most arid areas, such as the Sahara or the Sind deserts, there are usually ample supplies of subterranean water, often of course at considerable depths. It would not be economic to extract water from a very deep drilling for soil cultivations, but in the case of hydroponics, where careful conservation is practised, there is no doubt of the profitability of the outlay. At one site in Tanzania, the borehole water used in a hydroponicum had a salinity of 1080 ppm while another drilling in Rhodesia had only 310 ppm. In Fiji, well waters averaged from 1346 to 12,122 ppm salinity, but the bulk of the highest concentrations consisted of chlorides, which may be dispersed by exposure to air or filtration through organic matter.

Municipal supplies

City water supplies consist of filtered and treated water. The chlorine content should receive attention. For example, in Barcelona, this amounts to 230 ppm. In the River Lee-derived water, used for household supply in certain parts of Essex (England), chlorides total 40 ppm, while in west London municipal water they total only 27 ppm. In the city of Birmingham (U.K.), they average 8 ppm and in some areas of Lancashire 90 ppm. The residual chlorine in western London water ranges from 0.00 to 0.05 ppm. This is perfectly safe to use. In the same water, copper amounts to as much as 0.05 ppm. No deleterious effects have been observed with this concentration.

Rainfall

In theory, rain water is pure, but in actual practice it usually contains minute amounts of nitrogen compounds, oxygen, and carbon dioxide, as well as certain impurities, especially near large industrial cities, where the fumidity of the air is well known. These impurities are not generally of any great significance in hydroponics.

Sea water and brine

After distillation, these waters may be utilised for soilless cultivation. It is also possible to add several parts of ordinary sea water to quantities of fresh water without producing inhibiting effects upon plant growth. Halophytes are, of course, capable of withstanding greater concentrations. New techniques have been evolved for utilising very saline waters.

Other sources

Water from mines, effluents, springs, and miscellaneous sources may prove satisfactory. In cases of doubt, it should always be examined before use. Some waters contain excessive concentrations of sulphides, but these can be dispersed by allowing the water to stand in shallow open troughs, well exposed to the air, for two or three days. In cases where the boron, manganese, fluorine, or other minor element content exceeds the limit of safety, it is not advisable to employ a water until it has been treated. These ions may be removed by treatment with one or other of the synthetic resins used in ion exchange techniques, such as permutits or amberlites. The resins may be obtained from any of the firms which manufacture them, together with literature on their use.* Ready-made iron and manganese removal filters can also be purchased, together with such useful items as sedimentation tanks, sterilising gear, water testing equipment, and ion exchange apparatus, from water engineering firms. Permeable membranes are now available for purifying saline waters.

Apparatus

The choice of apparatus for any irrigatory system will normally be governed by the topography of the site in question. Amateur gardeners and housewives can make use of ordinary jugs, cans, and hosepipes. In commercial installations, every effort should be made, on the grounds of economy alone, to utilise gravity flows. Where this is not possible, pumps will be required. For many units, especially those dependent upon boreholes, windmills are a good investment. Electrical, diesel, petrol, and paraffin or TVO driven engines may all be employed with success as sources of power. Where a plentiful supply of cheap wood or other fuel exists, steam is quite satisfactory. In the East, the Persian wheel is commonly to be seen. This consists of a large vertical wheel, fixed in the mouth of a well, while over it a looped chain of pots is suspended. The lowest of these vessels reach into the water below. As the wheel revolves, one length of the chain is continually rising with pots full of water, which discharge themselves into a trough fixed at the summit, and then return empty to be filled again. The apparatus is worked by means of bullocks harnessed to a beam and a smaller horizontal wheel. The *shadoof* of Egypt and Arabia, which is referred to in the Old Testament of the Bible, works on the principle of the seesaw. A long stout pole is balanced over the well or river bank. Several persons walk up and down this beam, the heavier end of which dips into the water and brings up a supply in the buckets or bags attached to it. These are then emptied into the adjacent channels connecting with the patches to be

---

*Rohm and Haas Co., Chemical Process Co., and Dow Chemical Co., U.S.A.
The Permutit Co. Ltd., London (England).
Monsanto Chemical Corporation.
These firms have local agents in most countries, whose addresses may be obtained through the appropriate trade organisations.

irrigated. In India, a large bag made from bullock-hide is often suspended over a well by means of a pulley. A pair of oxen draw this up full of water at regular intervals. The path trodden by the beasts is set at an incline, to facilitate more rapid raising and lowering of the bag. Home-produced methane gas can also be used to provide heat for steam engines.

Terracing is generally employed in mountainous regions, like parts of Japan, and the Himalayan foothills, to enable irrigation by gravity feed to be carried out. The terraces consist of a series of contour banks and channels. The water flows from the highest down to the lowest spreading over the surface of each plot, whence it escapes through regular outlets to the next in order of descent. Terraced vineyards may be seen in Syria, France, Italy, and many other countries. In China, rice is commonly cultivated in terraces. An important principle of irrigation is that the water should not be too rapid in its flow.

Where water is stored in large tanks or reservoirs, evaporation can be reduced substantially by treatment with cetyl alcohol. This process is most beneficial in arid regions. Evaporation losses have been cut by as much as 70 per cent in some cases. Cetyl alcohol (hexadecanol) should be spread as a thin film over the surface of the water. It does not prevent the uptake of oxygen, and so will not interfere with the freshness of the storage reservoir. It prevents to a great extent the transfer of water to the atmosphere, and experiments have shown that something like $4\frac{1}{2}$ million litres may be saved from evaporation over the course of a year in a tank having a surface area of a $\frac{1}{2}$-hectare.

Water consumption

The water requirements of hydroponic installations vary greatly depending upon the size of the plants, the wind velocity, and the local relative humidity. On the average, it is best to allow for a consumption of between 0.20 litre and 1.25 litre per 0.093 square metres of trough space daily. In damp areas, the former figure will be more accurate, while in hot, dry regions, the latter one will approximate to the amount

---

FIG. 35. *(Opposite)*
What happens when salt water is used for irrigation in hydroponic growing media.

KEY   Root hairs or feeders ◯   Broken or patchy salt water film ● ● ●

Particles of sand or aggregate ▦   Substratum dew ○ ○ ○

Salt water (sea/ocean/underground saline) ■   Air ▭

A

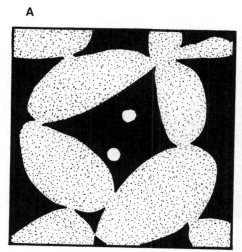

A. Spaces between the sand or aggregate particles filled up by salt water immediately after flooding or irrigation

B

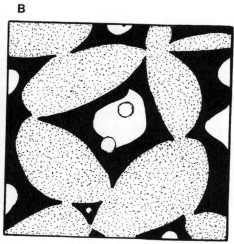

B. Because the water percolates swiftly, the root hairs are soon largely exposed to the air in the air pockets which form in the growing medium

C

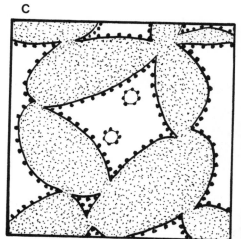

C. These root hairs or feeders being so small are only in partial contact with the salt water or solution. The thin film of liquid breaks up into patches, so that the roots are not suffocated

D

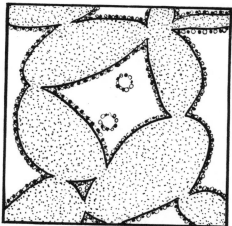

D. The air in the pockets remains moist, and during night time, when temperature falls, substratum dew is formed giving fresh water.

required. However, the usual average is about 0.50 litre per 0.093 square metre per diem in most units.

Using salt waters

Trials undertaken in many parts of the world, especially those initiated by Dr H. Boyko, of the World Academy of Art and Science, Rehovoth, Israel, have shown that very saline waters, even of oceanic strength, may now be used in hydroponics, provided that the passage of the liquid through the growing media is fairly rapid. It is also necessary that there should be fall in temperature at nights, to permit the formation of subterranean dew free from salts. Figure 35 shows what happens when such saline waters are employed in irrigating troughs.

Very alkaline waters may be improved by adding 0.5 to 1 cubic centimetre of sulphuric acid to every 500 litres of water. Acidic waters can be treated with dilute alkali. (*Note*: water should never be poured into sulphuric acid – always add the acid slowly to the water with due care.) It is quite common to adjust the pH value of a water by these means.

PART THREE

Nutrient Formulae

9. Hydroponic grass production. On left, grain or seed spread out for germination; on right, green fodder after seven days culture.

CHAPTER 13

Mixtures

Several hundred different formulae have been proposed for, and used in, hydroponic cultivation over the years. Despite the considerable amount of work that has been carried out in various areas on the soilless growth crops, it is not possible to say that any one 'best' solution or mixture for hydroponics exists. This is because conditions may be dissimilar and reactions that inevitably take place within hydroponic cultures, combined with the selectivity exercised naturally by plants, enable a very wide range of compositions to produce satisfactory and profitable results.

General limits

The main determinant from the nutritional point of view in the growth, development and production of soilless-cultured plants is the total ion concentration in solution in terms of the osmotic value. Here, of course, the optimum concentration must depend upon the type of crop and the local climatic conditions obtaining. In addition, account has to be taken of the influence of the ratio existing between the individual ions in the known favourable total ion concentration. In any nutrient solution, the various ions should be present in a free state. But when the concentration of two kinds of ions becomes so high that association occurs, then there will be precipitation of molecules, so that they go out of direct circulation in the solution. In consequence, the ion ratios will be restricted severely in any fixed total ion concentration.

It will therefore be apparent that the use of soilless cultures imposes certain practical limits upon the ion ratios in nutrient mixtures and solutions. This is of considerable importance in the preparation of formulae and the management and operation of hydroponic units.

In Chapter 1, a selection of nutrient solutions used by investigators in the field of laboratory water cultures has been given. It will be noted that there is considerable variation in these formulae and that the recommended total concentrations differ appreciably, with osmotic pressures of from 0.48 to 2.5 atmospheres.* It must of

---

*A. A. Steiner (1969) has recommended the following osmotic pressures for hydroponic tomato growth:
temperate regions with dark winters   Winter: 1.8 atmospheres   Summer: 0.7 atmosphere
                                        Spring: 1.1 atmospheres   tropical regions: 0.5 atmosphere

course be remembered that laboratory work implies the use of distilled water to make up the solutions and a steady controlled environment. Neverthless, the figures are significant and indicate the wide tolerance of plants and the inherent selective ability and contrasting needs of species. In Chapter 3, a general account is given of the physiological needs of plants and their requirements for different elements.

It is possible to define theoretical limits for ion ratios in solutions. There will be restrictions for anion ratio and also for cation ratio. But in practice, not very many formulae or compositions actually conform to these desiderata, being frequently outside the theoretical limits. However, once the formulae are dissolved in water and go into solution, the true composition may be said to come quite automatically within the accepted ion ratios because rapid precipitation will occur of certain surplus salts.

This fact is rather significant for practical hydroponic culture since it gives the grower far more freedom in preparing nutrient formulae.

Practical formulae

A suitable hydroponic mixture should provide a satisfactory total ion concentration, maintain proper balance and equilibrium in solution, represent an appropriate osmotic value, and offer a reaction within acceptable pH limits. It is far easier to secure all these desirable factors in controlled laboratory cultures, where distilled water is employed, than it is in the field, where many different sorts of water may have to be utilised.

Again, plants differ in their nutrient requirements, both according to type and the season of the year or climatic changes, as well as their stage of growth. The average hydroponic operator will be obliged to look for general formulae which can give satisfactory nourishment to a very wide range of crops and rely largely upon the inherent selectivity and adaptive ability of plants to adjust and accommodate themselves to conditions, provided of course that these offer all the necessary circumstances for optimum development.

We have already seen in Chapter 3 that plants utilise a considerable range of nutrient elements often within quite wide limits. It is worthwhile summarising the most important of these here, in terms of their desirable possible or acceptable concentrations in a hydroponic solution:

Element	*parts per million (ppm)* *in solution*	
	LIMITS	AVERAGE
Nitrogen	150– 1000	300
Calcium	300– 500	400
Magnesium	50– 100	75
Phosphorus	50– 100	80

Element	parts per million (ppm) in solution		
	LIMITS		AVERAGE
Potassium	100–	400	250
Sulphur	200–	1000	400
Copper	0.1–	0.5	0.5
Boron	0.5–	5	1
Iron	2–	10	5
Manganese	0.5–	5	2
Molybdenum	0.001–	0.002	0.001
Zinc	0.5–	1	0.5

The variability of cropping and environmental conditions make it impracticable to define any universal nutrient solution in precise terms, although it may be convenient to use many general formulae for ordinary soilless cultures. However, it is appropriate to aim for optimum nutrient solutions to suit particular situations and for a wide range of plants. A nutrient solution or mixture can be propounded by taking account of the following points: (1) a particular relative cation ratio; (2) a particular relative anion ratio; (3) a particular total ion concentration; and (4) a particular pH. In the actual preparation of the formulae it is necessary to consider the sources of the chemical fertilizers. Here the choice is quite large, in fact being mainly governed by the cost of the product in local circumstances. Commercial or technical grades of salts may be used in field work.

The quality of the irrigation water used to prepare solutions is important. It is very difficult to secure the correct combination of the elements for good nutrition if the water analysis is unknown. There may always be the danger of adding large amounts of certain nutrients to water already high in these same substances, thus increasing their concentrations beyond safety limits, so that the solution could reach toxic levels.

In certain advanced hydroponic installations, computers are employed to formulate optimum nutrient solutions for different crops. For the general grower, this may not be practicable. Quite satisfactory mixtures have however been prepared and may be made up by: (1) selecting the desirable limits of concentration of the different elements for crops with reference to the Table printed above; (2) aiming for a pH value in the resultant solution of between 5.5 and 6.5 (6.0 is generally the best value for all around cultivation); (3) checking the composition of water for salts already present in it and allowing for these when compounding the hydroponic formula. If certain elements are excessive in the water supply then they should be reduced accordingly in the fertilizer mixture.

Examples of typical hydroponic formulae prepared for different areas may be mentioned.

NETHERLANDS STANDARD COMPOSITION

This is based on

	Anions:	NO_3^-	:	$H_2PO_4^-$	:	SO_4^{--}
		60	:	5	:	35
	Cations:	K^+	:	Ca^{++}	:	Mg^{++}
		35	:	45	:	20

A part of the $H_2PO_4^-$ may be present as HPO_4^{--}, depending on the pH.

This combination is excellent for tomato, cucumber, freesia, paprika, lettuce, rose, Asparagus officinalis, Asparagus plumosus, radish etc., and is still suitable if the ratios are changed within the following ranges:

NO_3^-	50 to 70% of the anions
$H_2PO_4^-$	3 to 10% of the anions
SO_4^{--}	25 to 45% of the anions
K^+	30 to 40% of the cations
Ca^{++}	35 to 55% of the cations
Mg^{++}	15 to 30% of the cations

For calcifugous plants it is necessary to change the cation ratio into:

K^+	:	Ca^{++}	:	Mg^{++}
35	:	20	:	45

These include all Ericaceae, possibly all Araceae and some orchids.

The formula is:

	mg per litre H_2O
Potassium phosphate	136
Calcium nitrate	1062
Magnesium sulphate	492
Potassium nitrate	293
Potassium sulphate	252
Potassium hydroxide	22.4

Used with neutral or distilled water, represents an osmotic value of 0.7 atmosphere at pH 6.5 ± 0.1.

Trace element mixture, as for No. 7 below may be added.

(2) KUWAIT IV (D.W.1)

	gm per 1000 litres H_2O
Magnesium sulphate	339.30
Monocalcium phosphate	128.87
Calcium nitrate	2002.00
Potassium nitrate	264.00
Potassium sulphate	18.84

	gm per 1000 litres H_2O
Sodium chloride	156.60
Nitric acid (concentrated)	13.00 mls
Hydrochloric acid (concentrated)	20.00 mls

(3) KUWAIT IV (D.W.2)

	gm per 1000 litres H_2O
Magnesium sulphate	339.30
Monopotassium phosphate	131.69
Calcium nitrate	2096.00
Potassium nitrate	160.60
Potassium sulphate	18.84
Sodium chloride	156.60
Nitric acid (concentrated)	13.00 mls
Hydrochloric acid (concentrated)	20.00 mls

Used with neutral or distilled water for tomato culture, with pH around 5.5. Formulae (2) and (3) are identical with respect to concentrations and ratio of elements. The only difference is the substitution of monocalcium phosphate in (2) by monopotassium phosphate in (3), thus showing the possibility of preparing any nutrient solution with different fertilizers or chemicals depending on availability and relative prices of the substances concerned.

Minor elements were added to the main formulae as follows:

	mg per litre H_2O
Ferric ammonium citrate	1.00
Manganese sulphate	0.5
Copper sulphate	0.05
Zinc sulphate	0.05
Boric acid powder	0.5
Molybdic acid	0.01

(4) STANDARD FORMULAE FOR GRAVEL CULTURE IN JAPAN

		gm per 1000 litres H_2O
(*i*)	Potassium nitrate	810
	Calcium nitrate	950
	Magnesium sulphate	500
	Ammonium phosphate	155
(*ii*)	Potassium nitrate	810
	Ammonium nitrate	320
	Magnesium sulphate	500
	Superphosphate	580

Minor elements are added to both mixtures at the rate of 3 ppm of iron, 0.5 ppm of boron. The first formula is most suitable for fruit vegetables, whilst the second one is preferable for leafy greenstuff. These basic formulae should be used at proper strengths according to the kind of crop, the state of development and the growing season. For instance, with tomatoes, $\frac{1}{4}$ to $\frac{1}{2}$ strength is employed until the fruit-set of the third cluster, then full strength can be applied. For cucumbers, half to full strength is used in the early stages and $1\frac{1}{2}$ strength at the time of heavy picking during harvests.

(5) PENNINGSFELD'S CARNATION MIXTURE, WEST GERMANY

gm per 1000 litres H_2O

Calcium nitrate (15.5% N, 34.2% Ca)	868
Potassium nitrate (13.8% N, 46.6% K_2O)	416
Ammonium sulphate (21% N)	10
Monopotassium phosphate (35.8% K_2O, 51.7% P_2O_5)	284
Magnesium sulphate (16.4% MgO)	378
Iron sulphate (20.1% Fe)	20
Borax (11.4% B)	10
Manganese sulphate (32.5% Mn)	5
Zinc sulphate (22.7% Zn)	0.04
Copper sulphate (25.5% Cu)	0.04

(6) BASIC FORMULA, BENGAL, INDIA

gm

Sodium nitrate	170
Ammonium sulphate	85
Calcium sulphate	43
Superphosphate	100
Potassium sulphate	114
Magnesium sulphate	70
Trace elements mixture	0.5

The trace elements mixture is prepared from: 5 gm of zinc sulphate, 15 gm of manganese sulphate, 13 gm of boric acid powder, 5 gm of copper sulphate, and 19 gm of iron sulphate.

This formula may be used for dry application at the rate of up to 60 gm per square metre of trough surface space, or else dissolved in water to form a nutrient solution at the rate of 2–3 gm per one litre.

(7) RIVOIRA'S FORMULA USED AT SASSARI, SICILY

	mg per litre H_2O
Biammonium phosphate	200
Calcium nitrate	500
Potassium nitrate	200
Magnesium sulphate	100
Iron (EDTA)	5.13
Manganese sulphate	0.73
Zinc sulphate	0.06
Copper sulphate	0.06
Boric acid	0.59

(8) WROCLAW FORMULA FOR WATER CULTURE, POLAND

	gm per litre H_2O
Potassium nitrate	0.6
Calcium nitrate	0.7
Ammonium nitrate	0.1
Superphosphate	0.5
Magnesium sulphate	0.25
Iron sulphate	0.12
Boric acid	0.0006
Manganese sulphate	0.0006
Zinc sulphate	0.0006
Copper sulphate	0.0030
Ammonium molybdate	0.0006

This solution may be acidified by adding orthophosphoric acid at the rate of 100 ml per 1000 litres of solution. In winter time, ammonium nitrate may be omitted. During summer periods, the quantity of copper sulphate can be quintupled. Again, in winter 0.3 gm of potassium sulphate may be added to augment the amount of this element during dull weather when there is an insufficiency of light.

(9) VOLCANI INSTITUTE FORMULA, ISRAEL

	gm per 1000 litres H_2O
Potassium nitrate	450
Ammonium nitrate	350
Magnesium sulphate	50
Phosphoric acid	100 cc

Minor elements: Fe as sequestrene F13, B, Mn, Zn, Cu.
For use with fairly saline or calcareous waters.

(10) PENNINGSFELD'S NORTH AFRICAN FORMULAE

(i) for sweet water: *gm per 1000 litres* H_2O

Potassium nitrate	384
Calcium nitrate	217
Ammonium phosphate	46
Monopotassium phosphate	144
Magnesium sulphate	190
Iron sulphate	10
Borax	2.5
Manganese sulphate	2.5
Copper sulphate	2.5
Ammonium molybdate	0.75
Zinc sulphate	0.02

(ii) for salt water
+ 2500 ppm: *gm per 1000 litres* H_2O

Potassium nitrate	361
Ammonium sulphate nitrate	190.5
Monopotassium phosphate	144
Iron sulphate	10
Borax	2.5
Manganese sulphate	2.5
Copper sulphate	2.5
Ammonium molybdate	0.75
Zinc sulphate	0.02
Potassium bromide	0.01

(11) UNITED STATES DEPARTMENT OF AGRICULTURE'S FORMULA, MARYLAND

                                                              gm per 1000 litres H_2O

Potassium nitrate	525
Ammonium sulphate	88
Monocalcium phosphate	220
Magnesium sulphate	400
Calcium sulphate	435

(12) AGRICULTURAL EXTENSION SERVICE'S FORMULA, FLORIDA

                                                              gm per 1000 litres H_2O

Potassium nitrate	365
Ammonium sulphate	80
Monocalcium phosphate	170
Magnesium sulphate	160
Calcium sulphate	900

For (11) and (12),
18 gm of the following
minor or trace element
mixture should be
added:

		gm
Iron sulphate		113
Manganese sulphate		7.5
Copper sulphate		3.5
Sodium tetraborate (borax)		85
Zinc sulphate		3.5

These various formulae are fairly representative in composition and indicate the wide range of fertilizer salts and their combinations that may be employed in hydroponics.

It must be emphasised that for commercial soilless cropping – and indeed for advanced amateurs – the guiding principle should be to choose fertilizers that are easily available locally and which come in a favourable price range. The question of costs is important because it is often possible to use a reasonably priced nutrient in place of a more expensive salt with just as good results.

For the convenience of readers, a further list of suitable hydroponic mixtures is given here:

NOTE: To form nutrient solutions with these formulae add 2 gm of the stated mixture to one litre of water. This quantity can be increased to 3 gm if growth is slow. Minor or trace element formulae, which can be used together with the major salts compositions are given at the end of the list.

		gm
A	Sodium nitrate	355
	Superphosphate	200
	Potassium sulphate	113
	Magnesium sulphate	113

		gm
B	Ammonium sulphate	227
	Ammonium phosphate	156
	Potassium muriate	85
	Calcium sulphate	57
	Magnesium sulphate	113

		gm
C	Ammonium sulphate	280
	Potassium sulphate	71
	Superphosphate	170
	Magnesium sulphate	85

		gm
D	Potassium nitrate	538
	Superphosphate	184
	Ammonium sulphate	142
	Magnesium sulphate	156

		gm
E	Ammonium phosphate	71
	Sodium nitrate	227
	or	
	Ammonium nitrate	113.5
	Calcium nitrate	29
	Potassium sulphate	113.5
	Magnesium sulphate	113.5

		gm
F	Ammonium phosphate	199
	Potassium nitrate	964
	Ammonium sulphate	142
	Ammonium nitrate	85

For use where calcium and magnesium are already present in the water supply.

		gm
G	Ammonium phosphate	199
	Potassium nitrate	950
	Calcium nitrate	142
	Ammonium nitrate	157
	Magnesium sulphate	552

		gm
H	Superphosphate	510
	Potassium nitrate	964
	Calcium nitrate	765
	Magnesium sulphate	552

G and H are intended for use where the water contains insufficient or no calcium and magnesium.

		gm
I	Sodium nitrate	281
	Superphosphate	200
	Ammonium sulphate	72
	Potassium sulphate	89
	Magnesium sulphate	113

		gm
J	Sodium nitrate	794
	Potassium muriate	72
	Superphosphate	425
	Magnesium sulphate	241
	Ammonium sulphate	57

During a cloudy or wet period, the potassium muriate should be increased to 144 gm and the sodium nitrate reduced to 561 gm.

		gm
K	Ammonium sulphate	99
	Superphosphate	113
	Potassium sulphate	43
	Calcium nitrate	28
	Magnesium sulphate	85

		gm
L	Monopotassium phosphate	255
	Calcium nitrate	71
	Magnesium sulphate	212
	Ammonium sulphate	28

		gm
M	Sodium nitrate	212
	Monammonium phosphate	72
	Potassium sulphate	113
	Calcium nitrate	57
	Magnesium sulphate	99

		gm
N	Potassium nitrate	765
	Calcium nitrate	156
	Superphosphate	212
	Magnesium sulphate	185

		gm
O	Sodium nitrate	184
	Calcium chloride	71
	Monopotassium phosphate	114
	Magnesium sulphate	170

		gm
P	Potassium nitrate	454
	Ammonium sulphate	170
	Superphosphate	185
	Magnesium sulphate	143

		gm
Q	Potassium nitrate	58
	Magnesium nitrate	170
	Ammonium chloride	42
	Calcium nitrate	539
	Monopotassium phosphate	157
	Magnesium sulphate	42

		gm
R	Sodium nitrate	184
	Superphosphate	100
	Calcium sulphate	28
	Potassium sulphate	57
	Magnesium sulphate	57

		gm
S	Ammonium sulphate	170
	Superphosphate	170
	Potassium nitrate	156
	Magnesium sulphate	94.5

		gm
T	Calcium nitrate	127
	Monopotassium phosphate	341
	Magnesium sulphate	255

		gm
U	Ammonium nitrate	950
	Potassium nitrate	425
	Monopotassium phosphate	215
	Calcium chloride	387
	Magnesium sulphate	340

		gm
V	Ammonium sulphate	71
	Potassium nitrate	709
	Superphosphate or *Rock phosphate	284
	Calcium sulphate	850
	Magnesium sulphate	445
	Ammonium phosphate	99

*Must be very finely ground.

W	Sodium nitrate	*gm*
		255
	Ammonium phosphate	47
	Potassium sulphate	113
	Calcium nitrate	28
	Magnesium sulphate	128

X	Potassium nitrate	*gm*
		297
	Sodium chloride	113
	Calcium sulphate	85
	Magnesium phosphate	113
	Superphosphate	99.5

Y	Ammonium nitrate	*gm*
		99
	Potassium nitrate	297
	Monopotassium phosphate	283
	Magnesium sulphate	211
	Calcium sulphate	29

Z	Calcium nitrate	*gm*
		114
	Monopotassium phosphate	283
	Potassium chloride	113
	Magnesium sulphate	156

AA	Potassium nitrate	*gm*
		282
	Superphosphate	240
	Magnesium sulphate	184

AB	Magnesium nitrate	*gm*
		255
	Potassium sulphate	142
	Superphosphate	185

AC	Magnesium nitrate	*gm*
		294
	Monopotassium phosphate	269
	Calcium sulphate	57.5

AD	Potassium nitrate	*gm*
		312
	Magnesium phosphate	295
	Calcium sulphate	72

		gm
AE	Calcium nitrate	212.5
	Magnesium phosphate	227
	Potassium sulphate	184

		gm
AF	Nicifos	560
	Potassium sulphate or muriate	184
	Magnesium sulphate	171

		gm
AG	Ammonium sulphate	227
	Bonemeal	705
	Potassium sulphate	128
	Calcium chloride	35
	Magnesium sulphate	128

		gm
AH	Calcium cyanamide*	198
	Monopotassium phosphate	227
	Magnesium sulphate	85

*When using calcium cyanamide, care must be taken to keep it from direct contact with plants. It is best with a filler of dry silver sand, and should be well mixed with this and other salts of the formula.

		gm
AI	Ammonium hydroxide	72
	Phosphoric acid	104
	Potassium hydroxide	43
	Calcium oxide	37.5
	Nitric acid	241
	Sulphuric acid	47
	Magnesium oxide	47

		gm
AJ	Potassium nitrate	213
	Ammonium sulphate	467
	Magnesium sulphate	255
	Superphosphate	397

		gm
AK	Sodium nitrate	218
	Ammonium sulphate	47
	Potassium sulphate	114
	Superphosphate	209
	Magnesium sulphate	123.5

NOTE: It will no doubt have been observed that the various formulae given in this chapter contain only fairly small individual or total quantities of nutrients. This is quite normal practice in listing mixtures and is done so that growers may test them out, if desired, on small plots first, before embarking on larger cultivation programmes, to see if they produce optimum results in the particular conditions, taking account of the local water supply and other factors. Major operators and commercial installations, wanting to prepare substantial amounts of nutrient mixtures or solutions at one time, can easily increase the bulk of any formula by multiplying the individual quantities in it. Care must be taken, of course, to employ a constant number for this, so that the relative proportions of the various ingredients remain unaltered, otherwise a lack of balance would occur.

For example to prepare a sizeable stock of the following formula, one could simply multiply each individual amount of the listed fertilizers as shown. Thus, though the quantities of the various nutrients are far bigger, the ratios between them remain unchanged and the bulk stock corresponds exactly to the original formula given.

Example: NETHERLANDS STANDARD COMPOSITION. To produce enough formula to form a nutrient solution of 1000 litres; multiply throughout by 1000, giving:

	gm per 1000 litres H_2O
Potassium phosphate	136
Calcium nitrate	1062
Magnesium sulphate	492
Potassium nitrate	293
Potassium sulphate	252
Potassium hydroxide	22.4

One milligramme (mg) equals $\frac{1}{1000}$ of a gramme (gm).

To provide enough formula to use with 100,000 litres of water, multiply the above figures by 100 and convert to kilogrammes (kilos). One kilo equals 1000 grammes. The quantities would then read:

	kg
Potassium phosphate	13.6
Calcium nitrate	106.2
Magnesium sulphate	49.2
Potassium nitrate	29.3
Potassium sulphate	25.2
Potassium hydroxide	2.24

Similar calculations may be made without difficulty for other nutrient mixtures, up to any total quantity of compound or solution required.

Minor or trace element mixtures

In addition to the formulae already noted, the following compositions may be used:

		gm
1	Zinc sulphate	6.00
	Manganese sulphate	16.50
	Boric acid powder	13.00
	Copper sulphate	6.00
	Ferrous or iron sulphate	17.75

Add at the rate of one gramme to every 1000 grammes of major salt mixture. The quantities used are only small because certain amounts of trace elements are generally present already as impurities in the main salts or in the water supply.

2	*Stock solution*	*gm*
	Manganese chloride	0.10
	Zinc chloride	0.05
	Boric acid powder	0.05
	Copper chloride	0.01
	Ferric sulphate	0.20

Dissolve the above noted quantities of salts in one litre H_2O, and add up to 20 cubic centimetres (cc) of this stock solution to each 1000 litres of the main nutrient solution.

Alternative processes

So far we have described the formulation of nutrient mixtures composed of standard fertilizer salts. These are the simplest and most commonly employed means of nourishing crops in hydroponics. However, various alternative nutritional processes exist or are under investigation. These include:

(*a*) The use of different slow-release fertilizers, such as synthetic resins, porous carrier materials made from siliceous and diatomaceous substances, urea-form fertilizers, compounds for graduated crop nutrition, the sequestrene chemicals, and glass frits, as well as other nutrient vehicles of slmilar types and objectives.

(*b*) Nourishment through the employment of sludges, treated sewages and wastes, and a number of related materials.

Because the majority of such nutrients normally reach the hydroponic operator in prepared or processed forms, their usage will be discussed in Chapter 14.

Ready-made fertilizer compounds
In order to save hydroponic growers the trouble of weighing out and mixing up their own nutrient formulae for soilless cultivation, various manufacturing firms in different countries have marketed ready-made or prepared mixtures for use. These should be composed of standard hydroponic prescriptions or recipes and will often be designed for employment in particular regions or under different climatic conditions. Some, however, can be utilised as general formulae over a wide range of circumstances and for all sorts of crops. It is important, before using such nutrient mixtures, to read the manufacturers' descriptions of their compositions or to ask for analyses. Furthermore, always check on prices or the final cost of using a prepared formula might well turn out to be far more expensive in large scale work than the purchase and blending of one's own formulae.

The following compound fertilizer mixtures have been tested in hydroponic culture and found very satisfactory for general growth:

(*a*) *Phostrogen* Manufactured by Phostrogen Ltd., London Road, Corwen, Merioneth, Wales, United Kingdom. Available direct from the makers or through local agents in different countries.

(*b*) Hydroponic Chemical Co., Inc., Box 97-C, Copley, Ohio; and

(*c*) Hydroculture Inc., P.O. Box 1655, Glendale, Arizona; and

(*d*) City Green Hydroponics Ltd., 6471 Northam Drive, Mississauga, Ontario, Canada, make prepared formulae for soilless cultivation.

(*e*) Others.

(The reader can enter here any more suitable hydroponic growing compounds that may come to his or her notice.)

CHAPTER 14

Usage and application

The fertilizer chemicals or other nutritional materials for hydroponics are a very important part of the apparatus of soilless cultivation. For this reason, much care should be taken in their selection and purchase. They should also be stored in dry conditions and not exposed to damp. In wet weather, some salts can liquefy, if proper precautions are not taken. Products manufactured in different areas sometimes contain diverse percentages of particular nutrients. Normally, analyses are supplied by the makers. Some fertilizers contain two or more major nutrient elements. This can save time and trouble in compounding formulae. In choosing hydroponic chemicals, do not hesitate to select those which are available at the lowest cost, bearing in mind of course the questions of quality and nutrient content.

Common fertilizers

Ordinary agricultural, horticultural or technical grade fertilizer salts are the most satisfactory and cheapest for general work. The following substances are generally available in most areas:

For nitrogen Sodium nitrate, ammonium sulphate, ammonium nitrate, calcium nitrate, calcium cyanamide, urea, ammonium chloride, ammonium hydroxide.
For phosphate Superphosphate, monocalcium phosphate, basic slag.
For potassium Potassium sulphate, potassium muriate, potassium hydroxide.
For magnesium Magnesium sulphate.
For calcium Calcium sulphate.
For iron Iron sulphate.
Compounds Monoammonium phosphate, potassium nitrate, monopotassium phosphate, potassium magnesium sulphate.

In addition, there are numerous proprietary fertilizers, produced by different manufacturers under various trade names, which contain two or more nutrients. Most single salts and compounds also carry, as impurities, several other major or trace elements. For full details, books on fertilizers should be consulted.

The following salts should not be mixed together in formulae:

Ammonium sulphate or ammonium phosphate with basic slag or calcium cyanamide;
Basic slag with superphosphate, calcium nitrate;
Calcium cyanamide with superphosphate or calcium nitrate;
Oxide of lime with superphosphate, calcium nitrate or ammonium phosphate.

Mixing

After being carefully weighed out, the nutrient salts should be well mixed together, any lumps being broken up into a fine powder. A reliable balance or scale should be employed. All fertilizers or formulae must be stored in dry conditions or containers until needed for use. The complete mixture should be added to the stated quantity of water in the solution tank or reservoir, unless it is being used for dry application, and the whole thoroughly stirred until it is dissolved.

Application

The nutrient solution will require checking and testing in most large hydroponic installations every week. Further details about these procedures will be found in subsequent chapters of this book. The quantities of formulae to be used are generally given below each recommended mixture, but in general the rate of usage is from 2 to 3 grammes of a formula per one litre of water. Where the nutrients are applied dry and then watered in, the normal amount given is about 30 grammes of mixture to each square metre of trough surface space every week or ten days, though this can be increased to 60 grammes if growth is slow. Care must be taken to ensure that dry fertilizer mixtures are distributed evenly over the whole area of the beds, and immediately watered into solution in the substrate.

Variations

Cloudy or winter weather means that plants need more potassium, so during dull and wet seasons it is advantageous for growers to increase the quantity of this element in nutrient mixtures. In prolonged dull weather it can be safely doubled, by raising the quantity of whatever potassium-containing salt is used. At the same time, in order to economise, the nitrogen supply can be reduced proportionately. On the other hand, in bright summer periods, the crops will require much more nitrogen and less potash. Experience has shown that the osmotic pressure of the nutrient solution should be higher in winter time than during the summer. Similarly, greater pressure is demanded in temperate regions than is desirable in tropical and sub-tropical localities. All the same, it is important to bear in mind that it is the environmental effects, such as the light conditions, the prevailing temperatures, the aeration of the root zone and related factors that exercise very strong influences upon the absorption of the nutrient ions. Absence of oxygen, in particular, in the solution and the root area, is especially damaging to good growth and development. In addition, for optimum production it is essential that pH values for hydroponics should, in general, not be lower than 5.0 and nor much over 6.5 (see Chapter 13 page 171, and Chapter 17 pages 243–5).

Slow-release and other nutrients

Instead of common or standard fertilizer programmes in hydroponics, use can be made of alternative processes for supplying the essential nutrients. These have been mentioned briefly in the preceding chapter. However, it must be pointed out that, in some cases, although such procedures may save time and labour, some of them are still in their infancy and may be costly to utilise. A good deal of further research and investigation is still called for in these instances.

Synthetic resins

Work in hydroponics has been undertaken with synthetic carrier resins supplying plant nutrients in adsorbed form. The advantages of using such materials, which come under different trade names, such as amberlites or permutits, include the fact that sufficient nutrient ions may be incorporated in the growing media at the beginning of the season to last all through the cropping period, only the addition of water at subsequent periods being usually necessary. This obviates the frequent application of standard fertilizer formulae. Many of the complications of nutrient management may be eliminated; there can be a reduction of losses due to leaching during rainfall in open air units; and there is the possibility of varying single ion concentration with simultaneous variation in ions of opposite charge. Depending on the preparation, synthetic ion exchange resins of the amberlite or permutit types have either anion- or cation-exchange properties. The former is an amine-formaldehyde resin, while the latter are phenol-formaldehyde resins in which hydrogen of phenolic group is exchangeable for other cations.

The suggested amounts of synthetic resins for use in basic work are:

Synthetic resin	gm	Synthetic resin	gm
$K+$	2040	SO_4--	141
$Ca++$	1048	H_2BO_3---	28
$Mg++$	510	$Fe++$	1.75
NO_3-	1134	$Mn++$	0.45
H_2PO_4---	72–85		

Mix the above quantities in with each one square metre of the aggregate before planting or sowing. There is enough for a period of approximately 4 to 5 months.

It has been found that the use of a potassium nitrate solution as the source of potash and nitrogen, with consequent omission of potassium and nitrate ion-exchangers from the beds, reduced any adverse contact effects. The operator is therefore advised, should he or she find that growth is unsatisfactory, to leave out these synthetic resins from the mixture, and substitute instead a watering of 57 grammes of potassium nitrate in 450 litres of water, two or three times weekly, as required. Or if preferred, the salt may be applied dry at the rate of 14 to 28 grammes per square metre of trough surface space every week or ten days, sprinkled evenly between crop rows and well watered in.

The use of synthetic resins is still in the early stages, and further investigation continues at the research centres, but the results so far obtained indicate that these carriers have a promising future in hydroponic culture, if their cost can be reduced for commercial purposes.

The grower is recommended to make trial of them, starting on a small scale, and watching progress carefully. Supplies may be obtained for trial from the Rohm & Haas Company, Washington Square, Philadelphia 5, Pennsylvania, United States, or the Permutit Company Ltd, Gunnersbury Avenue, London W.4., England, and local agents. Pamphlets which give details of the conversion processes are also available from these firms. (See also Chapter 17, page 234.)

At the University of Sassari, Sicily (Istituto di Agronomia Generale e Coltivazioni Erbacee), the value of ion-exchange resins has been tested by stratifying four kinds of these carrier materials in hydroponic growing beds at a depth of 20 cm. The resins employed were IR-50, IR-120, and IR-45.

Compounds

Magamp K is a mixture of magnesium-ammonium phosphate and magnesium-potassium phosphate. As a commercial fertilizer it has an average composition of 7% N, 40% P_2O_5, 6% K, and 12% MgO. Floranid-nitrophoska is a complex fertilizer, containing 10% Isodur, 10% ammonium and nitrate nitrogen, 5% phosphoric anhydride soluble in water and ammonium citrate, 8% potassium oxide, 2% magnesium oxide, and 1% iron sulphate. These nutrients are both slow-release compounds. The Magamp K is slowly soluble, and Floranid-nitrophoska is slowly available, to plants. The nitrogen in the latter substance is partly present as isobutyldendiurea, called Isodur, in trade terms.

Urea-form fertilizers are often employed as sources of slowly soluble nitrogen in soilless culture. Various trade names exist to designate the products of different manufacturers. Ranges of compounds made by certain firms are now available which give graduated nutrition to crops over fairly long periods. These fertilizers can be employed to supply also phosphorus, potassium, magnesium, and other essential elements. Often a single slow release material may provide a combination of several plant foods in stated proportions, as has been already noted in the cases of Magamp K and Floranid-nitrophoska above.

The sequestrene or chelated nutrients, such as ferric potassium ethylenediamine tetra-acetate, have been used for supplying iron, in cases where there may be dangers of this element reacting with other elements in solution. For example, the proprietary 'Chel 330', which is sequestrene 330 Fe or monosodium ferric diethylenetriamine penta-acetate, has given good results in growing tomatoes in calcareous media in the Bahama Islands. Chelated trace elements, packed in convenient quantities, are available for hydroponic use, from various horticultural sources.

Sustanum is a porous carrier material manufactured from diatomaceous and siliceous substances, in which the nutrient elements are embedded. When incorporated in hydroponic troughs and properly watered, it supplies crops with adequate amounts of both the major and the trace elements over a considerable period of time. Successful results have been obtained in many parts of the world by using sustanum slow-release fertilizer in soilless culture units. It is available in two formulae, one for tropical, and the other for temperate zone work, based upon standard hydroponic formulae.

Sustanum combines most of the advantages of synthetic resins in hydroponics with the added value of being cheaper to buy. For general use, 455 grammes of this fertilizer mixed into each square metre of trough space will provide sufficient nourishment to last most crops for 5 months. Both large and small quantities of sustanum for hydroponics, together with full instructions for application, may be obtained from the manufacturers: Trace Element Fertilisers Ltd, 118 Ewell Road, Surbiton, Surrey, England, or through local horticultural stores.

Various other techniques of nutrient usage have also been developed. In British Columbia, certain nutrients for a cropping season have been mixed in with sawdust growing medium, so that there was a reduction in the amounts of fertilizers to be applied through the irrigation system. At the Saanichton Research Station, all the plant food requirements, except nitrogen and potassium, were incorporated in the substrate in the troughs of the hydroponic installation. The amounts used per cubic metre were:

Ground dolomitic limestone for calcium and magnesium   4 kg

Single superphosphate (19%)   2.4 kg

Minor elements: B 8.4 gm, Mn 21.2 gm, Zn 1.6 gm, Cu 0.53 gm, Mo 0.35 gm, and Fe 27.9 gm, were dissolved in 17.7 litres of water and added.

Normal N and K levels were fed in the nutrient solution.

Pine tree and other barks have been impregnated with essential nutrient ions and used as growing media. The elements are released slowly during the period of plant development.

Glass frits, which provide partial or complete formulae for hydroponic culture, are another interesting prospect. Ascorbic acid, released by the crops' roots, slowly dissolves the glass of the frits, thus making gradually available the nutrient ions contained in the material. The frits are, of course, mixed in with the aggregate in the soilless troughs.

Further ingenious developments in the field of hydroponic crop nutrition may be expected in the future.

Assessing fertilizers

All fertilizer salts contain stated proportions of the essential nutrient(s) that they will supply. These should be printed on the bags or will be shown in the analyses. Operators should take care to note these, because different salts may vary in their nutrient content. Superphosphate, for example, often comes in several grades – single with from 15 to 20% P_2O_5, concentrated 36 to 42% P_2O_5, and triple or treble with from 48% P_2O_5 upwards. Other fertilizers may differ similarly, although there are general standards laid down. In this book, where superphosphate is indicated in formulae it may be taken to be the triple or treble type, unless noted to the contrary. Granular fertilizers are not very suitable for hydroponics – they are often difficult to dissolve and contain much waste matter and residues. It is best to use powdered forms of nutrients, as finely ground as possible.

If it should be found that a given salt newly selected for use in a formula should contain a higher percentage than might normally be employed, a reduction should be made in the weight of fertilizer used, worked out by reference to the percentage of the element in the standard substance. The converse would apply where the percentage was lower than normal and in such cases the weight would have to be increased as might be necessary.

Compound fertilizers are designated by the percentage of nutrients that they contain, as well as by the relative proportions of the ratios of these nutrients. A simplified list will read:

Type	% nutrients			Plant food ratio		
	N	P_2O_5	K_2O	N	P_2O_5	K_2O
N.P.K.	10	10	15	1	1	$1\frac{1}{2}$
	12	12	18	1	1	$1\frac{1}{2}$
	6	15	15	1	$2\frac{1}{2}$	$2\frac{1}{2}$
	9	6	18	$1\frac{1}{2}$	1	3
	12	8	8	$1\frac{1}{2}$	1	1

Type	%nutrients			Plant food ratio		
	N	P_2O_5	K_2O	N	P_2O_5	K_2O
N.P.	8	12	8	1	$1\frac{1}{2}$	1
N.K.	9	18	—	1	2	—
P.K.	16	—	16	1	—	1
	—	10	20	—	1	2

Unit system

With this method the number of units of a particular nutrient in 50.80 kg of a fertilizer is the same as the percentage of that nutrient in the fertilizer. Thus 5.80 kg of ammonium sulphate (at 21% N) contains 21 units of nitrogen; the same quantity of 48% superphosphate will supply 48 units of P_2O_5; and a similar amount of potassium muriate of 60% K will provide 60 units of potash (K_2O). A bag of compound fertilizer made up of 12.12.18 N.P.K. would contain 12 units of N, 12 units of P, and 18 units of K. To make up a quantity of compound mixture to equal the three separate lots of individual fertilizers, which total together 152.40 kg, it is necessary to multiply first the 12 units of N to bring them to 21 units: 12 × 1.75 equals 21. This will also give us 21 units of phosphate and 31.50 of potash. With 1.75 bags of compound mixture we would than have the correct number of units of nitrogen and be short of 27 units of phosphate and 28.50 of potassium. It would be necessary to make up these deficiencies with extra straight salts, approximately 13.7 kg of P salt at 48%, and 14.45 kg of K salt at 60%. Adding together: 1.75 bags compound (88.90 kg) plus 13.7 kg and 14.45 kg straight salts gives us a total of 117.05 kg.

It is therefore apparent that it would be more profitable, in terms of weight, to use a proportion of compound fertilizer than to rely on all straight nutrients, since we will need 35.35 kg less for providing the same number of units.

Where compound fertilizers can be used conveniently in hydroponics to provide more than one nutrient it frequently pays to employ them, as well as saving time and labour.

Element concentrations

Conversion tables may be worked out to help in choosing nutrient formulae in hydroponics. In Chapter 13 (pages 170–71) the average and possible or acceptable concentrations of nutrient ions in solutions have been given. The following table lists a number of fertilizers and the quantities of each that would be needed to produce an approximate concentration of 1 ppm in 450 litres of water. Such tables* are useful in enabling

---

*Calculations for further types of fertilizer salts could be supplied without difficulty by the chemistry departments of universities or research institutions to growers.

growers to calculate how much of a salt they will require to produce a desired parts per million value of a given element in a solution.

Fertilizer	Number of grammes required per 450 litres of water to give concentration of 1 ppm
Sodium nitrate	2.9 N
Calcium nitrate	3.8 N
Ammonium sulphate	2.1 N
Potassium nitrate (for N)	3.5 N
Potassium nitrate (for K)	1.2 K
Superphosphate (16% P_2O_5)	7.5 P
Monocalcium phosphate	3.3 P
Magnesium sulphate	4.8 Mg
Potassium sulphate	1.1 K
Potassium chloride or muriate	0.9 K
Calcium sulphate	2.1 Ca
Ferrous sulphate	2.5 Fe
Manganese sulphate	1.8 Mn
Boric acid powder	2.6 B
Monopotassium phosphate	2.0 P
Ammonium phosphate	3.5 N
Ferric ammonium citrate	4.0 Fe
Copper sulphate	1.8 Cu
Zinc sulphate	2.0 Zn

To obtain the desired ppm concentration, multiply the quantity listed by the ppm required. For example, to secure 300 ppm of nitrogen in a mixture:

Using sodium nitrate: 2.9 × 300 = 870 gm
Using ammonium sulphate: 2.1 × 300 = 630 gm

Ammonium sulphate averages 20% N, against sodium nitrate's 16%, so less fertilizer will be needed.

To obtain 80 ppm of phosphorus, with monocalcium phosphate; 3.3 × 80 = 264 gm.

For iron, at 5 ppm, with ferrous sulphate: 2.5 × 5 = 12.5 gm and with ferric, ammonium citrate: 4.0 × 5 = 20 gm.

Readers interested in further information on the subjects of plant nutrition, ion proportions and antagonism, may consult books on plant physiology, which continue these studies to a higher level than would normally be necessary for general commercial hydroponic practice.

PART FOUR

Cultural Operations

10. Young tomato plants in hydroponics. Note the overhead and vertical strings for tieing, around which the stalks are wound as they increase in height.   (Dr. Cyril Pustan).

CHAPTER 15

Planting

The term 'planting' includes a number of cultural practices, which although mainly mechanical in technique, nevertheless contribute largely to the ultimate success of any soilless cropping programme. Correct storage, treatment, and germination of seeds, satisfactory propagation, hardening off and transplanting, together with proper spacing and anchorage of plants, are vital to the efficient operation of the hydroponicum.

Seed storage

All seeds have a limited life span, even under the most favourable storage conditions. Under less satisfactory circumstances, the vitality of seeds may be reduced to a matter of weeks or possibly days. It must be appreciated that the seed is a living organism, the energy for its vital processes being furnished through respiration. Within the seed, there is a stock of stored food material. In conditions of low temperature, the dry, dormant seed respires at a greatly reduced rate, and the food requirements are correspondingly small. As soon as it absorbs moisture, however, the processes are accelerated, and if the temperature is high enough, growth associated with germination may begin.

The economic life of a representative list of seeds of some useful species is given below:

Plant	Economic longevity of seed in years
Cucumber	5
Onion	1
Lettuce	5
Peppers	2
Radish	4
Tomato	4
Muskmelon	5
Wheat	5–10
Oats	10
Timothy	1–2

Plant	Economic longevity of seed in years
Barley	8
Rye	5
Soyabeans	5
Sorghum	7
Maize	4–6

These figures apply, of course, only to seeds kept under good storage conditions. In many cases, the vitality of a small percentage of a particular sample may remain unimpaired for very much longer periods, even up to 100 years or more. The most important factor is moisture, followed by temperature. Seeds will survive exposure to temperatures of from 27 to 39°C for long periods, if the relative humidity is so low that they remain dry. Where the air is damp, viability may be lost within a few days. It is essential, therefore, under tropical conditions to ensure that every precaution is taken. In cold countries, potato seed tubers must be protected against frost. In addition, safeguards should be provided to exclude insects and rodents. The best storage temperatures for most seeds range from 2 to 5°C. The atmosphere should be dry, and free from noxious fumes or gases.

In the case of onions, the seed keeps better if placed in sealed containers in a refrigerator in hot areas. Other seeds may be put into glass jars or tin cans with tight fitting lids. Even in temperate zones, the paper packets used by most seed merchants are quite unsuitable for storage purposes. When removing seeds from a container care should be taken to bring it to room temperature before opening so as to prevent any condensation of moisture on the contents. Unused seeds should be returned to storage as soon as possible.

Germination tests

In commercial work, it is often advisable to test batches of seed periodically for the germination capacity. Various unscrupulous seed firms are known to fill up their stocks and offerings with sterilised weed seed. This is frequently very hard to distinguish in outward appearance from the genuine article, and as it never comes up in any case, the purchaser is none the wiser. Complaints of bad germination merely elicit a rebuff: the fault being invariably attributed to the grower's lack of skill.

Germination tests can be carried out very simply by using either the 'rag doll' technique, or the plate method. With the former, from fifty to a hundred seeds are carefully counted and laid out on wet towelling which is then loosely rolled up into a cylinder. Filter paper can also be utilised. The rolls of seed are kept in a moist place at a temperature of from 18 to 27°C for several days. They should be inspected daily to determine when the seed germinates. As soon as this has occurred, the number of germinated seeds are counted, and the percentage of germination calculated. In the plate method, a piece of wet filter paper, towelling, or white cloth, should be placed at the bottom of a soup plate, a large watch glass, or a Petri dish. Up to a hundred seeds are counted out and placed on the paper or cloth. Another plate should then be inverted over the lower receptacle, and the apparatus stood in a warm room. It must be kept moist at all times, but there should not be any free water standing in the dish. As the seeds germinate, they must be counted, and the percentage calculated in the usual manner.

The rapidity of germination, and the vigour of the seedlings, should also be noted, because seeds that germinate very slowly, and well over the normal time for the species in question, may fail to produce good plants. Any germination value below 75 per cent is unsatisfactory. The seed of warmth-loving crops, like tomatoes, rice, peppers, maize, or cucumbers, germinates most rapidly at temperatures of between 21 and 32°C. At temperatures of over 32°C, seedlings may suffer some damage. Plants which prefer cooler conditions, such as lettuces, radishes, and a number of the cereals and brassicas, produce seed that will germinate at 4°C.

Seed treatment

Some seeds, like lettuce, germinate poorly at high temperatures. This difficulty may be overcome by placing them in a refrigerator for twenty-four hours, or by treating them with thiourea as follows:

Wrap the seed in a piece of muslin or cheesecloth, and allow it to soak for about five hours in a 0.5 per cent solution of thiourea at 21 to 27°C. Once every hour, the bag of seed should be lifted from the solution, gently squeezed, and then returned to soak. After five hours, the seeds should be removed from the solution, washed with plain water, and well dried. Storage for two weeks after treatment improves the germination capacity.

There are several types of diseases which may be carried on the testa. After germination, these can attack the young seedling. Treatment of the seed before sowing with fungicide is a good practice. Red copper oxide dust is often used for this purpose, the dry seed being placed in a tight container, with a supply of the dust, and the whole then shaken. Various seed disinfectants, such as the organic mercury fungicides, are available in proprietary packages from horticultural merchants and shops. Full instructions for the use of these materials are always given on the containers, or in attached leaflets, and these directions should be strictly adhered to.

Seed germination

There are several techniques for starting seeds. In water cultures, the germination net may be used profitably. With sand and aggregate cultures, a tray filled with fine medium can be employed. Wick devices are also useful, while a porous brick covered with a thin layer of sand and partially immersed in a basin of solution is often valuable in difficult cases. Very small seeds need special attention and treatment. Good results have been obtained with vermiculite as a medium for germination. Except when sowings are made directly into the main beds, it is always desirable to set aside one part of the hydroponic installation for propagation purposes.

Plant propagation

The amount of seed to be sown depends upon the number of plants that will be ultimately required. It is advisable to use about three times as many seeds as there will be plants needed, to allow for culling and failure to germinate. All small seeds should normally be started in separate propagation boxes, troughs or beds, filled with substrate for later transfer to the main troughs, unless there are special reasons to the contrary. Larger seeds, like those of the cereals, peas, beans, and okra, will generally be sown *in situ* in their permanent places, if only to save extra labour. The usual depths of sowing are: celery, tobacco, and very small seeds, about 3 millimetres; lettuce,

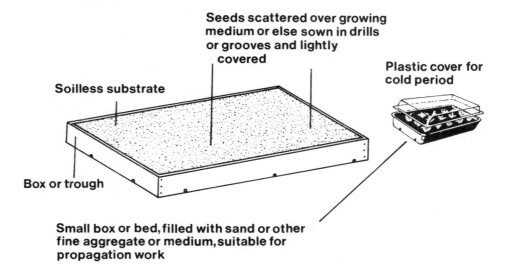

FIG. 36.
Small box or bed, filled with sand or other fine aggregate or medium, suitable for propagation work.

tomato, peppers, the brassicas, and some flower seeds, about 5 millimetres; beetroot, radish, and similar sized seeds about one centimetre; and the larger types like beans, peas, and the cereals, about 2.5 centimetres. Setts, bulbs, corms, rhizomes, and tubers, have to be placed about 2.5 to 7.5 centimetres below the surface of the substrate, and of course such propagation material would naturally be planted out in the main beds initially. Sowing or planting in rows is most satisfactory.

Before sowing certain seeds, they should be soaked in water for twenty-four hours to hasten germination. Others, with very hard seed coats, will need immersion in boiling water for up to five minutes, treatment with acid, or filing of the testa.

It is important to ensure that seeds and other propagation material, whether in litter, on a germination net, or in sand and aggregates, are in contact with the water held as a film around the particles of the growing medium, or the support. The water has to be retained tightly enough by surface attraction to prevent free movement, but at the same time it should be readily available for the tissues to absorb. In addition, the conditions of germination must be such that the developing embryo, tuber, or cutting, receives adequate aeration. Excessively wet, over-watered seedbeds are not conducive to good propagation.

Sand or fine aggregate beds intended for propagation work should be levelled off by passing a board to and fro' across the surface of the growing medium. Litter trays need to have the contents carefully disposed so as to form a flat and even top. After this, the medium must be well soaked with water, and permitted to stand for a day. It should then be about as moist as a damp sponge that has been lightly squeezed out. A series of grooves about 7.5 centimetres apart are made across the beds by pressing a piece of wood, about 9 millimetres thick into the medium to the required depth. This will, of course, depend upon the type of seed to be sown. The damp bedding material will stay in place quite satisfactorily until the seed is sown. Individual seeds should be dropped into the declivities at the rate of about four to 2.5 centimetres. After sowing, the litter or aggregate is drawn over the seeds in the grooves by re-passing the levelling board over the surface of the medium. A covering of newspapers or sacking will help to keep the beds moist. With very small seeds, it is simplest to mix them with a filler of fine silver sand, before spreading, in order to ensure even distribution. The beds should be checked twice daily during hot, dry weather to see that there is adequate moisture present. A light watering can be given as often as may be required, but care has to be taken to ensure that they are not permitted to become excessively wet, otherwise there may well be some incidence of 'damping-off', or mildew. When seed is broadcast in the propagation troughs, it should be scattered up to 1.75 centimetres apart, and covered with paper, burlap, or cardboard. It then germinates on top of the growing medium, but the radicle soon descends into the litter or the aggregate. The covering has to be removed as soon as the seedlings form their cotyledons, otherwise they will become etiolated, and tend to adhere to the paper or canvas.

When seeds are sown directly into the main beds, they should be spaced out properly as for the mature crop. Sometimes, it is quite a good scheme to sow two or three seeds in each place, and to remove the weaker specimens after germination, leaving the strongest one only to develop. Overhead shades are necessary for newly seeded troughs, and these also serve to ward off heavy showers of rain. Light mulches, of straw, hay, wood wool (excelsior), shavings, or shredded asbestos, are often beneficial, and help to keep the growing medium damp. As the seeds come up, the mulch is pushed back.

On germination, most seedlings should be supplied with nutrients at half strength (0.5-X). This is most essential for seeds that do not contain any great quantity of stored food materials; where there is, however, a substantial amount of endosperm within the seed-coat, nutritive salts may not be needed for a week or two. Between waterings with solution, or spreadings of dry salts, ordinary irrigations with plain water should be given to keep the beds moist. In water cultures of the Gericke tank type, the level of the solution in the basin has to be brought very nearly to the top of the container, so that the air space between it and the bottom of the litter tray is narrow enough for the roots of the developing seedlings to cross.

Culling and thinning

After germination, the seedlings should be thinned out, the weaker ones being discarded, to a distance of about half-an-inch apart in the propagation trays. Pricking out may also be undertaken. In that case, the young plants are moved to a new part of the troughs, the growing medium being properly levelled, and small holes prepared. For making the drills for pricking out, a multiple dibber can be usefully employed. This consists of a strip of 2.5 × 5.0 centimetres wood as long as the width of the bed. Small 1.75 to 2.0 centimetre dowels, about 2.5 centimetres in length, are affixed to this board, either with screws or by gluing them into previously prepared apertures. The dowels should be spaced out at 7.5 or 10 centimetre intervals. Small cork stoppers may also be utilised. The tool is pressed onto the growing medium, thus making rows of small holes, into which seedlings may be dropped conveniently. The young plants are lifted from the beds with a knife blade or flat thin strip of metal. As each seedling is transplanted, the medium is pressed gently but firmly around the stem. The surface is then smoothed and dampened with water. After pricking out, irrigation with plain water may be given for two days, and thereafter solution or salts at 1-X strength. With good pricking out, no wilting will occur. Where synthetic resins or diatomite carriers are employed for supplying the nutrient ions, the normal amounts will have been mixed into the growing medium beforehand, and in such cases, no extra waterings or applications of nutrients will be needed. In sub-irrigation propagation cultures, the aggregate may be settled around the roots of the seedlings by the use of the regular irrigation cycles. Flooding has to be carefully controlled to prevent wetting of the root crowns.

Hardening-off

Before the final transplanting to the main troughs, all seedlings should be hardened off to prevent possible wilting, and to ensure that they will become established quickly. Unhardened seedlings are liable to show a high percentage of mortality. Removal of the overhead shades in out-of-door units tends to increase transpiration and so 'firm up' the plants. In greenhouses, the concentration of the nutrient solution may be temporarily raised to as much as 4-X strength in steps of four days at a time, about ten days before transplanting. Alternatively, the frequency of irrigation with solution, or of dry application, may be increased to produce similar effects. In areas where wind velocity is fairly strong, or when the sun is on the meridian irrigation or surface watering with 4-X concentrations should only be undertaken in the evening just before dusk, otherwise the foliage may be burnt by drops of solution drying on the leaves. If it is necessary to feed during the daytime, the plants should be lightly sprayed with plain water immediately afterwards.

Cuttings

These will strike well in beds of sand or vermiculite, or a mixture of both. It is desirable to choose firm and sufficiently ripened shoots for taking the cuttings from. A close and warm atmosphere will ensure quick rooting, and a good percentage of 'takes'. For that reason, the beds or pots are best covered with polyethylene or glass. The cuttings may also be treated with root-forming hormones, such as Seradix A or B. The growing medium should be pressed firmly around the cuttings, which are best inserted in a sloping position, care being exercised to see that they are the right way up. The end of the shoot that is to be in the aggregate should be cut across with a clean slanting excision just below a node or leaf-bud. The lower leaves should be removed, leaving three or four buds to be under the medium when planted. The upper leaves, if large, may be reduced in size. Cuttings of too young and immature growth are liable to decay. Laticiferous plants often strike best if the lower end of the cutting is first plunged into almost boiling water. Generally speaking, vegetative propagation is best carried out at the commencement of the active growing season.

Cuttings need careful shading at all times. They should not be allowed to dry out in the beds, nor to become waterlogged. Ornamentals, like *Crotons* and *Panax* spp., can be struck in standard jar water cultures. Aquatics, both as cuttings and seeds, are usually propagated in pots of aggregate placed just under the surface of a basin full of 0.5-X nutrient solution.

Other propagation techniques

Fern spores should be sown on trays of fine sand, and covered with glass. In striking cuttings of cacti it is often best to partially dry the sections in the sun first, so that they become slightly shrivelled. This prevents rotting in the moist aggregate. Layering, and propagation of runners, rhizomes, and crowns, as well as the division of rootstocks and bulbs or corms, may be carried out in hydroponics, using beds of fine growing medium or vermiculite, without difficulty. The same applies to the bulbils of *Agave* and *Furcraea*, and also the tubers of potatoes, yams, arrowroot, artichoke, and the sweet-potato (*Ipomoea Batatas*). Root-suckers, and stem-suckers (ratoons) or 'gourmandisers'; eyes or buds; leaves from *Begonias, Gloxinias,* and *Bryophyllum*; aerial and subterranean roots; all these start satisfactorily in soilless culture. Hydroponics is especially advantageous for the raising of citrus stocks, and the germination of seeds of forestry trees and plantation crops.

11. Young lettuces thriving in a nutrient film layflat unit.

Orchids

These are usually propagated from cuttings, divisions of the rootstock, or by means of pseudo-bulbs, only very expert growers attempting to raise them from seed. Orchids are characterised by the presence of a microscopic fungus (*mycorhiza*) mycelium growing on their young roots and taking the place of the root hairs of other plants. This supplies the epiphytes with moisture and food materials through the medium of its hyphae. In vegetative propagation, orchids usually carry with them sufficient of the mycelium for their needs. For raising them from seed, it is necessary to infect the germinating medium with the appropriate fungus. Pure cultures of these fungi are available for the purpose. Sphagnum moss, old bark, peat, well-leached coir fibre, or chopped up coconut husks, make good propagation media. Orchids can now be propagated using meristem cultivation techniques in hydroponics.

Transplanting

It is recommended that young seedlings should be transferred normally from the propagation trays or pots to the main beds with a ball or cube of growing medium left intact around their roots, if possible (except for layflats). Before transplanting, the sand or aggregate should be well irrigated. A hole is scooped out in the medium or substrate in the main bed for each plant individually with a small trowel, and after the roots have been carefully inserted, the sand or gravel must be gently but firmly drawn back around the stem. Seedlings should not be set so deeply that the root crowns will be submerged by the periodic waterings of the trough. Sometimes, a light spray or sprinkling of water may be given after transplanting has been finished. It is often advantageous to supply new transplants with plain water only for a few days, until they have become well established. Excessive watering should be avoided: it hinders the development of new roots. In very hot areas, gravel beds can be shaded or mulched with some suitable litter to keep the surface cool.

In water cultures, where a litter bed is employed, it is essential to set seedlings so that their roots can penetrate through the wire mesh bottom of the tray into the solution in the tank below.

Sowing and planting in situ

When sowing seeds of crops like maize, beans, and peas, or in the planting of potatoes, bulbs, and corms, it is usual to position them in the places that will be eventually occupied by the mature plants. For intercropping work, small seeds are often sown in between the lines of the permanent plants by making a series of narrow grooves with the end of a long pointed stick in the growing medium. The seeds are sprinkled in these declivities, after mixing with a filler, and the whole then smoothed over to cover them up. Peas and beans should be soaked in water for twenty-four hours before placing in the beds, this encourages speedy germination. Setts should be planted with a good 'eye' uppermost. If holes for bulbs are made with a dibber, it is important to see that no pocket of air is left between the bottom of the hole and the base of the bulb. A little fine sand or aggregate sprinkled in the aperture before planting will prevent this from occurring.

In litter beds for water culture it is often desirable to examine the the troughs closely after a few days to see that none of the seeds have been raised above the surface of the medium by their developing roots. With vermiculite, seeds should not be sown by pressing them down into the aggregate with a finger or a stick, otherwise they will simply 'pop up' again in a short space of time. Dibbers should always be employed in beds of light or spongy media.

Spacing

Main sowings or plantings in hydroponic troughs can be as much as fifty per cent closer than they would be in conventional horticulture. The only limiting factors are those of light and air, since provided the roots are assured of adequate anchorage, the quantity of nutrients can be adjusted to meet all demands.

In growing hydroponic vegetables, the aim should be to secure as large a yield as possible from a given unit area; with floriculture the object is to achieve the 'massed bank' effect. The commercial production of flowers has, of course, the same end in view as has any other business enterprise.

To calculate the number of plants required to set out a particular area, multiply the distance apart that they are to be spaced in the rows by the distance between the rows, and then divide the result into the number of square centimetres in the area in question.

EXAMPLE: How many tomato seedlings will be needed to plant up a bed area of 278,640,000 square centimetres, if the plants are to be set out in rows 36 centimetres apart at intervals of 36 centimetres between each plant?

CALCULATION: $36 \times 36 = 1296$
$278,640,000 \div 1296 = 215,000$ (number of seedlings required)

Calculations may be performed in larger units in square metres (m^2) to save time and to suit individual convenience.

The exercise of skill, and the possession of some experience, are fundamental to good spacing of commercial or ornamental plants. The questions of light intensity, periods of sunshine or of dull cloudy weather, and the relative humidity of the local atmosphere, are all of paramount importance when selecting planting distances. Naturally, in regions of good light and low humidity, spacing will be as close as possible, whereas in damp, dark situations, it is essential to allow room for proper illumination. Under the latter conditions, artificial lighting would be of great advantage. Each case has to be judged according to local circumstances.

Seed quantities

To assess the amount of seed required to sow in order to get enough plants to fill any particular bed or beds, it is simplest to weigh out a small quantity – say from 3 to 30 grammes – of the seed, and then count the number of seeds in that lot. This figure should then be divided into that of the actual number of plants needed at the chosen spacing. According to the result, the grower will be able to estimate the weight of seed needed. All weights should be multiplied by 2, to allow for failures, and culling.

Pre-treatment of seeds and planting material

It is often advantageous to pre-treat seeds and cuttings with a nutrient solution prior to sowing or planting. The elements absorbed during the process of soaking assist the embryo plant to develop more quickly and to turn into a stronger seedling. They also provide a certain reserve store of foodstuff. Ordinary nutrient formulae at low strengths may be employed, but good results have been obtained with single salt solutions. The volume of solution should not exceed an amount above that which can be absorbed by the seeds in twenty-four hours. The cereal grains, for example, absorb about one quarter of their weight of solution. Wet grains must not be stored in a damp condition, otherwise they will 'heat up'. Soaked seed should, therefore, either be sown at once after treatment, or else dried at a temperature of not over 21°C.

Triple superphosphate is a valuable salt for general use. Of the minor elements, manganese is sometimes the most difficult to supply to certain seedlings. A solution of manganese sulphate may be used with considerable advantage for pre-treatment of seeds in such cases. This introduction into the seed of both the major and the minor elements in a readily available form so as to carry the young plant through its early stages before its root system is sufficiently developed to make full use of the normal source of supply, has everything to commend it.

CHAPTER 16

Daily work

The practice of hydroponics combines the features both of an art and of a science. Like every other applied science, soilless culture of crops is based upon a solid groundwork of fact and knowledge. Many years of experiment and research have supplied the necessary data for the application of what were once only laboratory techniques to the field of practical plant production. Scientific principles alone would be of little aid to the ordinary person; they must be first translated into working projects before they can become of real utilitarian value. This is where the artisan skills are so essential. In hydroponics, a great deal depends upon a range of subsidiary activities and operations which may be grouped most conveniently under the heading of general cultivations. This term includes such subjects as unit management, cropping programmes, continuity of supplies, treatment of beds, and other aspects of successful plant growth.

Unit management

Hydroponic farms and gardens should be so managed that they deliver a constant supply of produce throughout the year. In warm or tropical areas, where an equable climate prevails throughout most of the year, this can be arranged without a lot of difficulty in open air installations, but in colder regions, greenhouse and cloches will be required for the growing of tender plants during winter. If the extra capital outlay can be afforded, it is usually well worthwhile to install these contrivances, since the off-season prices for high grade produce are always considerably better. Given good planning and management, the additional cost of glasshouses can be paid off or amortized within a few years by selling luxury crops, like strawberries, tomatoes, lettuces, as well as the flowers of carnations, roses, and chrysanthemums, in wintertime. In the monsoon areas, too, produce of this nature fetches much higher prices during the rainy seasons, when it is impossible to grow it in ordinary soil, than it does at normal periods.

   The following operational suggestions are intended to serve as a general guide to growers. They may need modifying in the light of local conditions or demand.

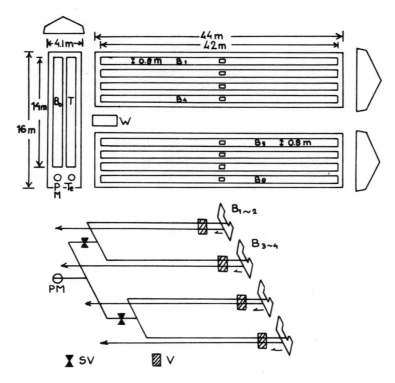

FIG. 37.

Design of a hydroponic installation for gravel culture in Kochi prefecture, Japan, showing the convenient arrangement of the troughs and apparatus, facilitating easy unit management. Protection is provided by plastic covered greenhouse. Vinyl house area 666 m^2 in total; B_0: nursery beds, 1.2 × 14 m, 2 rows; B_1—B_8: growing beds, 0.8 × 42 m, 8 rows in sets of two; T: underground tank for solution storage, capacity 42 m^3; T_e: entrance of the tank; PM: feeding pump and motor, 60 mm 1.5 HP; H: end box for feeding and drainage; SV: solenoid valve 60 mm; V: reciprocating valve 60 mm; W: boiler for heating.

Calendar of sowings and plantings for a year's working

NOTE: Some plants are listed more than once under each month. This refers to different varieties, or to dissimilar treatments. The times of the seasons alter according to the latitude and longitude of the place in question.

A. Winter months

MONTH 1

Requiring warmth:

Vegetables – Early beans, lettuces, tomatoes, asparagus.
Flowers – Begonias, gloxinias, various bulbs.
Fruits – Strawberries.
Cuttings – Chrysanthemums, carnations.

MONTH 2

Requiring warmth:

Vegetables – French beans, cress, carrots (short varieties), lettuces, leeks, mustard, onions, potatoes (early), radishes, seakale, rhubarb, tomatoes.
Flowers – Achimenes, antirrhinums, begonias, cannas, clivias, gloxinias, hyacinths, hippeastrums, bulbous irises, lilies, narcissi, roses, streptocarpus, salvias, sweet peas, tulips, verbenas, vallotas.
Fruits – Early vines.
Cuttings – Anchusas, chrysanthemums, carnations, gaillardias, oriental poppies, phlox decussata, romneyas, statices, verbascums.

MONTH 3

Requiring warmth:

Vegetables – French beans, broad beans, brussels sprouts, carrots (short varieties), cress, cucumbers, celery, cauliflowers, leeks, lettuces, mustard, onions, radishes, seakale, tomatoes.
Flowers – Achimenes, antirrhinums, ageratum, anagallis, begonias, brachycome, balsams, cobaea, cosmeas, cannas, celsia, celosia, clivias, clerodendron fallax, carnations, dahlias, dianthus, eccremocarpus, fuchsias, gloxinias, impatiens, kochia, hyacinths, hippeastrums, irises, lilies, narcissi, lobelia, marigolds, marguerites, mimulus, nicotianas, nemesias, phlox, petunias, pelargoniums, rehmannia angulata, roses, streptocarpus, salvias, sweet peas, salpiglossis, schizanthus, statices, stocks, trachelium, tulips, vallotas.
Fruits – Melons, strawberries.
Cuttings – Begonias, chrysanthemums, carnations.

Requiring Shelter:

Vegetables – Onions, early peas, parsnips, parsley, turnips, potatoes.

Tolerant: Vegetables – Artichokes (Jerusalem), chives, cabbage, garlic, onion sets.
Flowers – Anemones, some lilies, certain roses, ranunculuses, and various shrubs.
Fruits – Grape vines.

B. Spring months

MONTH 4

Requiring warmth: Vegetables – Brussels sprouts, broccoli, cress, celery, celeriac, cucumbers, cauliflowers, herbs, mustard, radishes, tomatoes.
Flowers – as for (3) above, also – asparagus plumosus, asparagus sprengeri, aspidistras, coleus, crotons, cacti, ferns, chrysanthemums, heliotropes, palms, smilax, asters, zinnias.
Fruits – Vines.
Cuttings – Ageratum, dahlias, delphiniums, coreopsis, fuchsias, heliotropes, lobelias, marguerites, pelargoniums, salvias, lupins, scabious.

Tolerant: Vegetables – Brussels sprouts, broccoli, broad beans, carrots, cabbages, cauliflowers, lettuces, leeks, onions, peas, parsnips, chives, garlic, mint, potatoes, horseradish, rhubarb, shallots, seakale, spinach, spinach beet, turnips.
Flowers – Alyssum, bartonia, alpines, climbers, carnations, canterbury bells, daises, forget-me-nots, gladioli, montbretias, clarkias, calendulas, candytuft, collinsia, convolvulus, coreopsis, cornflowers, escholtzias, godetias, gypsophila, larkspurs, lavatera rosea, linums, limnanthes, lupins, malopes, nemophilas, nigellas, phacelias, poppies (shirley and cardinal), rudbeckias, roses, saponaria, sunflowers, virginia stocks, viscarias, polyanthuses, sweet peas, tigridias, wallflower.
Fruits – strawberries.

MONTH 5

Requiring warmth: Vegetables – French beans, runner beans, celery, cucumbers, vegetable marrows, tomatoes.
Flowers – primula kewensis, primula obconica, primula sinensis, popular annuals, achimenes, azaleas, begonias,

carnations, chrysanthemums, camellias, cyclamen, dahlias, eupatorium, gloxinias, pelargoniums, haemanthus, jasminum, luculia.

Fruits — Melons, late vines.

Tolerant:
Vegetables — Asparagus, artichokes (globe), beetroots, broad beans, broccoli, brussels sprouts, cabbages, carrots, cauliflowers, cress, endive, kale, kohl rabi, lettuces, mustard, parsley, peas, radishes, salsify, savoys, spinach, turnips, onions, potatoes.

Flowers — Alpines, antirrhinums, gladioli, montbretias, pansies, pentstemons, sweet peas, violas, violets, nicotianas, aster, dahlias, canary creeper, calandrina, dimorphotheca, jacobea, layia, leptosiphon, mesembryanthemum criniflorum, nasturtiums, salpiglossis, sweet sultan, tagetes, signata, pumila, ursinia, venidium, zinnias.

MONTH 6

Requiring warmth:
Vegetables — Cucumbers, tomatoes.

Flowers — Cinerarias, primulas, begonias, carnations, chrysanthemums, gloxinias, streptocarpus, pelargoniums, fuchsias.

Fruits — Melons.

Tolerant:
Vegetables — Beetroots, French beans, haricot beans, broccoli, brussels sprouts, celeriac, celery, leeks, onions, chicory, ridge cucumbers, lettuces, mustard, cress, endive, kohl rabi, marrows, peas, radishes, spinach, turnips, potatoes, other root tubers.

Flowers — Asters, zinnias, antirrhinums, alpines, aquatics, chrysanthemums, dahlias, magnolias, pansies, pentstemons, violas, violets.

C. *Summer months*

MONTH 7

Requiring warmth:
Flowers — Cinerarias, calceolarias, certain primulas, auriculas, chrysanthemums, carnations.

Tolerant:
Vegetables — French beans, coleworts, carrots, cress, endive, lettuces, mustard, peas, parsley, spinach, turnips, radishes, brussels sprouts, broccoli, runner beans,

celeriac, cabbage, ridge cucumbers, marrows, leeks, some tomatoes, kale, maize.

Flowers – Alyssum, anemones (St. Bride's), aubretias, aquilegias, canterbury bells, coreopsis, campanulas, daisies, delphiniums, foxgloves, forget-me-nots, holly-hocks, lupins, oriental poppies, iceland poppies, stocks, sweet williams, abutilons, begonias, cannas, helio-tropes, flags, flowering maize, polyanthuses, primroses, ricinus, saxifrages, salvias.

MONTH 8

Requiring shelter: Flowers – Tender primulas, cinerarias, calceolarias, pelargoniums.

Tolerant: Vegetables – Carrots, coleworts, cress, cabbage, endive, lettuces, mustard, parsley, peas, radishes, turnips, celery, kale, leeks, cauliflowers, broccoli, brussels sprouts.

Flowers – Stocks, forget-me-nots, colchicums, crocuses (late flowering), lilium candidum, sternbergias, brooms, ceanothuses, roses, wisterias, helianthemums, phila-delphuses, diervillas,

Fruits – Papayas.

Layering and budding – Strawberries, carnations, clematis, roses.

MONTH 9

Requiring warmth: Flowers – Cyclamen, mignonette, stocks, schizanthus, some begonias, lachanalias, calceolarias, cinerarias, freesias, hyacinths (Roman), arums, some primulas.

Tolerant: Vegetables – Cabbages, red cabbage, cress, endive, lettuces, mustard, onions, radishes, spinach, spinach beet, broccoli, coleworts, kale.

Flowers – Hydrangeas, pelargoniums.

Fruits – Strawberries.

Cuttings – Pelargoniums, hydrangeas, and shrubs.

D. *Autumn months*

MONTH 10

Requiring warmth: Vegetables – Cress, endive, lettuces, mustard, radishes,

Flowers – Popular annuals, cyclamen, daffodils, narcissi,

hyacinths, irises, lilies, tulips, violets.

Cuttings – Calceolarias, pentstemons, pelargoniums, mesembryanthemums, pansies, verbenas, antirrhinums, violas, violets.

Tolerant: Vegetables – Brussels sprouts, cabbages, kale, savoys.

Flowers – Anemones, crocuses, daffodils, alyssum, calendula, candytuft, clarkias, coreopsis, cornflower, godetia, larkspur, nigella, poppies, scabious, viscaria, lilies, snowdrops, scillas, muscaris, narcissi.

Fruits – Strawberries.

MONTH 11

Requiring warmth: Vegetables – Mint, lettuces.

Flowers – Bulbs, cinerarias, calceolarias, primulas.

Cuttings – as for (10) above.

Tolerant: Vegetables – Cabbages, coleworts, savoys.

Flowers – daisies, forgetmenots, wallflowers, polyanthuses, tulips, hyacinths, lily of the valley, sweet peas.

MONTH 12

Requiring warmth: Vegetables – Peas, broad beans, lettuces.

Flowers – Azaleas, brooms, deutzias, hydrangeas, lilacs, roses, astilbes.

Cuttings – as for (10) above.

Crops mature earlier in soilless cultures than they do in soil. A sowing and planting programme should take account of this, so as to ensure that a continuous supply of produce is available at the most profitable times, or when needed for home consumption. Florida commercial growers have obtained maturity of their hydroponic tomatoes within 70 days as compared with up to 160 days in conventional horticulture. Lettuces raised without soil in Surrey, England, were reported to produce good hearts seven days earlier than controls planted in soil. The average period for tomatoes to ripen is about 85 to 95 days, and these figures have been achieved in outdoor beds, without any special equipment, in Bengal. Some average times for different crops are given here, as reported by the United States War Department, and from experiments carried out at Kalimpong and Mirik, West Bengal.

AVERAGE TIMES FROM SEEDING TO FIRST HARVEST UNDER FAVOURABLE CONDITIONS	*Crop*	*Days*	
		U.S. Army	*West Bengal*
	Tomatoes	80–90	85–91
	Cucumbers	55–65	44–50
	Muskmelons	90–110	
	Chillies	70–90	
	Lettuces	45–55	33–37
	Radishes	30–40	
	French Beans		35–39
	Maize		71–78

W. F. Gericke, working in California, has produced marketable tomatoes in 60 days from sowing of seed.

The germination periods of seeds vary greatly according to local conditions. The following times are normal under reasonable circumstances.

AVERAGE GERMINATION PERIODS OF VEGETABLE SEEDS	*Crop*	*Days*
	Beans, broad	7–12
	Beans, French	9–14
	Beans, runner	9–14
	Beetroot	17–24
	Beet seakale	17–24
	Borecole	6–11
	Broccoli	6–12
	Brussels sprouts	6–12
	Cabbages	6–12
	Carrot	16–22
	Cauliflower	6–12
	Celery	17–23
	Cress	4–7
	Cucumber	5–12
	Endive	12–20
	Kale	6–12
	Kohl Rabi	6–12
	Leek	19–22
	Lettuces	7–12
	Mustard	4–6
	Onion	10–20
	Parsley	25–35
	Parsnip	18–25
	Peas	6–10

Crop	Days
Radishes	5–8
Savoys	6–12
Spinach	8–14
Spinach beet	16–22
Swede	6–12
Tomato	6–12
Turnip	6–12
Vegetable Marrow	5–9

T. Eastwood has recommended certain crops as well suited to soilless culture, and divided them into two lists:

Vegetable crops: Tomato, green beans, cucumber, eggplant, pepper (chillies), radish, green onion, lettuce, turnip greens, mustard greens, Chinese cabbage greens, chard, celery, spinach.

Floral crops: Roses, gardenias, yellow daisies, pansy, carnation, chrysanthemum, stocks, aster, antirrhinums, lily, sweet pea, feverfew, begonias, pelargonium, calendula, larkspur, marigold.

Cropping

INTERCROPPING. Some crops take up more space with their foliage than with their roots, thus leaving a free area of growing medium at surface level. Between such tall subjects, lines of plants that appreciate shade may be sown or intercropped. Examples are lettuces between rows of tomatoes, radishes amongst peas, and endive interspersed with runner beans.

CATCH CROPPING. While large plants are developing, seeds of quick growing catch crops may be sown in the troughs. These latter will be ready for harvesting before the former need the extra room. Cases that might be cited include salad greens amongst beetroot, dwarf beans with cabbages, or mustard and cress with celery.

MULTIPLE CROPPING. Crops of different habits may be grown together in the same trough with success, so saving an appreciable amount of space. Pumpkins and maize, tomatoes and potatoes, or climbing beans and various root vegetables lend themselves to this combination.

Cropping programmes

The cropping programme should be decided in the light of specific requirements. These will depend upon the nature of the installation; whether it is designed for commercial production or for domestic use. The aim should be to grow a succession of essential or saleable crops, so that the hydroponicist will have regular supplies whenever they are needed. Yields of produce in soilless cultivation are often greater than they may be in soil, and this should be taken into account when preparing working plans.

The cropping scheme is best set out in the form of a chart, as given below:

CROPPING PROGRAMME TO PRODUCE (WEIGHT) OF CROP PER WEEK							
Crop	A Required Weekly Production (weight)	B Immediate Establishment (troughs)	C Successive weekly sowings or plantings (weight)	D Crop periodicity* (time)	E Maximum number of beds required (B × D)	F Nutrient requirements (weekly)	G Seed requirements

*length of time from sowing, planting, or transplanting to completion of harvest.

Continuity of supplies

In warm areas, it will be possible to grow crops all the year around, provided the proper cultural techniques are employed. Similarly, in cold regions, the installation of glasshouses will enable operators to produce whatever fruits, vegetables, and flowers they may need, irrespective of the season, if heating is available. Artificial lighting is also a valuable aid in many cases.

With open air cultures in temperate climates, where there is heavy frost or snow in winter, some limitation is necessarily placed upon production of fresh vegetables. The times at which greenstuff would be available direct from outdoor hydroponic troughs in such areas is shown in the continuity chart, prepared for general guidance, and reproduced here. Naturally, these periods could be extended with careful management, and the use of cloches or other protective devices. (See table opposite.)

Treatment of beds

Routine sterilization of hydroponic troughs is desirable, at any rate in commercial work. When crops have been grown for long and extended periods of time in any aggregate or medium, a tendency develops for the accumulation of pathogenic micro-organisms to arise in the beds. These may be dust-borne, or carried by human agency. Chemical treatment will prevent the incidence of such disease organisms. Formaldehyde can be employed at not under a 7500 ppm concentration of commercial formalin. It is, however, rather expensive. Chlorine, applied as calcium or sodium hypochlorites, at a concentration of 10,000 to 20,000 ppm of available chlorine is also fairly satisfactory. The most convenient method of sterilization is probably to make use of the sodium chlorophenates. These are obtainable as sodium trichlorophenate, sodium tetrachlorophenate, and sodium pentachlorophenate.

Sterilization procedures

(A) SODIUM CHLOROPHENATES. First, thoroughly wash or clean the growing medium free of dead roots and any rubbish and drain the bed. Fill a suitable container(s) with water and add sodium hydroxide or lye at the rate of 300 ppm (284 grammes to 1130 litres of water). Add the sodium chlorophenate to the lye solution in the container or tank, also at the rate of 300 ppm (again 284 grammes to 1130 litres of water) and stir until thoroughly dissolved. Pour or pump this solution into the beds until the growing material is covered completely. See that the material is levelled off carefully before sterilization is commenced to ensure even coverage. Let the solution stand in the beds for from twelve to sixteen hours. Then drain it off by discharging it into the walks or aisles. Now wash out the tank and troughs with plain water, followed by a further irrigation for 12 to 16 hours with a fresh 300 ppm solution of lye only.

CONTINUITY CHART FOR TEMPERATE ZONES WITH SEVERE WINTERS
(OPEN AIR CULTURE ONLY)

Month

Crop	J	F	M	A	M	J	J	A	S	O	N	D
Artichoke												
Beetroot												
Beans, broad												
Beans, French												
Beans, runner												
Broccoli												
Brussels Sprouts												
Cabbages												
Carrots												
Cauliflowers												
Celery												
Coleworts												
Endive												
Kale												
Kohl Rabi												
Leeks												
Lettuces												
Onions												
Parsnips												
Peas												
Potatoes												
Savoys												
Shallots												
Spinach												
Spinach beet												
Turnips												
Turnip greens												
Vegetable marrows												

Finally, drain this away, and wash out all parts of the unit with plain water. Water should be allowed to stand in the troughs for another 12 hours to wash away all traces of the chemicals. Two more flushings will then complete the operation.

As the chlorophenates are extremely toxic to plants, great care must be taken to wash out the beds and flush the growing material thoroughly after sterilization. They are also injurious to human beings and animals and should be handled with rubber gloves. Masks will provide additional protection.

(B) FORMALDEHYDE.   To one part of commercial formalin, add a hundred parts of water. In practice, 11.25 litres of formalin may be diluted with 1125 litres of plain water. The growing material should be soaked with this solution for about sixteen hours, during which period the beds must be covered with a tarpaulin to confine the fumes. The formalin solution is then drained or drawn off and beds and media well flushed two or three times with fresh water. If in any doubt, up to four or five such flushings may be given. When handling formalin, rubber gloves, a rubber apron and a mask should be worn.

(C) HYPOCHLORITES.   Calcium hypochlorite is commonly available in the powder form, while sodium hypochlorite is usually obtainable as a liquid. To prepare a 10,000 ppm concentration, dissolve 68 grammes of pure calcium hypochlorite $(Ca(OCl)_2)$ in 4.5 litres of plain water; in the case of sodium hypochlorite $(NaOCl)$ 80 grammes will be required in 4.5 litres of water to give the same concentration. As the commercial preparations of these chemicals are not, however, one hundred per cent pure, care should be taken to ascertain the degree of purity (sometimes it may be only 50%) and alter the weights accordingly when mixing up solutions. To prepare a 20,000 ppm concentration, equivalent to a 2% solution, the quantities used should be doubled. Chlorine solutions need to have the pH adjusted to from 8.0 to 10.0. Concentrated hydrochloric acid should be added for this purpose. About 71 grammes of acid to each 4.5 litres of solution are generally adequate for the task.

Seed sterilization

Seeds may also be sterilized by using a 1% formaldehyde solution, made up from 30 grammes of commercial formalin (37% formaldehyde) in 1.25 litres of plain water. The seeds should be soaked in this solution for about fifteen minutes, after which they should be dried on a piece of muslin before sowing. Stirring of the liquid every five minutes during soaking is desirable. Another method is to immerse seeds with fairly hard testas in hot water (44°C) for up to half-an-hour. Chlorine solutions, prepared as for bed or growing media sterilization, using commercial bleaching powders or aqueous solutions, are also satisfactory. When using chlorine solutions for seed disinfection care should be taken to dry the seeds before thay are propagated.

Counteracting acidity and alkalinity

It may be of interest here to refer also to typical treatments for checking excessive acidity and alkalinity in growing materials in hydroponic beds. Acidity can be a serious worry in the growth media. Alkalinity, too, is often a cause of concern. To counteract acidity in growth media, the application of various forms of lime, such as ground limestone, dolomitic limestone, calcium chloride, agricultural slag, and calcium carbonate, are efficacious. They may be mixed in with the existing media or aggregate, to raise the pH. The following amounts form a good basis for work:

Requirements RAISING pH OF GROWING MATERIAL	Rate of application	
	AMOUNT OF CALCIFEROUS MATERIAL IN KILOS	AREA IN SQUARE METRES
from 5.0 to 6.0	2.25	10
5.0 to 6.5	2.70	10
6.0 to 6.5	0.45	10

Quantities may be increased by 50% to 100% if necessary. When using hydrated lime, the above weights may be reduced by about one-third. After mixing with the media, the beds should be well watered.

Flowers of sulphur, or the sulphates of aluminium and iron may be utilised for lowering pH. This is of course the counteracting of alkalinity. The undernoted quantities offer a good basis for work:

LOWERING pH OF GROWING MATERIAL	Requirements MATERIAL	AMOUNT IN KILOS	Rate of application AREA IN SQUARE METRES
from 8.0 to 7.0	Aluminium sulphate } Iron sulphate }	2.00	10
8.0 to 6.0	Aluminium sulphate } Iron sulphate }	4.00	10
8.0 to 5.5	Aluminium sulphate } Iron sulphate }	6.30	10
8.0 to 7.0	Flowers of sulphur	0.75	10
8.0 to 6.5	Flowers of sulphur	1.30	10
8.0 to 6.0	Flowers of sulphur	1.80	10

These materials may be mixed with the growing media, and the beds well watered. Iron and aluminium sulphates act in about two to three weeks, and flowers of sulphur in from six to nine weeks.

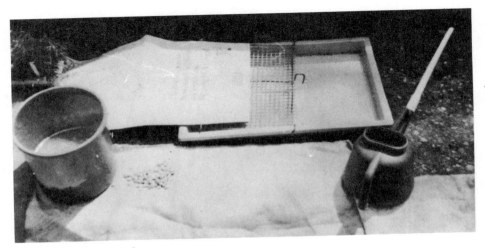

12.A. Materials required.

12.B. Unit sown with grain or seed.

12. Essential equipment for soilless grass growing.

12.C. Grass after seven days – rye and oat green fodder for livestock.

When employing any of these substances to counteract either acidity or alkalinity in hydroponic media, it is best to check the final results before planting the beds, by the usual pH tests with an indicator. When the treatment is finished, the beds should be well flushed through several times with fresh water to remove any accumulated residues.

As a safety measure, it is often a good plan to add about 1.30 kilos colloidal rock phosphate to each 283 cubic decimetres of media (450 kilos), so increasing the buffer action. Alternatively, peat moss at the rate of one-fifth by volume gives valuable results. Calcareous sands may also be treated with potassium permanganate (28 grammes to 4.5 litres of water), formaldehyde (one part to fifty of water), or chloropicrin. The growing media or substrates should be aired and flushed for up to seven days after using either of the last two named chemicals.

Flushing

As long as no unusual circumstances arise, hydroponic beds need not be flushed more often than once every three months. The normal procedure is to flood and drain them several times with fresh water to remove any accumulations of salts. However, should a high concentration of certain extraneous ions develop, or toxicity symptoms make an appearance, more frequent or immediate flushing will become essential.

Removal of roots

All debris on the surface should be removed before attempting to extract the roots of old plants. It is best to cut off large plants about 15 centimetres above the level of the growing medium, so that the severed stem makes a sort of handle that can be grasped for ease of removal.

A thorough cleaning of the growing medium is needed after each harvest in normal circumstances. All that is necessary is for the main root system of old plants to be pulled out, and well shaken over the troughs, so as not to carry away an excessive quantity of the media. The surface should then be raked smooth, and any rubbish carted to a distance and burnt.

Surface compacture

In out-of-door beds, after heavy rainfall, some binding of the medium on the surface of troughs may occur, especially in the case of fine media or of vermiculite. When this happens, beds should be very lightly raked over, otherwise root aeration may be affected adversely. Care must be taken not to damage any surface feeding roots during the operation.

Irrigation

During irrigation in soilless troughs, the nutrient solution fills the voids in the aggregate, driving out air that has a relatively low content of oxygen and a high proportion of carbon dioxide. While drainage is proceeding, on the other hand, fresh air is drawn into the growing medium. This new air contains more oxygen and less carbon dioxide. The more rapid the movement of solution in the beds (commensurate with non-injury of the roots) the greater will be the speed of air displacement. Too much free water in the medium for too long a period will lower the supply of oxygen to the roots.

Carbon dioxide

Where extra carbon dioxide is supplied to greenhouse crops from cylinders or from dry ice, care should be taken that the circulation facilities are functioning properly. The lower the light intensity the less carbon dioxide will be necessary, while when illumination is good more of the gas can be utilised by plants with results beneficial to growth.

Routine inspections

When making routine inspections during the course of the daily work, growers should check among other details, the following points:

(i) Condition of the growing medium; (Moisture content, any waterlogging, proper functioning of drainage apertures, correct aeration, and overheating or coldness.)

(ii) Appearance of crops; (Aeration, incidence of pests, vermin, and diseases, correct sowing and planting, proper tieing, right spacing, dirt or dust on the foliage, satisfactory pollination and fruit formation, any deficiencies, chlorosis, and necrosis.)

(iii) Watering and irrigation;

(iv) Nutritional requirements;

(v) Environmental adjustments, as necessary;

(vi) Other details.

It must be emphasised that however great the degree of technical control may be, very much still depends upon the daily observations of the grower. It is possible to work out in theory the exact water and nutrient needs of any given crop during its growing season, from germination to harvest, but any such programme which ignores that basic biological principle – change – will not succeed. Living organisms, such as plants, are subject to many changes, often from day to day, depending upon the needs of the moment. The interpretation of these requirements is part of the daily job of the hydroponicist. To assess the needs of crops calls for skill and experience. Once an operator has got the 'feel' of soilless culture methods, he can tell almost at once how the plants are responding to the current environmental and nutritional conditions. Irrigation is another subject that demands some sensitivity on the part of the grower. To know just how much water to give, or when to give it, are matters of real practical significance. The experienced hydroponicist, whether an amateur or a professional, should be a careful and conscientious observer, ready to carry out the daily work with intelligence and initiative.

Day by day observations of water requirements are essential. These may vary considerably according to the local climatic conditions, such as the prevailing wind, the relative humidity of the atmosphere, and the rainfall, if any. The aggregate substrate or other growing medium should usually be as moist as a damp sponge that has been lightly squeezed would be. Excessive wetness stops proper aeration, while submersion of the root crowns will cause death of the crop. Improper aeration soon becomes apparent in hydroponic troughs. The plants assume a tired look – that of age prematurely imposed upon youth. It is easily detected by the experienced grower. In water cultures care must be taken to adjust the air space between the surface of the solution and the base of the plant support from day to day. This rises or falls according to the intake of solution by the crop, the rate of evaporation, or the incidence of precipitation. Nutritional status of the cultures will need attention as the seasons advance, and the natural processes of growth and development alter the requirements of the plants.

Certain adjustments, based upon regular assessments of local light conditions, temperatures, and other environmental changes, are necessary for the efficient operation of hydroponica. In very hot dry weather, the shades must be well fitted over the beds. Similarly, when heavy rain showers occur, the canopies should be carefully secured so as to stop excessive flooding of out-of-door troughs. In glasshouses, attention will need to be paid to the daily light conditions, particularly in smoky or cloudy areas, as well as to the period of the illumination. Where artificial lighting has been installed, this is especially important. Thermometers, rain gauges, wet and dry bulbs, and other instruments should be checked daily, if not more frequently.

Wind barriers and screens may require raising or lowering, or their positions altering as circumstances dictate. Pumps, valves, taps, sprinklers, and other machinery or equipment, will need regular attention, and daily inspection.

As the time of harvest approaches, the grower should make frequent observations of the condition of the crop, and decide on the approximate date of the commencement of picking. Catch crops and intercrops should also be watched carefully in order to ensure that they are removed at the right moment.

Hard manual labour plays no part in hydroponics. The ordinary operations of tillage, which are so essential for successful growth in soil, are never required in soilless cultivation. Digging, ploughing, harrowing, weeding, and similar work, become things of the past once it has been decided to change over to the hydroponic technique. For the small grower who may be unable to afford the luxury of hired labour, these are very important considerations, as anyone who has been compelled to have to follow through a programme of trenching, ridging, or compost-making (so popular in all orthodox textbooks!) will appreciate. Nevertheless, the daily work of the hydroponicum calls for the exercise of a certain degree of technical control and artisan skill. In small household units, the amount of competence needed is of the minimum standard, but in large commercial installations the greatest care and efficiency are required at all times.

Phytosanitary precautions

The importance of keeping hydroponic installations spotlessly clean cannot be over-emphasised. Dirt is always conducive to the spread of disease, and it encourages the incidence of pests. Decaying organic matter, such as vegetable refuse, must never be left lying about in or near soilless cultures. Flies soon gather in the vicinity of rubbish dumps, while vermin take refuge underneath heaps of filth. Flies and moths are often the vectors of certain plant diseases. In dirty greenhouses, red spider is very liable to make an early appearance. For these reasons, all rubbish should be burnt regularly in an incinerator, and the paths, beds, storage rooms, and offices must be cleaned at frequent intervals. Water and solution tanks or reservoirs are best kept covered to exclude dust, and also to prevent the growth of algae.

Smoking should never be permitted in hydroponica. Virus diseases are often carried on dry tobacco leaf. A smoker's hands and face become contaminated, with the result that even an accidental touch may bring about the infection of susceptible plants, such as tomatoes. Cases have been known where viruses have remained in dry tobacco for up to sixty years. Before smokers enter commercial hydroponic units, they should wash their hands and faces, and put on clean overalls. If there is any likelihood of forgetfulness on the part of visitors – such as absent-mindedly lighting a cigarette while inspecting the plants – they may be asked at the point of entry, to leave pipes, cigarettes, and tobacco in a safe place until their departure.

In areas where diseases are known to be rampant, it is a good precaution to provide buckets of disinfectant for the washing of the workers' boots or feet each morning before they commence duty. Hands, especially under the finger-nails, should be well scrubbed with soap and water.

Regular fumigation of greenhouses, and the washing down of paths, are other desirable precautions. In outdoor units birds, fowls, dogs, cats, and rodents should be driven away with the usual protective measures. Crows may be discouraged by hanging up a stuffed black stocking shaped to look like a dead *Corvus* in a prominent position, while 'glitter-bangs' will frighten away small birds. Pigeons are often a nuisance, especially just after peas and beans have been sown, or are starting to germinate. To guard against attacks by these pests, a few peas rolled in red lead (Pb_3O_4) should be scattered on the surface of the growing medium.

Sanitation means the systematic elimination of sources productive of plant injuries. Biological agents are the main factors involved. One of the main duties in the daily work in hydroponica is to check carefully on all possible causes of trouble. Soil infested with micro-organisms, diseased native vegetation, and any foliage harbouring insects should be eliminated from the vicinity of installations. It is desirable to cut back trees, shrubs, and large herbaceous plants to a distance of at least fifteen metres, and even further if possible, around units. The first signs of disease in any of the crop plants should be noted. Destructive insects need watching for. The leaves and other portions of plants attacked, or the entire plant, if necessary, should be removed immediately in order to prevent further infection of the crops. Diseased vegetation must be removed to a distance and burnt without delay. Quite often large worms, insects, and molluscs, can be destroyed by hand picking in the early stages of an invasion. Fungi-affected foliage or stems must be cut out, while the presence of virus diseases calls for the destruction of the whole plant together with its root system. After touching diseased plants, the hands should be scrubbed with carbolic soap and hot water, before doing any other work. All tools, apparatus, and equipment will also need cleansing.

Records

Daily records and notes are vital matters in hydroponic cultivation. Nothing is too insignificant to enter on these charts. A well kept notebook becomes in course of time almost a textbook in itself and constitutes a valuable guide for future work. Some specimens of useful record sheets are given here.

Crop:
Variety:
Number
of plants:
Area:
Reference:

I. GENERAL REC

Date	Temperature Max °C	Min °C	Relative humidity	Rainfall in mm	Light conditions	Hours of sunshine	Length of daylight	Artificial lighting	Condition of crop Indifferent (I) Fair (F) Good (G) Excellent (E)	Date sown	Da plan
TOTALS (where applicable)											

II. RECORD OF NUTRIENTS USED (SIMPLIFIED)

Crop:
Variety:
Area:

Date	Formula	Quantity	Nutrient variations	pH	Remarks
TOTALS					

(where applicable)

HART

Date picking commenced	Produce harvested	Date harvesting ceased	Formula used & rate	Irrigation(s) amount & number	pH value	Deficiencies, pests & diseases	Any special attention	Remarks and comments

III. RECORD OF NUTRIENTS USED (SUB-IRRIGATION)

Crop:
Variety:
No. of trough:
Water tank
capacity:
H_2O pH:

| Date | Macronutrients | | | | | Micronutrients | | | | | | | Macronutrients | |
| | Quantity of element in solution | | | | | | | | | | | | Quantity of eleme | |
	Salt 1 ppm weight	Salt 2 ppm weight	Salt 3 ppm weight	Salt 4 ppm weight	Salt 5 ppm weight	1	2	3	4	5	6	7	Salt 1 ppm weight	Salt 2 ppm weig

TOTALS
(where applicable)

ded to solution			Micronutrients							pH before adding acid	pH after adding acid	Amount of H_2SO_4	Remarks
Salt 3 n weight	Salt 4 ppm weight	Salt 5 ppm weight	1	2	3	4	5	6	7				

CHAPTER 17

General cultivation

Experience is a good guide to the successful management of all the various aspects of hydroponic cultivation, particularly in the cases of those subsidiary, but nevertheless, highly significant practices that contribute so much to the smooth operation of any installation devoted to soilless growth of plants.

Labelling

The dates of sowing or planting should be inscribed upon labels affixed to each trough. It may also be advisable to leave a space on these for such details as the formula in use, number of irrigations required and similar information.

Temperature of media

The temperature of the growing medium should generally never exceed 37°C. This high figure will not be suitable for many crops, and in such cases, it is far better to keep the temperature down to about 21 to 26°C. Good shading should accomplish this in hot climates, as well as close planting, so that the aggregate, sand, or litter is well protected from the rays of the sun by a thick coverage of foliage. Germinating seeds, young seedlings, and transplants are most affected by excessive heating of the media. In greenhouses, the aim should be to keep the solution or medium at the same temperature as that of the surrounding air. Should it be of a lower temperature than is the atmosphere in the houses, then wilting may occur, due to retardation of water uptake by the plants.

Heating power

In cold climates, the growing medium or solution in the tanks can be warmed by installing electric heating cables. The ordinary ones supplied for hotbeds are satisfactory if coated with asphalt emulsion or passed through black iron pipes. They are usually placed 10 to 15 centimetres apart. Otherwise hot air or steam pipes can be employed. Electrically operated thermostats will control and regulate the range of

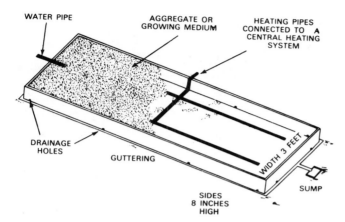

WATER PIPE   AGGREGATE OR GROWING MEDIUM   HEATING PIPES CONNECTED TO A CENTRAL HEATING SYSTEM

DRAINAGE HOLES   GUTTERING   WIDTH 3 FEET   SUMP

SIDES 8 INCHES HIGH

FIG. 38.
Heating in a hydroponic trough. Various forms of power can be used. (8 in. = 20·32 cm; 3 ft = 91·44 cm.)

temperature. Part of the daily routine should be to check all heating apparatus, as well as the temperature conditions. Subnormal temperatures will give rise to sudden wilting, slowing down of the growth rate.

Crops must be supplied with the right amount of heat if optimum growth is to result. The temperatures appropriate to different species and varieties can be ascertained by consulting a horticultural encyclopaedia. Experiments have shown that for every 5° rise in heat the rate of photosynthesis increases from about 2 to 2.3 times until 29.5° to 35°C has been reached, beyond which no further rise in the rate occurs, as far as normal plants are concerned. A very excessive temperature may in fact cause a decrease.

Heating is valuable in cold areas for propagation work, and the forcing of certain crops. It can be applied by various means, such as hot water pipes, oil burners, warm air blowers, and electric lamps or by heating cables. These apparatuses are regularly advertised in the horticultural press, and their capabilities and potentialities are well known. All the methods can be used in hydroponica. It is always advisable to consult a suitably qualified engineering organization before embarking on a big programme of heating or lighting.

Several electrically powered implements, as well as solufeeders – devices for diluting a concentration solution automatically before it reaches the beds – and purificators – instruments for purifying sand for soilless culture – have been designed for hydroponic usage. These types of equipment all have their respective advantages, and may often be employed with profit under suitable conditions. They are available as the proprietary products of different manufacturers. Tablet-making machines, and dry fertilizer mixers, are other useful appliances to have in the commercial installation, being both labour saving and economical of time.

Conversion and regeneration for ion exchange resins

The preparation of resins for hydroponics is best carried out in 7.5-centimetre pyrex tubes, 1.30 metres in length. The resin bed may be held by stainless steel or monel gauze. Downward displacement is best. A full load for one such tube is $2\frac{1}{2}$–3 kilos of resin. Alternatively, single pairs of ion exchange units with semi-automatic control valves and regenerating tanks may be employed. Where elaborate apparatus is out of the question, resins or other carriers can be converted or regenerated *in situ* in the hydroponic troughs, provided these have been thoroughly flushed and cleansed beforehand.

Solar distillers

These appliances are of considerable importance in hydroponics, because it is through their agency that supplies of otherwise unsuitable saline water can be used effectually. Brine or salt water exists in appreciable amounts in arid areas, and also beside the sea-shore, as well as in some coral islands. It is mostly found in hot and sunny regions. In places where illumination is poor, solar distillers are not practicable, and reliance has then to be put in ordinary stills. These apparatuses require expensive fuels, like coal, wood, oil, or electricity. Solar distillation, on the other hand, is extremely cheap to operate. However, saline waters can now often be used in the raw state in hydroponics (see Chapter 12, p. 166).

The Mildura solar still, which incorporates suggestions made by the Australian Division of Industrial Chemistry (C.S.I.R.O.) consists of a glass sheet roof, forming a sealed tent-like compartment, fitted over a shallow tray of waterproof plastic material. Brine is siphoned into the tray, and evaporated by the heat of the sun. The resulting vapour condenses on the inside of the panes of glass, and runs into small gutters on either side of the tray, from whence it is collected. The water is delivered into the still by means of a floating-ball valve. A solar still built to this design can deliver 1400 litres of fresh water per annum to each square metre of tray space. The Mildura still measures just over 4 square metres in size, and can produce an average of 22.5 to 27 litres daily. The best results occur during periods of bright sunshine, but under Australian conditions, the still will operate on cloudy days. The warm temperatures of the State of Victoria in which Mildura is situated, are comparable to many other regions of the world. Solar distillation, of course, reaches maximum efficiency during hot, dry periods, when fresh water is most needed by plants. The Mildura still was first built in 1956.

For several years before this Australian development occurred (which has been followed by American work in the Gulf of Mexico area, and recently the production of new units in other countries) solar distillers were used successfully with hydroponics

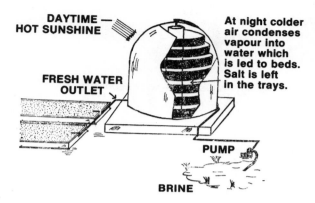

DAYTIME — HOT SUNSHINE

FRESH WATER OUTLET

At night colder air condenses vapour into water which is led to beds. Salt is left in the trays.

PUMP

BRINE

FIG. 39.
Solar distiller for producing fresh water from brine or saline ground-water in soilless units.

in other arid areas of continental climate. The basic parts of a typical apparatus employed comprise: (i) a condenser, (ii) a series of trays and (iii) a container for the outpouring water. The arrangement depends upon the fluctuations in temperature which take place in some regions. During the hot period of the day, the saline water is evaporated inside the condenser to vapour, which by the late afternoon and throughout the following night is delivered as fresh water due to the chilling of the dome. It is desirable for the condenser to be made of metal or glass, with a large enough surface to cool the brine. In the centre of the apparatus is situated a core of paraffin wax or calcium chloride. The apparatus can be produced as a portable set. A vacuum increases distillation by $1\frac{1}{2}$ times for every cycle, and enables water to be pumped through the outlet pipe to a height of up to six metres. The nightly distillation (from 6 pm to 6 am – half of the complete cycle) can be expressed in the following formula:

$$D_{H^-} = \frac{K\left[AM_1C_1 + M_2(T_1 - T_3)C'_2 + M_2(T_3 - T_2)C''_2 + AM_3C_3 + IM_2\right]}{L}$$

Where:

K = coefficient of the useful working of the apparatus, or part of the process of warming needed for distillation. Apparatus containing only brine K:0.3–0.35; with paraffin wax or calcium chloride K: 0.40; with vacuum K: 0.6–0.7 (examples only).

A = amplitude of temperature changing inside the apparatus under the glass from warming during sixteen hours to cooling during four to five hours (example 25–30°C).

M_1 = amount of brine inside apparatus in kg for number of days of working taking average 0.7 for first filling.

C_1 = specific capacity of heat of the brine 0.95.

M_2 = amount of paraffin wax or calcium chloride.

C_2 = specific capacity of the heat of M_2.

T_1 = temperature of melted M_2 in the apparatus when warmed during sixteen to seventeen hours.

T_3 = temperature of hardening.

C''_2 = specific capacity of the heat of liquid M_2.

C'_2 = specific capacity of the heat of hard M_2.

T_2 = temperature of cooling M_2 at 5 or 6 am.

M_3 = mass of the material, trays, glass, metal, ground inside apparatus.

C_3 = specific capacity of heat of M_3 (average 0.2 cal/kg).

L = latent temperature of melting/hardening M_2: 40–50 cal.

I = latent temperature of condensing/evaporating of water: 585 cal.

Lighting

The importance of lighting cannot be too highly stressed. Although good light intensity is of vital significance in hydroponics, owing to the close spacing of the crops, care must be exercised to see that plants get enough 'rest period'. In dull, cloudy climates, artificial lighting has several advantages. It hastens flower formation thereby shortening the time that crops occupy valuable space in the glasshouses. It also increases the number of flowers and fruits produced per individual plant, and it encourages greater stem length and size of flowers like carnations.

In the average home, the level of illumination on sunny days ranges from about 10 footcandles to 70 footcandles. Indoor plants therefore benefit greatly from extra light, of from 100 to 300 footcandles for perhaps five hours per diem. In commercial cultures, the fitting of lamps to provide an illumination of some 500 footcandles on the tips of the plants for up to 10 hours daily in very dark weather is advantageous. Fluorescent lighting has proved quite suitable. Intermittent lighting is better than continuous burning. 400 watt H-1 mercury lamps, used in ordinary 500 watt filament RLM reflectors spaced at a distance of 1.25 metres along a one metre wide trough, may be alternated with incandescent filament lamps. The former could be burned continuously for four to six hours, while the latter may be burned intermittently on a thermostat. They also supply part of the heating in greenhouses. The two types of lamps need to be wired on separate circuits.

Aeration

Adequate movement of air through the root substrate is essential at all times. This applies both to culture in solutions and in solid media. Under this heading, a few words on the subject of ventilation would also be appropriate. Plants will not tolerate noxious fumes and gases. Many industrial gases are injurious to crops. Epinasty may be caused by illuminating gas leaks in the house. Fumes from coal or coke furnaces can give trouble, while oil burners need to be well trimmed at all times. Some agricultural fumigants and gases give rise to necrosis if proper precautions are not taken. If obnoxious gases should penetrate the growing media in hydroponic beds, they may be dispersed by flooding of the trough. Greenhouses and rooms used for cultivation purposes should be fitted with a proper system of ventilation. This is desirable, not only for the sake of the plants, but also for the human beings who may have to work or live in them.

Wind

Drying winds cause excessive transpiration and increase the water requirements of crops. Shelter against wind is very desirable for hydroponic crops.

Rain

Mention has already been made of the use of rain water in irrigation. Very heavy rain will batter down delicate crops like lettuces. The shades which are usually provided in open air units are of considerable value in preventing such damage.

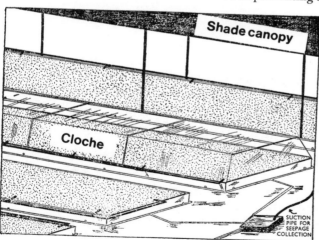

FIG. 40.
Protection of hydroponic troughs by means of shades and cloches against rain or inclement weather.

Labour

It is essential to give regular care and attention to hydroponic units if good crops are required. Soilless culture is a branch of plant growing which calls for intelligent forethought. It is surprising, however, in what a short space of time comparatively inexperienced persons can master the day to day routine of operations. M. Bentley (1955), working in South Africa, has reported that his units have been satisfactorily maintained by local labour during his absence. Provided that skilled supervision is assured in commercial installations ordinary workmen, if they have an interest in the task and a feeling for plants, can perform routine duties. The average householder should have no difficulty in running a small hydroponicum. Above all, it is vital to follow the rules laid down with care and to exercise commonsense. Normally, one hectare under soilless culture requires about 40 hours per month in labour.

Replacing media

Most of the growing media will last indefinitely, except for vermiculite, which breaks down after some time, and the litter used in Gericke-type cultures, which needs renewal periodically. Where any detriments or toxicities arise in sands or aggregates, they can affect the growth rate, and cause defoliation, root damage, and necrosis. These symptoms should be watched for at cold times.

Refrigeration equipment for cooling growing media is sometimes installed in tropical regions. It may be fitted either in the beds or in the water reservoirs. This should be inspected regularly.

Humidity

The relative humidity of the atmosphere bears directly upon a number of matters, such as water losses from the plants and from the troughs, and the incidence of diseases like damping-off, black spot, mildew, leaf mold, and rust. Wet and dry bulbs should be read daily. In large units a hygrothermograph is a great asset.

Atmospheric environmental conditions

These really embrace all the factors inherent in the climatic surroundings of any locality, the sum total of which produces a state more or less favourable to good growth of crops. Every effort should be made during daily inspections to become acquainted with the prevailing growth environment. Regular readings of a barometer will prove of help to growers in deciding what precautions to take against stormy weather.

Pollination

In glasshouses, pollination of plants is often necessary. This may be done by gentle spraying with clean water at warm air temperature or by the use of a rabbit's tail or cottonwool.

Irrigations

In gravel or sub-irrigation cultures, the height of the flooding depends to some extent upon the age of the plants. Young seedlings will need high irrigation – up to the surface of the medium, but not over the root crowns. Older plants manage very well with an irrigation to about 2.5 centimetres below the top of the aggregate. It is essential to ensure that the bases of the leaf petioles of small seedlings and rosette plants are not allowed to become saturated with solution or water.

The solution in water culture tanks may be circulated by passage over a baffle, or by injection of air into the troughs. Movement of the liquid past the roots of the plants should be slow, otherwise injury may occur. Circulation twice weekly is adequate.

With sub-irrigation and semi-spray cultures, daily work includes control of the

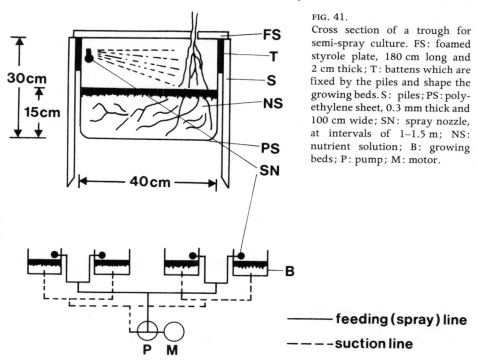

FIG. 41.
Cross section of a trough for semi-spray culture. FS: foamed styrole plate, 180 cm long and 2 cm thick; T: battens which are fixed by the piles and shape the growing beds. S: piles; PS: polyethylene sheet, 0.3 mm thick and 100 cm wide; SN: spray nozzle, at intervals of 1–1.5 m; NS: nutrient solution; B: growing beds; P: pump; M: motor.

pumping operations. Where these are automatic, inspections and setting of the time clock will be necessary. In manually operated units, the pump will require starting and stopping. Pumping times and frequencies, the speeds of flooding and drainage, and the variance of growth by manipulation of the pumping schedule all need attention. Excess pumping in hot zones may retard development of lettuces and radishes. Chrysanthemums also do not like too frequent irrigations. For small seedlings one pumping daily will suffice initially, but for large plants two to four floodings may be demanded depending upon local conditions. Usually not more than three are necessary. The appearance of the crop is the best guide to the arrangement of the pumping cycle. There should be an interval of four hours between each irrigation. In the tropics, flooding of the troughs should be done at least once during the warm part of the day. Night pumping is unnecessary. The aims of irrigatory practice should be first, to fill the troughs rapidly; second, to drain them reasonably quickly; and third to get all the solution away after each flooding. Considerable interest is currently being shown in semi-spray cultures, which can economise in water usage.

The skill and commonsense of growers are most called into question in connection with the operation of watering. While the different methods of soilless culture vary in the manner in which the water is supplied, as far as the mechanical handling of the fluid is concerned, the requirements of the plants change only with their age, stage of growth, and responses to the local climatic and environmental conditions. Variations may occur from day to day. Too much water will kill crops, while undue dryness will lead to wilting and the destruction of delicate membranes. Thus, although necrosis brought about by lack of aeration and the submersion of the root crowns has to be avoided at all costs, it is equally important to prevent desiccation. New units should be tested for water needs before planting or sowing begins. This may be carried out by flooding the beds and making notes on such factors as evaporation or seepage over a few days. Growing media should always be slightly moist, just like a damp sponge that has been wrung out. Proper drainage systems are essential for all installations.

The frequency of irrigation will vary according to the system used, and local conditions. In cool periods, watering once or twice a week is quite practicable with sand or mixed aggregate culture. This may be increased to once a day at hot times, or in warm glasshouses. Vermiculite beds hold moisture exceptionally well – in fact this power of water retention may well prove a drawback in humid areas, unless special drainage devices are employed. Sub-irrigation units usually require flooding two or three times daily, the operation being controlled in many cases by a time clock. Some installations may use a recycling technique.

In open air hydroponic units during wet periods it is necessary to ensure that good aeration is provided and no water logging occurs. Protective devices are most desirable. It is also most essential that the drainage holes should be in good working order, and that if any nutrients are lost through leaching they should be replaced in

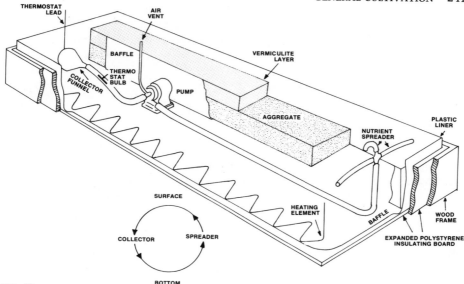

FIG. 42.

Recycling automatic collection technique for spreading and applying nutrient solution. No tank is required with this method. The liquid plant food is passed continuously from bottom to surface of the growing medium.

time to prevent any check to the growth of the crops.

By and large, it can only be stressed that watering is very much a matter for the judgement of the individual grower, involving studies of the condition of the media, the appearance of the plants, and the local climatic conditions obtaining at the hour in question.

Feeding

The rates of application for plant nutrients are discussed in chapters 13 and 14, but it is important to remember that crops are living organisms, which make known their needs through exhibiting certain symptoms. If hunger signs appear, extra nutrients must be given. The feeding schedule should be carefully worked out to suit the needs of individual crops, which may vary according to the season.

Vermin

For hydroponic purposes, these include rats, mice, birds, dogs, and cats. They should be rigorously excluded from units. Soilless cultures are self-contained systems needing careful control. A cat chasing a mouse in a bed of tomatoes can do far more damage in a few minutes than will be the value of the death of its quarry. Traps for rodents are a useful part of the unit equipment. A wire fence of one or two centimetre gauge mesh will protect crops from such depredations. Nets or other devices will prevent birds from pecking at small seedlings.

Weeds

These do not constitute any problem in hydroponics, since the inert growing media does not encourage their development. Furthermore the controlled conditions of operation, the close spacing, and the full coverage by the cultivated plants all tend to check the infiltration of weeds. Strict sanitary precautions should always be applied.

Shading

Shades protect crops from excess light or sun scorch, and also ward off heavy showers, cloudbursts, or falls of hail. The requirements of individual crops should be studied when erecting shades. They are, of course, mainly designed for growth in tropical areas. The aim should be to provide the plants with the maximum amount of 'filtered' light, while excluding the strong noonday sun. Morning and evening sunshine should be admitted to the beds.

Climatic factors

Every effort must be made to choose different varieties of crops according to their tolerance of heat and other conditions. This is basically an ecological problem, although the additional protection given to cultivated plants against the vagaries of nature by the hydroponic technique is of profound significance. In open air units, the manipulation of shades can do much to alter local temperatures. Where cloches and greenhouses are employed, it is possible to control even more effectively the day to day growth and development of the crops. Lowering of the temperature slows down the rate of growth. This is conducive to bud formation. When the buds are definitely set, the heat may be appreciably increased, with the result that blossom formation is hastened. There should normally be a variation between day and night temperatures for good growth.

Evaporation may often be a factor of some importance. The average daily water losses from a trough area of 20 square metres may range from nil to 135–40 litres, according to the region or season in question. The last figure can be greatly reduced by the use of protective devices. Snow, frost, and ice should also be considered. Hydroponic crops have been known to withstand being frozen solid in the beds for several weeks without harm, but naturally if it is suspected that such conditions will be encountered varieties capable of tolerating them must be selected. Hail storms and other meteorological phenomena need guarding against by suitable protection of troughs and units.

pH checks

In commercial units, and in some amateur installations – if the owners are so disposed – it is desirable to undertake checks of pH values weekly or fortnightly. The moisture present in the growlng medium, or the solution in the tanks, should be tested. It is advantageous from time to time to test the water supply as well, in order to see if any variations occur. Generally speaking, most crops thrive best when the pH of the nutrient solution absorbed by the roots is between 5.0 and 7.0. Under ideal conditions, plants differ in their preferences for pH values, but in actual practice crops are remarkably tolerant. pH 6.0 to 6.5 are the average figures.

The following chart indicates the preferences of particular crops but it must be emphasised that these may vary according to locality, stage of growth, season, and variety of plant. Numerous workers have studied the effects of the reaction of the medium or solution upon plant growth, and their conclusions do not always accord. (See also Chapter 13, p. 171, Chapter 15, p. 189 and Chapter 22, pp. 292–3).

SOME OBSERVATIONS OF HYDROGEN ION CONCENTRATIONS (pH) FOR VARIOUS SPECIES

NOTE: Variations within a limit of 0.2 either way are of no consequence. Too low a pH can give rise to calcium deficiency, since the absorption of that element may be interfered with, as well as injury to the root system, marginal burning, wilting, and necrosis. Too high a pH may precipitate iron, thus causing chlorosis. Where recommendations differing from the average have been made, they are noted with the date and the name of the worker concerned. Despite the maxima noted below, growers are recommended to try and keep within the limits 5.0 to 6.5 for most purposes.

Vegetables

Plant	Maximum pH
Artichokes	7.5
Beans	6.0–6.5
Beetroot	7.0–7.2
Broccoli	6.5
Cabbages	7.5
Asparagus	7.5
Tomatoes	6.0
*(E. M. Emmert 1931)	8.4
Carrots	7.5
Celery	7.5

Vegetables	Chives	6.5
	Aubergine	6.5
	Watercress	6.5
	Brussels sprouts	6.5
	Garlic	6.5
	Lettuces	7.0
	*(E. M. Emmert 1931)	7.5
	Kale	6.8
	Onions	7.5
	*(A. L. Wilson 1930)	6.0–7.0
	Parsnip	5.0
	Groundnuts	6.0
	Sweet potatoes	5.5
	Radishes	6.5
	*(E. T. Wherry 1924)	7.0
	Shallots	6.0
	Squashes and Gourds	6.0
	Swiss chard	6.5
	Turnip	6.0
	*(E. T. Wherry 1924)	4.0
	Cantaloupe (muskmelon)	6.8
	Cauliflowers	7.5
	*(P. H. Wessels 1932)	5.5–6.6
	Chicory	6.5
	Cucumbers	6.5
	Endive	6.5
	Horseradish	6.5
	Leeks	6.5
	Parsley	7.5
	Peas	6.0
	Potatoes	5.5
	*(O. Arrhenius 1929)	5.0
	*(P. H. Wessels 1932)	4.8–5.4
	Pumpkins	5.0
	Rhubarb	6.0
	Spinaches	6.5
	Rutabaga (Swedish turnip)	7.0
Fruits	Pineapples	5.0
	Strawberries	6.0
	*(C. S. Waltman 1931)	5.3–5.5
Cereals	Oats	7.5
	*(E. T. Wherry 1924)	5.0

Cereals

*(O. Arrhenius 1929)	5.0
Rye	5.0
Barley	7.0–7.2
*(E. T. Wherry 1924)	8.0
Wheat	7.0
Maize	5.8–6.0
Rice	6.5–7.0

Miscellaneous

Timothy	6.0
*(E. T. Wherry 1924)	9.0
*(O. Arrhenius 1929)	5.0
Alfalfa	7.0
*(E. T. Wherry 1924)	8.0
*(W. L. Powers 1927)	5.6–6.0
*(O. Arrhenius 1929)	7.2
Lupines	6.0
Red clover	6.0
Hungarian vetch	5.3
Spearmint	6.0
Flax	7.0
*(E. T. Wherry 1924)	4.0
Alsike clover	6.0
*(E. T. Wherry 1924)	7.5
*(W. L. Powers 1927)	5.6
Buckwheat	5.0–6.5
Nelumbo lutea	4.5–9.0
Lemna trisulca	4.9–7.3

Spraying

Should a very prolonged spraying operation be required, it may be advisable to flood the troughs with water, so that if any dripping of the spray materials from the foliage into the growing medium occurs, they will become highly diluted. This avoids the danger of root injury. After completion of the work, the beds must be drained, and the liquid discarded. Dusting and fumigation, if of lengthy duration, also call for similar precautions. Occasional sprayings and dustings can, however, be carried out quite safely without any special preparations. The use of proper spraying equipment will eliminate all need for flooding of troughs, unless special reasons dictate otherwise.

Training

Supports for plants in hydroponics are of necessity based rather upon the walls of the troughs than upon the root substrate, since the shallowness and density of the growing media employed militate against the insertion of stakes. Tall plants and vines should be trained to climb up wires or strings. Where galvanised metal rods are used, as sometimes occurs in glasshouse work, the portions in contact with the aggregate or sand must be painted with asphalt emulsion.

Sprinkling and syringing

The foliage of indoor, household, or greenhouse plants needs gently syringing with tepid water from time to time. This removes dust from the leaves and stems. Sprinkling controls the relative humidity of the atmosphere to some extent, and may be of value in certain circumstances. Water used for syringing and sprinkling must be distributed through a fine sprayer, so that it settles on the leaves, and does not run down the stems in excess quantities into the growing medium where it could dilute the nutrient solution, and flush nutrient ions from the pots or troughs.

Supporting of crops

Raffia or bass is not suitable for tying plants such as tomatoes, where pollination is often carried out by syringing of the flowers, since it tends to rot fairly quickly in a damp atmosphere or when saturated with water. String, preferably thatching twine, makes good supports and ties. Wire strainers are best. When securing the stems of plants with ties, care should be taken to ensure that enough room is left in the loops for future development of tissue. Various supporting devices for crops are available on the market or from manufacturers under proprietary names.

General precautions

Always check regularly:

(1) Equipment and apparatus.
   Proper functioning, good condition, tools well cared for.
(2) Environmental conditions.
   Temperature, humidity, water supply, light intensity and duration, shading, protection, wind, frost.
(3) General.
   Wilting, excess salts, presence of noxious fumes and gases, toxic materials, inattention by labour to instructions, careless mixing or application of nutrients, ventilation, slow growth, etiolation, 'bolting' of plants, phytosanitary precautions, proper pollination techniques, dripping of moisture from overhead galvanised pipes, etc.

CHAPTER 18

Deficiencies

Deficiencies or defects in plants growing in soilless cultures may arise from any one or more of a variety of causes. Numerous physical, chemical, and biological factors exist which tend, if not checked, to inhibit (even prevent) the satisfactory development of crops. These factors may be divided into three general groups:

(a) NONPARASITIC DISEASES

Injuries due to climatic factors, such as abnormal temperatures, sun scorch, excessive humidity, and wind;

Nutrient element excesses;

Nutrient element deficiencies;

Toxicities caused by the presence of non-nutrient substances in injurious concentrations in the solution or media.

(b) PARASITIC DISEASES

Injuries caused by insects, fungi, bacteria, algae, nematodes, seed plants, birds, rodents, and molluscs.

(c) VIRUS DISEASES

These are systemic and internal diseases of plants, caused by infectious principles, apparently complex protein molecules.

(Latin, *virus*, venom; Greek, *Ios*, Sanskrit, *visha*, poison)

Systemic diseases are those in which the causal factor directly or indirectly affects the growth and development of the whole plant, while localized diseases are so termed because they appear only in certain organs or parts such as the roots, stems, leaves, flowers, or fruits. Physiological diseases involve physical and chemical factors relating to plant nutrition.

Nonparasitic diseases

Injuries caused by climatic factors. The adverse effects of abnormal temperatures may be mitigated by the usual protective measures. In hot areas, good shading will prevent overheating of growing media, or sun scorch. Under cold conditions, the usual warm greenhouses will be necessary to protect delicate and exotic plants from the effects of the elements. The relative humidity of the atmosphere often has detrimental consequences for some crops. Excessive dryness may be combated by syringing or spraying with water. Among the disturbances that may result from low humidity is blossom-end rot of tomatoes. High humidity often encourages 'damping-off' of seedlings, or mildews and other fungi to appear. Good aeration is essential for healthy growth, and discriminative defoliation of leafy species is frequently advantageous since it permits the free flow of gentle air currents past the stems and fruits of large plants. Wind, if too strong, is liable to break and damage tender plants, as well as causing wind rock of tall types of crops. The usual guards and barriers are effective as preventive measures against normal winds. Injury to crops may also be caused by unbalanced water supplies, due to faulty irrigation or inefficient pumping. It is important to ensure that the water relations of plants are not subjected to improper disturbance.

Nutrient element excesses. High total salt concentration, if excessive, causes symptoms of hard and stunted growth, accompanied by the exhibition of very dark green colouring in plants. Usually, concentrations can be raised to three or four atmospheres without any specific injurious effects on growth, other than slight hardening. Above this maximum, inhibiting symptoms soon appear. Under conditions of low light intensity, or when hardening off seedlings for transplanting, it may be desirable to employ a 2-X to 4-X solution. During periods of high light intensity when rapid absorption and utilisation of nutrient ions takes place, the concentration can range from 0.5-X to 1-X.

In tomatoes, high total salt concentrations will encourage the incidence of blossom-end rot, indicating a water deficit. The fruits will be small in size and will ripen unevenly. Lettuce leaves formed by plants feeding on such solutions will exhibit a tendency towards accentuated marginal curling, and will be tough to eat. Radishes usually become woody and pungent, with small roots. At times, these symptoms are accompanied by chlorosis.

The usual remedy for excesses of major nutrient elements is to reduce appreciably the amount of the salt(s) concerned in the formula in use, or else to change over to another mixture. It may also be advisable to flush the beds through with plain water, and to leach the growing medium for a few days.

An excess of boron may be corrected by adding a solution of commercial sodium silicate (12 gm to 450 litres of water) to the water used for flushing of media. In the cases of other minor elements, like iron, manganese, copper, and zinc, treatment of the troughs with a 10% solution of sulphuric acid is often beneficial. The soaking may be of twenty-four hours duration.

As a class, the macronutrients in moderate excess do not produce any very sudden or startling symptoms of toxicity, like violent chlorosis or immediate necrosis. In extremely powerful concentrations, they would of course give rise to early death of the plants, but this is not a normal occurrence in soilless culture, except in the case of accidents, such as the upsetting of a sackful of fertilizer into a trough. However, if the concentration of one major element is abnormally high, the absorption of other ions may be decreased so severely that deficiencies of certain elements may arise. Potassium and calcium are liable to interfere with each other's absorption. With the exception of reduced forms of nitrogen, the main effect of high concentrations of the macronutrients is, as has already been mentioned, a hardening of growth. Sodium and chloride, which are relatively non-toxic, may be classed with the nutrient elements in this respect.

Where nitrate nitrogen is the sole source of nitrogen, it is difficult to cause an over-assimilation of that element under conditions of high light intensity and favourable temperatures, though very great concentrations of nitrate salts, which would raise the total osmotic concentration of the solution, will of course produce the effects of salt hardening, with stunted growth and other characteristic symptoms. If ammonium nitrogen or urea are used, over-assimilation can easily occur with high concentrations bringing about rank top growth, weak stems, low ratio of roots to tops, and suscepti-bility to wilting. In tomatoes, fruit set may be reduced, and the fruits may fail to develop proper colouring. In lettuce cultivation, care must be taken to avoid the excessive application of nitrogen, or else the leaves will fail to stand erect and may wilt quickly. With radishes, there will be a large growth of dark green succulent tops and little root formation.

Excessive phosphorus in a nutrient solution will bring about precipitation of iron, with consequent symptoms of iron deficiency. For this reason, the phosphorus level is usually kept as low as is consistent with satisfactory growth of crops in hydroponics.

Generally speaking, excesses of the micronutrients are extremely difficult to diagnose. Considerable trouble is often experienced in soilless cultures when the minor elements are present in too high concentrations. The main offenders are likely to be iron, manganese, boron, copper, and zinc. High levels of these elements, in the range of over 10 ppm to 100 ppm, depending upon the nutrient ion in question, and the manner of supply, will produce serious chlorosis followed by root injury and com-plete necrosis of the plants. Crops can often tolerate a high concentration of a particular trace element if all the other micronutrients are present in adequate amounts, but should they be available only in relatively small quantities, then toxicity symptoms will appear. For example, in water culture, tomatoes have been known to tolerate copper at over 1.0 ppm when supplied with normal concentrations of all the other minor elements; however, in cases where these were deficient, injury resulted with copper at a level of as low as 0.2 ppm.

Iron at too high concentrations is toxic to plants. It injures the root system, and interferes with the absorption of manganese, thus causing a deficiency of that element in the shoot. It may also produce phosphorus deficiency. Phosphorus is precipitated

13. Hydroponic installation in the Canary Islands. A volcanic ash substrate is used.

by a high level of iron in the solution, so that the first symptom of excess iron in an otherwise normal nutrient solution is a shortage of phosphorus.

Copper is severely toxic to crops when present in concentrations above 1 ppm to 5 ppm, as a rule. The toxic level of this element varies with the method of culture; apparently toxicity is reached at lower levels in water culture than in sand. Plants soon show interveinal chlorosis, and exhibit a light green foliage colouring. Toxic levels of zinc are also identified by the incidence of interveinal chlorosis.

Severe injury to plants is caused by boron in excess of 20 ppm in the nutrient solution. Dead areas develop along the margin and between the veins of leaves. In tomatoes, the necrosis shows as transparent patches in the early stages, the areas later turning brown. In serious cases, all leaves may be affected. Lettuces display a similar pattern, though the transparent stage is not usually obvious, and the foliage shows browning on the edges, and later on the interior portions. However, many nutrient irregularities produce a browning of leaf margins in lettuces, so these symptoms are not especially characteristic of boron toxicity.

Of the other elements, sulphur, which is utilised by plants in large amounts, can be tolerated in relatively high concentrations provided that the total salt level of the nutrient solution is not raised excessively. Chlorine can often be accepted by plants in appreciable strength. Its main effect in excess seems to be one of hardening principally on account of the osmotic concentration.

Nutrient element deficiencies.   It is possible to form quick preliminary diagnoses of nutrient element deficiencies by careful observations of hydroponic crops. The following are the main points to look for:

Symptoms	*Indicating a deficiency of*
Slow growth, poor development and light green or yellowish foliage	Nitrogen
Dull, abnormally dark green leaves, sometimes with grey or purple discolorations	Phosphorus
Mottled lower leaves which later become brown and appear scorched	Potassium
Stunted plants with dark and crinkled leaves	Calcium
Yellow leaves, delayed blooming, and slight spotting turning later to white and finally brown	Magnesium
Leaves yellow between the veins, followed by severe burning	Iron
Poor bloom and weak growth. Leaves appear chequered	Manganese
Veins turning yellow with dead areas of a purple colour forming at leaf bases	Sulphur
Brittle stems	Boron
Stunted growth	Zinc

Confirmation of these symptoms in serious cases, where remedial action by increasing the deficient nutrient is ineffective, should be sought through the usual testing procedures, discussed in Chapters 22 and 23.

Parasitic diseases

Insect pests.   The control of insect pests depends upon the application of common-sense methods based on special knowledge of the insects concerned, and of any particular circumstances under which they may occur. The various means of control may be grouped under four headings:

(a)   CULTURAL

These aim at checking undue increase of pests rather than at actual elimination, and comprise such measures as the growing of mixed crops, changing the times of sowing or planting, the use of insectivorous birds, stimulation of plant growth, good irrigation and drainage, selection of resistant varieties, and removal and destruction of attacked plants.

(b) MECHANICAL
These are intended to stop any increase in attacks by pests. They include the removal of affected parts of plants, the trapping of insects by means of baits, nets, burning, and similar techniques.

(c) INSECTICIDAL
Insecticides are usually applied either as stomach poisons, or as contact poisons, depending upon the types of insects in question. The former are taken into the alimentary tract of the insect, and are intended to destroy biting, chewing, and swallowing pests. They are also effective against those insects that abrade the plant surfaces and suck out the pulp, lap up food or moisture from leaves and stems, feed on baits, or use their mouth parts to clean their bodies and appendages. The latter are for use on other kinds of pests, and act by contact with the insect. Their residual toxicity may last for days or weeks.

(d) SPECIAL
Under this heading may be included fumigants and ant exterminators, as well as a number of auxiliary agents for pest control.

Fungi.   These may be destroyed by the use of fungicides. Two general classes of fungicides are known: eradicants, and protectives. Eradicant fungicides kill by direct action at the time of application, while protective fungicides prevent invasion of plant tissues. The former must be applied to all infested areas simultaneously when the fungus is in a susceptible stage in its development. The latter are for use before plants have been attacked, and must either persist throughout the danger period or be frequently renewed. Several materials are employed as both eradicant and protective measures.

Both sprays and dusts are used, containing copper, sulphur, inorganic and organic mercury compounds, organic iron-sulphur compounds, and chlorinated quinone.

Bacteria.   Control measures include the use of sulphur, copper, zinc, and certain organic materials, made up into commercial sprays and dusts. In some cases, removal and burning of affected plants is the only remedy. Good lighting and aeration will check the growth of bacteria. Fungi and bacteria cause such diseases as the downy and powdery mildews, rusts, anthracnose, blight, damping-off, bacterial ring, and similar conditions.

Algae.   The green 'slime' of algae may be a nuisance in hydroponica. It should not arise if the amount of copper in the nutrient solution or mixture is adequate, and the solution is not allowed to remain standing on the surface of the growing medium.

Nematodes.   For the control of nematodes, the following remedy has given effective results:

Use a water dispersion of a dichloropropylene-dichloropropane mixture, or ethylene dibromide, to obtain complete control of root-knot nematode (*Heterodera marioni*) in sand or aggregate culture. In the case of the former, a concentration of 600 ppm is best, and as regards the latter one of 1250 ppm is satisfactory (parts by weight). The treatment consists of soaking the growing medium in the solution of chemical and water for at least twenty-four hours. The beds should be covered during this period. Tanks, cisterns and sumps will need similar attention. After the soaking period is over, drain out all appliances, wash them well, and flush three times with plain water. Then leave fresh water standing in the beds for twenty-four hours, after which they will be ready for use again.

Seed plants.   Parasitic seed plants should be destroyed.

Birds, rodents, and molluscs.   The usual traps and protective measures will eliminate these pests. Slugs and snails can be destroyed with metaldehyde or Paris Green bait.

OTHER PESTS.   Lizards can be trapped by mechanical methods, or poisoned with suitable baits. Cats can be driven away by leaving a bottle of strong ammonia with the top unscrewed in any area that they may frequent. Locust attacks can be prevented from destroying hydroponic crops by surrounding the beds with screens of mosquito netting secured to the shade poles.

Virus diseases

The systemic nature of viruses makes control difficult. The following measures will often prevent an outbreak:

    (i)   removal of any infected plants (roughing),
    (ii)   removal of any other hosts,
    (iii)   control of vectors,
    (iv)   use of tolerant, resistant or immune varieties of plants,
    (v)   employment of disease-free seeds.

Plant viruses may be transmitted in several ways, such as during contact with carriers, in building or grafting, by parasitic seed plants, through cigarette or pipe tobacco, and by other means. Common vectors include white fly, aphis, and similar insects. Viruses vary greatly in their ease of transmission and infectious capacities.

The common symptoms of virus infection are: alteration in the colouring of plants, like clearing of the veins, general chlorosis, yellowing, mottling of the foliage, mosaic, lesions, streaking, internal and external necrosis, nanism, and distortions. Vigorous plants are usually more badly affected than are weak and inactive ones. Strict phyto-sanitary precautions are the best preventive against the incidence of virus diseases. All infected plants should be immediately removed from the troughs and burnt. After touching any plant showing symptoms of a virus infection, the hands and face should be well washed with carbolic soap and water before further work is attempted.

CHAPTER 19

Vegetable growing

The term 'vegetable' is derived from the Latin word *vegetabilis*, meaning 'animating'. Fresh greenstuff is an essential constituent of all balanced diets.

The popularity of the salad vegetables has increased steadily, so that today there are few households in which tomatoes, lettuces, and cucumbers do not find a place. Correspondingly, the interest in the basic greenfoods – cabbages, brussels sprouts, kale, spinach and cauliflowers, has also risen, since once accustomed to the taste of fresh vegetables people are loath to do without them in some form or another at times when their first choice may be unavailable.

In hydroponics the exact selection of vegetable crops depends upon local climatic conditions in out-of-door installations. It is not possible to predict accurately in all cases, except in closed units especially where a locality has not previously been used for vegetable production, exactly what varieties will give the best results in particular combinations of outside climatic factors. Only field tests can provide the required information. The problem of disease resistance is another significant point to consider. Some varieties are less susceptible to diseases than are others. No arbitrary and fixed recommendations can be made for the cultural practices best adapted to each crop under all native climatic conditions. Each installation must necessarily be treated as a separate problem, and the details of operation adjusted to the locality in which it happens to be situated. For example, high wind velocities may make the use of 'self-topping' varieties of tomatoes desirable, or the vining of cucumber plants horizontally instead of vertically. The humidity of the atmosphere may govern the outside spacing of crops, as well as the need for defoliation or pruning. These, and many other factors have to be taken into account when working out the management and treatment of different species of vegetables in outdoor soilless cultures. The timing of crops is important in all commercial work. It is necessary to plan ahead in order to have an adequate supply of viable seed on hand, and to have each section of a unit ready for planting at the best periods. As one crop is ready to come out of the beds, another should be ready to go in, so that there is no wastage of time or labour. In protected and environmentally-controlled units, these considerations do not of course apply.

Main crops

The main vegetable crops will now be briefly considered, and their responses to hydroponic cultivation discussed.

ARTICHOKES
Cynara scolymus – Globe or French
This is a perennial vegetable, which continues to reproduce for several years without replanting. The plant appreciates good irrigation, but it cannot stand extremes of temperature. It needs protection from frost, and shading in very hot weather. Artichokes use appreciable amounts of potassium in their development. Cropping is most profitable in the second and third years.

Helianthus tuberosus – Jerusalem
Although a plant of the temperate zone, this artichoke often does exceptionally well in the tropics, provided it receives a modicum of shade, and adequate care and attention. The Jerusalem artichoke is well suited to sand culture. As growth proceeds, a little extra medium should be drawn up towards the stems, to make sure the tubers are properly covered.

ASPARAGUS
Asparagus officinalis
Asparagus was used by the Romans, at least two centuries before the Christian era, not only for food, but also for its medicinal properties. Propagation is usually by seed, though crowns may be obtained for transplanting. As it does not begin to crop until the third year, catch crops of lettuce or radish or some other salad vegetable should be sown between the rows until the space is needed by the asparagus. The plant is a gross feeder, and will respond well to the maximum concentrations of phosphorus and potash. The growing medium should be fairly loose in texture, and well aerated. For good white stems, blanching of the shoots is necessary. Celluloid or plastic collars may be employed.

AUBERGINE (Egg-plant, garden egg, or brinjal)
Solanum melongena
There are numerous varieties of aubergines, differing chiefly in size, shape, and colour of fruit. The purple garden eggs are generally preferred to the white or grey ones. The plant thrives best in a warm place, with a dry atmosphere. It is a gross feeder, and uses large amounts of nitrogen, phosphorus, and potassium. Excessive nitrogen will, however, encourage the growth of the leaves at the expense of the fruits if supplied at a late stage. The quantity of this element in the nutrient formula should be reduced by about one-third as soon as the fruits are well formed. It may be necessary

to do this several times in the season, since plants will bear more than a single series of eggs, while restoring the concentration to normal in between fruiting periods. To secure the largest fruits, the points of growth may be reduced in number by pinching out. Aubergines require ample irrigation. It is essentially a warmth-loving crop.

BEANS

Vicia faba – Broad
Phaseolus vulgaris – French
Phaseolus multiflorus – Scarlet runner
Phaseolus lunatus – Lima
Vigna sesquipedalis – Asparagus
Mucuna nivea – Velvet
Glycine hispida – Soya and other species

The culture of beans is not difficult. Generally speaking, these crops require good aeration, and should never be allowed to become waterlogged. Their tolerance of extremes of temperature varies greatly according to species and variety. All beans need ample supplies of phosphorus, potassium, and sulphur, but their requirement of nitrogen is not as high as it is in other crops.

BEETROOT

Beta vulgaris
Propagated by seed, beetroots are transplanted into the main troughs when 5 or 7.5 cms high. The germination percentage is usually rather poor. Plants benefit from a good supply of calcium and potassium in the solution, and can also utilise sodium and chlorine. As growth proceeds, a little extra aggregate should be placed around the roots. Beetroots are well adapted to hydroponics. Their light requirements are moderate.

THE BRASSICAS

Brassica oleracea botrytis – Broccoli and cauliflowers
Brassica oleracea var. – Cabbages
Brassica oleracea gemmifera – Brussels sprouts
Brassica chinensis – Pe-Tsai
Brassica oleracea capitata rubra – Red cabbage
Brassica oleracea acephala – Kale
Brassica caulo-rapa – Kohl-rabi
Brassica rapa – Turnips

All these vegetables are sensitive to lack of aeration in the growing medium. They should be supplied with frequent irrigations, and adequate concentrations of nitrogen

14.A   Dr. William F. Gericke with wheat plants grown in his hydroponic solution culture unit in California.

14.B.   A Gericke-type water or solution culture tank showing a fine lot of just harvested potatoes. (G. Gericke).

14.   Gericke-type water or solution culture.

and phosphorus. Iron is also important. The drainage system of a unit growing brassicas needs to be kept in good working order.

Cabbages in particular are gross feeders, and should not be left short of nutrients. In hot areas they need regular protection against insect pests, especially caterpillars. This vegetable has been cultivated from the earliest eras, and the ancient Greeks and Egyptians held it in high esteem. It was certainly grown extensively around Jerusalem at the time of Christ.

The iron supply of turnips in water cultures needs careful watching, since their lack of side roots makes it relatively more difficult for them to absorb sufficient quantities of this element than may be the case with other crops.

Cauliflowers do best when growth is quick and uninterrupted.

CARROTS
Daucus carota
Carrots need considerable care and attention if they are to do well. The short varieties are best for soilless culture, since they penetrate better into the aggregate, or litter bed in Gericke method installations. Once the seedlings have 'taken hold', good growth will result. Potassium and phosphorus are needed by this plant in adequate amounts, while the aggregate should not be too coarse or heavy.

CELERY
Apium graveolens
For ease of sowing, the seeds may be mixed with a filler of sand. The plant needs a cool and partially shaded site, and will require blanching before harvest. It responds well to an adequate level of nitrogen, and will benefit, as far as its table qualities are concerned from the presence of sodium and chlorine in the nutrient solution. Good aeration is essential for celery production in hydroponics.

CHILLIES (Sweet and hot peppers)
Capsicum grossum
Capsicum annuum
Capsicum frutescens
Capsicum minimum

Chillies demand a high level of nutrition and good management, as well as ample irrigation. They do best when the humidity of the atmosphere is relatively low. Light shading should be provided in very hot areas, and care taken to shield crops from strong winds.

The crop is essentially a warm season one, and if grown in cold countries should be planted under glass for best results.

CHICORY

Cichorium intybus

Several varieties of chicory are available, intended for different culinary purposes. Some are grown for their roots, which are cooked like carrots, while others are eaten as salads after forcing and blanching. In both cases, seeds may be sown in sand beds, and the young plants moved to the main troughs as convenient. For forcing chicory, the plants can be covered up with inverted flower pots, but a better method is to lift the crowns and trim off any side roots. The crowns should then be stacked in small boxes filled with aggregate. The growing medium must be kept moist with solution, and the whole apparatus has to be kept in complete darkness at a temperature of between 12.5 and 15.5°C. When the shoots attain a height of about 17.5 cm they may be cut off and used. It is important to ensure that blanching is thorough.

CUCUMBERS

Cucumis sativus

The cucumber plant is a native of the East Indies, and has been cultivated in oriental countries for about 4000 years. It is a warm season crop, but its culture is not difficult provided a few simple rules are observed. Cucumbers grow most vigorously at day temperatures of 24 to 30°C, and will stand over 38°C, provided the humidity is high. Seeds should be sown in sand troughs or boxes, and subsequently transplanted to the main beds, making sure that no check in growth occurs. Direct seeding can sometimes be practised. It is necessary to provide a system of supporting wires for the vines to climb up. A careful programme of terminal bud pinching is needed to ensure proper development of female flowers. As the lateral shoots develop, the terminal buds of the lateral branches must be removed just beyond the first female flower, which is usually one or two nodes from the main stem. The lateral branches are trained onto the trellis as they develop. As the laterals branch further, the removal of each branch terminal bud should be undertaken as with the primary branches. This keeps the plant branching and producing female flowers.

Cucumber flowers are imperfect, but both staminate and pistillate flowers are borne on the same plant. The staminate flowers, which produce pollen but no functional pistil, form in the axils of leaves and appear before the pistillate flowers. The latter, which produce a functional pistil but no pollen, arise in the axils of the secondary branches. Ridge cucumbers need fertilizing to produce fruits but in the case of the 'frame' cucumbers, the male flowers should be removed, as it is undesirable that the female flowers of these types should be fertilized. The cucumber plant has a high water requirement as compared with other species. It needs frequent irrigations, a high atmospheric humidity, shelter from wind, shading during bright periods, and a good level of nutrition.

ENDIVE
Cichorium endivia

This easily grown salad vegetable may be propagated either by direct seeding as an intercrop, or by transplanting. The culture is similar to that of lettuce. For blanching, draw the leaves together and tie them up, so as to exclude light from the heart of the plant, or else cover with an inverted flower pot, adjusted so that some air goes through the bottom.

LEEKS
Allium porrum

The leek is a gross feeder, and for best development requires ample supplies of phosphorus, nitrogen, and potash – in that order. Seed is sown in a sand bed, and the seedlings are transplanted later to their permanent positions. The stems may be blanched with celluloid collars, and it is often a good plan to cut the tap root with a sharp knife in tropical areas to prevent early running to seed.

LETTUCES
Lactuca sativa

This is one of the oldest vegetables known to man. Historical references exist which record that lettuce appeared at the royal tables of the Persian kings more than six centuries before the birth of Christ. There are two main types – cabbage, and cos. To give superior results, lettuces should be grown quickly, without any check during their development. Seed may be sown in sand boxes, and the young seedlings subsequently removed to their permanent positions in the main troughs, or else direct sowing may be carried out for intercropping. In the latter case, the seed may be mixed with a filler of dry sand to ensure even distribution.

In hot areas, lettuces need good shading, and every effort should be made to keep the beds fairly cool. It is also important to see that the solution in the troughs does not saturate the lower leaves of the plants nor submerge the root crowns.

MELONS
Cucumis melo – Cantaloupes or Musk
Citrullus vulgaris – Water melon

The musk melons are suited to hot, dry climates, and although they need ample irrigation, they are susceptible to high humidity. It is a good plan to place a small collar of damp excluding material around the base of the plant's stem to keep it dry during growth. Water melons also prefer a warm area. They are more hardy than cantaloupes. Both types may need hand pollinating.

OKRA (Lady's Fingers)
Hibiscus esculentus
These vegetables need a good supply of nitrogen, and warm conditions with satisfactory aeration and drainage. Before sowing, the seeds should be soaked in water for forty-eight hours, to encourage a better percentage of germination.

ONIONS
Allium cepa
Onions need reasonably dry conditions. Their requirements of potassium and nitrogen are fairly high, and care must be taken to see that the bulbs are not subjected to unnecessary dampness. For main crops, it is best to transplant seedlings, but for spring onions and catch crops, seed may be sown direct into permanent positions. With the larger varieties, when the onions have attained their full size, irrigation should cease, and the troughs be allowed to dry out. After the tops have died down, and the bulbs are properly ripened, they may be lifted for storage.

PARSNIP
Pastinaca sativa
The roots of parsnips are exceptionally long, and it may be necessary to provide this crop with a greater depth of aggregate than is normal. Phosphorus is important to good development, while calcium, nitrogen, and potassium are needed in fairly large amounts. To prevent forking of the roots it may be advisable to insert collars of fine metal gauze, painted with asphalt emulsion, into the growing medium around each plant. These will prevent branching of the roots and encourage them to grow straight down.

Parsnips are tolerant of cold conditions, and can withstand ordinary frosts.

PEAS
Pisum sativum
Peas are usually classified into early and main crop varieties. There are also dwarf and tall types. These plants require ample calcium, iron, and phosphorus. They need good aeration, and freedom from very humid conditions. Proper supports are essential. During dry weather, ample irrigation should be given.

Seed should be sown *in situ* in the main beds. To protect seeds from the depredations of mice or rats, they may be moistened with kerosene and rolled in red lead.

POTATOES
Solanum tuberosum
Very large yields of potatoes have been obtained in soilless cultures. Varieties are

grouped into three classes: earlies, second earlies, and maincrops. Compared with other field crops, potatoes need a shorter period for foliage development, hence they can be grown at high latitudes where short summers prevail. It is important to ensure that the tubers are provided with an adequate covering of aggregate, otherwise over-heating and greening may occur. The plants can stand very hot weather provided the root zone is kept cool.

Potatoes need ample supplies of potassium, phosphorus, and iron. Good aeration and drainage are vital. The pH of the nutrient solution should be on the acid side. Tubers or seed potatoes (setts) should be planted at the correct spacing directly into their permanent positions in the main beds.

RADISHES

Raphanus sativus

Often used for catch or intercropping, radishes can be grown easily in hydroponics by direct seeding. They do not withstand the shock of transplanting. In very hot areas, the plants may show some tendency to bolting, therefore good shading is important in such places.

Radishes were extensively cultivated in ancient Egypt, according to Pliny. They were also used by the Greeks in their sacrificial offerings to the god Apollo.

RHUBARB

Rheum rhaponticum

After planting, the crowns should just appear on the surface of the aggregate. A high level of nutrition is needed, with ample phosphorus. Forcing may be undertaken by covering with inverted barrels or boxes.

SPINACH

Spinacia oleracea

This crop needs ample irrigation and a cool, shady situation. It is quick growing, and can utilise plenty of nitrogen. Seed should be germinated in sand beds, and subsequently transplanted to the main troughs.

SQUASHES

Cucurbita pepo – Vegetable marrow
Cucurbita melo-pepo – Squash

The seeds may be sown in the propagation unit in containers filled with sand or vermiculite, and later removed to permanent positions in the main beds. The plants like warmth, but may be adversely affected by excessive moisture. During wet weather, a piece of flat stone or tile should be placed under each fruit to prevent it from rotting. Hand pollination is frequently necessary for good fruiting. Squashes are one of the easiest of the vine crops to grow in hydroponics.

SWEET POTATO
Ipomoea batatas
A warm area crop, the sweet potato does best in a reasonably dry atmosphere, with shading from hot sun. The requirements of this crop for potassium, calcium, magnesium, and phosphorus are high, but it is not a gross feeder. Sand culture is well suited to its development.

TOMATOES
Lycopersicum esculentum
The tomato is a native of tropical America, and was cultivated by the Aztecs and the Incas before the Spanish conquests of Mexico and Peru. It likes warm growing conditions, with day temperatures of from 24 to 29°C, though it will tolerate a heat of 49°C for short periods. Both determinate and indeterminate varieties exist. Tomatoes should be protected from strong winds and excessive humidity. They also need some shading, and good aeration.

Seed is best germinated in sand boxes, and the seedlings are transferred later on to the main troughs. Supports must be provided for the vines to climb up. Fairly deep planting is advantageous since roots form all along that portion of the stem which remains below the surface of the growing medium, so giving better anchorage. Regular irrigation is essential to prevent any check to development, because tomatoes soon become stunted and woody if growth is interrupted following frequent wilting. The plant's need for nitrogen is large during the first stages of growth; later on potash will be required in substantial amounts, as well as phosphorus and some iron. Pruning or defoliation is often advisable in damp areas. It should not, however, be attempted until plants are at least one metre in height, and then only two or three side shoots at a time should be removed to admit extra light and air. The bottom shoots may also be pruned back so that they are a few inches above the surface of the growing medium. A single main stem should be taken up to the fourth truss, after which it is cut, and a side shoot then carried on, thus restoring pristine vigour. Suckers must be removed as they develop in the axils of the leaves.

During periods of hot, dry weather pollen is often not viable. Likewise in times of high relative humidity the pollen tends to stick to the anthers and is not shaken readily onto the stigma. It may be necessary to syringe the flowers gently with a fine spray of water, or to shake the supporting wires slightly to encourage pollination. Hand fertilization may also be practised, using a camel hair brush or rabbit's tail. In difficult cases, one or other of the growth-regulating materials available as pastes, emulsions, or solutions, can be employed to set the fruit artificially.

YAMS

Dioscorea

These crops are well suited to sand culture. The beds should be quite deep, about 30 to 45 centimetres being best. Shading is essential. Care must be taken not to over irrigate, or the tubers will rot. The setts should be planted about 25 centimetres below the surface of an extra deep trough, and supports provided for the vines to climb on.

CHAPTER 20

Floriculture

The soilless growing of flowers can be carried out very successfully. There are many thousands of householders who raise blooms without using soil on a small scale in order to beautify the home or decorate the drawing room, while on the other hand there are the big 'flower-factories' of the English carnation growers and the extensive layouts of the American professional hydroponicists, notably near Chicago, and at Sanford, North Carolina. These commercial units may turn out several thousand bunches of perfect blooms regularly each week throughout the year for sale in near or distant markets. Naturally, the successful operation of such large scale installations calls for the exercise of a high degree of technical skill and organisational ability.

Protection and care

Good growth of ornamental plants depends very much upon the amount of protection that it may be possible to give them against the effects of the elements – wind, rain, sun, and other factors – and the attacks of various pests and diseases. Flowers are delicate and exotic things, which need supreme care and attention if they are to achieve maximum beauty. Like a good complexion, a fine bloom will last only if it is looked after properly and well-protected from the ravages of life.

Many types of garden and outdoor or house flowers have been grown successfully in hydroponics. Perhaps the greatest amount of work has been carried out with carnations and chrysanthemums – two species that are especially well adapted to soilless culture. While much depends upon environmental conditions, and the variant factors of temperature, light intensity, and humidity, certain general rules can be laid down concerning the requirements of different flowers. These, combined with the results of observations and experience, form the basis of the notes given in this chapter on the cultivation of different ornamental plants. Before starting a hydroponic flower growing unit, growers should decide what type(s) of plants they intend to raise. Flowers are usually grouped into:

(a) Alpines, or strictly speaking, plants from mountainous regions, but loosely used to refer to all dwarf types suitable for rock gardens. They may be hardy herbaceous perennials, biennials, annuals, or shrubs.

(b)   Annuals (half-hardy). These complete their cycle of growth in one year, but need protection from cold in certain regions during spring time.

(c)   Annuals (hardy). They are resistant to cold.

(d)   Aquatics, or plants that grow wholly or mainly in water.

(e)   Bedding plants. This is a garden term only, having no botanical significance. It refers to those ornamentals that can be used for massed out-of-door beds.

(f)   Biennials, or plants which complete their cycle of life in two years. They do not normally flower the first year.

(g)   Bulbs. There are hardy and half-hardy bulbs as well as tender kinds.

(h)   Herbaceous perennials, or plants that live for a number of years, and have a comparatively soft growth. They may be hardy or tender.

(i)   Epiphytes, or plants that may grow on other plants without being parasitic.

(j)   Shrubs and climbers.

(k)   Roses.

(l)   Miscellaneous types.

Having chosen the species that it is intended to grow, the site for the unit should be selected with reference to the conditions of light, heat, and humidity, which favour the culture of the group to which they belong. Details of these requirements may be found in any good gardening encyclopaedia. Where the locality is unsuitable for the growth of a plant, the difficulty can be overcome by the erection of protective devices. The following notes have been designed to set out the main needs of some popular and representative flowers.

ANTIRRHINUMS (Snapdragons)

Antirrhinum majus

Seed should be sown in a tray of sand, and the young plants removed to their permanent positions with a ball of sand intact around their roots. Antirrhinums like a good level of calcium in the nutrient solution. The plants respond well to generous treatment. It is a good plan to pinch out the tops when the seedlings are several centimetres high – this discourages too early flowering, and results in better root growth with more blooms eventually. Cuttings are often used for propagation.

ASTERS

Callistephus chinensis

No great difference has been noticed between plants transferred with a ball of sand around the roots, and those transplanted with washed and clean roots, as far as ultimate development is concerned. Asters like moderate shading, and there should be no check in growth. Violent temperature fluctuations are undesirable. The plant is a gross feeder.

15. Examples of compressed air methods.

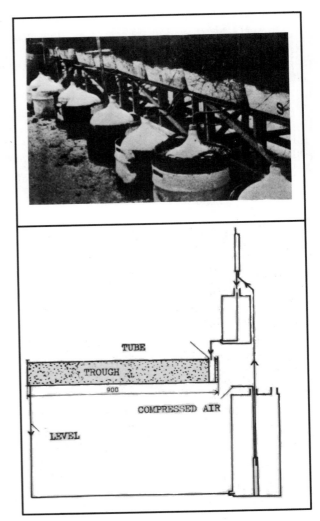

BEGONIAS

Begonias have low light tolerance, and need protection from direct sunlight. The beds should be kept moist, but not too wet. An air temperature of between 21 and 26°C is ideal. The plant has a low iron requirement, but needs a good supply of potash.

When grown from seeds, begonias need considerable care and attention for the first few weeks. The pans of sand or vermiculite should be covered with a sheet of glass, and watered from underneath by sub-irrigation or wicks. Surface watering is undesirable.

CANNAS

Canna indica

Often called the Indian Shot, this flower is the tropical gardener's stand-by. The seeds are very hard, and should be filed or treated with hot water before sowing, otherwise germination will be very slow. They can, however, be readily multiplied by division of rootstock. Cannas are gross feeders, but should not be given too much nitrogen, otherwise the foliage will develop at the expense of the blooms. The aim should be to secure heavy healthy heads on short stems.

CARNATIONS

Dianthus

These are one of the most extensively grown hydroponic ornamental plants. They are well adapted to soilless culture. The carnation is divided into two classes: the perpetual or early flowering, and the hardy or border carnations. The former is used for commercial production. Plants may be propagated either by seed or by slips. Seed needs careful handling, as it splits easily, while cuttings must be hardened off before they are transplanted. Carnations are gross feeders, but are intolerant of any imbalance in the nutrient formula. It is particularly important that the nitrogen/potassium balance should be correct. Excess calcium should also be avoided. Extremes in temperature, overwatering, and irregular irrigation should be avoided. These faults in technique will encourage the development of split calyx.

It has been found that the use of a solution of one part of boric acid powder in ten parts of water will improve the keeping quality of carnation flowers by three to seven days.

CALCEOLARIAS

A beautiful and elegant flower, but requires protection from damage by wind and rain. Shading is necessary in hot weather. It is easy to culture in hydroponics, provided that adequate heat is provided in cold areas.

CHRYSANTHEMUMS

These plants suffer most from lack of aeration. In hydroponics, good drainage is essential for chrysanthemums. They do very well in sand cultures. The need for an adequate level of phosphorus in the nutrient solution cannot be overemphasised. Propagation is normally by cuttings rooted-in trays filled with moist sand or vermiculite, but seed can also be used with the Cascade varieties. The principal types available include Large-flowered Exhibition, Incurved, Decorative, Single, Cascade, Border, and Korean.

Pinching out of the growing tips, or 'stopping', is essential to good production of flowers. Tables of the correct stopping dates for the different varieties are available in most books on chrysanthemums.

DAHLIAS

The dahlia plant is supposed to have been first discovered by Baron von Humboldt in Mexico in 1789. He sent a specimen to professor Cavanilles of the Botanical Garden at Madrid, Spain, who named the new plant in honour of Professor Andreas Dahl, a Swedish botanist and a pupil of Linnaeus.

Dahlias require a good level of potassium and phosphorus in their nutrition. Ample irrigation is required. The plants are tender and most susceptible to frost injury. Propagation is by cuttings, or root division using pot-tubers. They do well in hydroponics, but care must be taken to see that mildew does not occur, due sometimes to weakness caused by overstimulation. For exhibition purposes, growths of large flowered decoratives and cactus varieties should be reduced to one to three a stem according to strength.

GLADIOLI

Gladioli need ample potash and phosphorus. The plants are quite easy to grow, and respond well to care and attention. Any signs of iron deficiency should be watched for. Good lighting is important.

GARDENIAS

The culture of gardenias in hydroponics necessitates the maintenance of an acid reaction (pH 5.0–6.0) for optimum growth and production of blooms. Iron is also important, and extra amounts may be needed from time to time. Gardenias thrive on a certain amount of humidity in the atmosphere, and good irrigation. A high level of nitrogen and phosphorus is desirable. Propagation is normally by cuttings started in sand trays.

IRIS

Grows well in hydroponics, but may be susceptible to decay in the rhizomes, if not properly irrigated. In wet, damp areas, iris should be planted close to the surface of the growing medium, and in hot, dry places, a few centimetres lower down.

MARIGOLDS

Tagetes erecta – African
Tagetes patula – French
It may be necessary to make minor adjustments to accommodate the preferences of

different varieties of marigolds in hydroponics. The question of aeration is important. Some of the French types need more moisture and a finer aggregate than do a number of the African. The plants usually require a good level of potash in their nutrition.

NARCISSI (Daffodils)

Bulbs should be planted at a depth equal to about three times their own thickness. The plants need a cool climate, with air temperatures of not over 21°C if possible, for starting; later on they may withstand greater heat. A high light intensity often increases the iron requirement.

NASTURTIUMS

Tropaeolum majus

These flowers are very simple to grow, requiring only an ample supply of light and sunshine, and good aeration. They can be planted in hanging baskets or containers for verandah decoration.

PANSY

Viola tricolor

Seedlings must be transplanted with the ball of sand or other aggregate around their roots intact. Pansies need good irrigation, and ample nitrogen, phosphorus, and potassium in the nutrient solution. Shade is desirable, and they are not well suited to very dry places, unless kept fairly damp.

PELARGONIUMS

These do very well in coarse aggregates. Good aeration is important. The cuttings can be rooted easily in sand or vermiculite. A dry atmosphere is best, with adequate feeding, and reasonable shelter.

PETUNIAS

Seeds are small and need great care for successful germination. Over-watering should be avoided. The plants are well suited to growing in small boxes or troughs, because of their natural drooping habits.

ROSES

For the good growing of roses, a high level of potassium in the nutrient solution is needed. The pH should never fall below 5.5. Proper aeration and drainage are other significant matters of great importance in the rosarium. The best temperatures for roses range from 16 to 26°C though the range of tolerance is quite wide. Light intensity should be good, but sun scorch is dangerous.

The rose was the first ornamental plant to be grown in laboratory-style hydroponics

(W. F. Gericke 1927). For water cultures, short, stout varieties are the best, since they can be made to bloom several times each season. For sand and aggregate culture, many types are suitable. The rose is possibly more sensitive to the effects of environment than most other plants, and each locality has to be studied separately as to the most suitable hydroponic technique for employment there.

The principal types of roses grown for display purposes are: tea, hybrid tea, hybrid perpetual, pernettiana, polyantha pompon, hybrid polyantha, climbing polyantha, multiflora rambler, wichuraiana rambler, hybrid wichuraiana, climbing hybrid tea, noisette, and hybrid musk.

Regular pruning is necessary. Strong growths should be cut down to within three dormant buds of the surface of the growing medium, weaker ones to within one or two buds, and very thin shoots should be removed altogether. Propagation is by cuttings, budding, and sometimes seeding.

STOCKS
Mathiola annua
These plants present no particular difficulties, but they will not usually withstand temperatures of over 24°C. They are fairly tolerant of moisture, and a damp atmosphere. Seed should be sown in trays of sand or fine aggregate, and the young plants subsequantly removed to their permanent sites.

SWEET PEAS
Lathyrus odoratus
Direct seeding is best, and the aggregate should be cool and moist, with shading installed if the area is hot and dry. The seeds may be sown at a depth of 2.5 to 3 centimetres below the surface of the growing medium. Care must be taken when irrigating the seeds, since too much wetness will cause rotting, while excessive dryness will result in desiccation. The pH of the solution should be slightly alkaline. As the plants grow, more light and air must be given so long as the temperature around the roots does not rise unduly. A mulch of excelsior can be applied with benefit.
Sweet pea seeds may need 'chipping' to hasten germination.

ZINNIAS
These flowers are very tolerant of high light intensities, and can withstand considerable heat. Their popularity has increased by leaps and bounds during the past two decades. They are well suited to tropical areas. Zinnias use a fairly high concentration of nitrogen.

Numerous other species have been grown successfully in hydroponic units.

Decorative plants for offices

It is not often known that modern office blocks, with their larger window areas and central heating, offer suitable growing conditions for many attractive foliage plants. Current building designs in concrete and glass, following architectural trends, have influenced the type, size, and number of plants that can be kept inside offices. In some towns one can now see glass-enclosed patios in the middle of blocks and buildings, banks with gardens in the corners and airports or stations with planting wells inside the waiting rooms. The plants are supplied with high-intensity, illuminated, self-supporting facilities. A wide range of blooms and greenery may be used. Good growth and thriving results can be secured if the plants are well chosen and given reasonable care and attention.

In fact, whether offices are modern or not, plants grown in them must have optimum light, temperature and humidity for the particular kinds concerned. Offices dictate other necessary conditions, such as lower temperatures at weekends, when no staff are on duty, dust and draughts. In some offices, on the other hand, temperatures may soar very high at weekends, so that plants can become dangerously dry. Air conditioning may be quite favourable to many species, but when this is switched off conditions change rapidly.

The most important growth consideration in choosing a place for particular plants in offices is to ensure that it provides as much light as possible. Most large plants will use all the light they can get. They should not, however, be moved abruptly into direct sunshine from dark corners, but must be permitted to get more light gradually after a few days in intermediate conditions. Lack of humidity is another important factor, unless it can be provided artificially, avoid plants for offices with thin, soft, or hairy leaves, since these normally demand higher air moisture. Improper watering of plants in offices is frequently a cause of their decline and premature death. Often, watering may be governed by the widely differing opinions of staff members, each of whom bases his or her knowledge on experience with plants at home. In consequence, plants are either watered too freely, or not enough. It is hard to advise watering at definite intervals unless the actual environmental conditions are taken into account or known. Plants differ in their needs in different places. The most important factors in watering office plants are:

(a)   Location in the office;
(b)   Size of plant;
(c)   Root and top growth;
(d)   Needs of the plant group to which the particular specimen belongs.

A fairly good general rule is to water the plant well and then keep the top of the growing medium damp to touch. If in doubt, leave it until the next day. Water well again and repeat at appropriate intervals. Usually, twice or more weekly solution applications in hot and dry offices are adequate. For those interested in a more technical approach, a light hammer may be employed to tap the pots gently – if the sound given off is 'dull', then the plant has enough water, if 'hollow' sounding then water or solution will be required. However, this method only works best with earthenware or clay garden pots, it is unreliable with plastic containers or troughs.

Selection of office plants

The selection of plants for offices usually centres around tropical foliage types that will withstand high and fluctuating temperatures, low humidity and poorer light conditions. Three plants most tolerant of poor lighting, low humidity or neglect are:

- (i)   Cast iron plant or *Aspidistra elatior*;
- (ii) India rubber or *Ficus elastica*; and
- (iii) Snake plant or *Sansevieria trifasciata*.

Aspidistras suffered a decline in popularity, but are now making quite a come-back, especially the variegated form with large ovate leaves on long petioles arising from ground level. The rubber plant has ovate oblong leaves, formed on tall woody stems. The variegated types are the most attractive. The snake plant, sometimes called Mother-in-Law's Tongue, is Indian in origin, not African, and has stiff spear-like leaves that stand erect from the surface of the growing medium. Here again, the modern variegated forms are pleasant, with intriguing crossbands of lighter and darker shades of green, or sometimes marginal bands of yellow, for a change.

FICUS SPECIES.   In addition to the India rubber plant, other kinds of Ficus or fig types can be very dependable and offer variety of leaf form. These include:

> Fiddle-leaved fig or *Ficus lyrata*, with large fiddle-shaped leaves.
> Weeping fig or *Ficus benjamina*, with willow-like wavy-margined leaves.
> Java fig or *Ficus benjamina*, var. *exotica*, with a more refined and graceful form.
> Mistletoe fig or *Ficus diversifolia*, which has distinctive, smaller, obovate leaves and is very well adapted to office planting. This type forms a twiggy plant, slow growing and able to withstand quite adverse conditions, particularly poor light.

The Umbrella trees or *Scheffleras* can thrive in more dry conditions than most other tropical species for office use. There are three kinds common, all with large palmately compound umbrella-like leaves. They need ample light, but will withstand less favoured situations quite well.

The Palm family

Where graceful plants that will tolerate low light intensities and low humidity are desired, in very large offices, thought should be given to using members of the palm family. In these kinds of situations, the following should respond well:

> Sentry palm or *Howea belmoreana*;
> Paradise palm or *Howea forsteriana*;
> Neanthe palm or *Chamaedorea elegans* (Bella), possessing miniature proportions;
> Large lady palm or *Rhapis excelsa*, a very hardy species, tolerant of abuse, with a bamboo-like appearance and fan-shaped leaves.

In lobbies or places where there is warmth, but also draughts, *Philodendron sellowianum* and *Philodendron hastatum*, are to be recommended. In really cool conditions, variegated ivies and aucubas are best and will probably suffice.

Office plants should always have their names written on labels attached to them, both the popular one and the Latin or botanical description. This adds greatly to their interest and encourages staff to familiarise themselves with the different types. When buying plants from garden centres, nurserymen or other sources, always if possible stipulate the species and variety by both the botanical name and the popular one. This avoids misunderstanding and ensures you will get what you want, since popular names alter according to locality and can be a source of confusion. Look up the proper names and descriptions in a good horticultural or ornamental plant book, so that you know what you are getting, because armed with this knowledge one can let the nursery know that one will not be agreeable to accept inferior stock or other kinds instead of the species one ordered and stipulated. In the ornamental plant business, much substitution of types can occur, largely because of the public's unfamiliarity with each kind.

A little extra time and interest spent in getting acquainted with office plants will reap rewards in the form of refreshment at work, brighter and more cheerful surroundings – which in turn improves mental and physical well-being, and simplifies greatly the tasks of management – and contact with Nature throughout hours of duty.

For larger offices or whole blocks, special hydroponic systems of plant growing are now available. Entitled the Florever or Maramatic methods, these work well and batches of ornamental plants in different rooms can be cared for automatically from a central unit located in the basement or other convenient position.

The greater part of our lives is spent at work and so any improvement that it may be possible to make in our conditions of labour can exercise a good effect upon our minds and bodies. Persons employed in modern offices are perhaps more cut off from Nature and the enjoyment of country things than any other class of people. Today, office work can be very monotonous and boring, due to repetition of similar tasks day after day. The loss of individuality experienced in the impersonal atmosphere and surroundings discourages extra effort and lowers general productivity. Therefore there is a real need to look after the mental and physical welfare of office workers and to bring them into regular contact with natural life when on duty, and there is no better way for this than the presence of hydroponic plants and flowers.

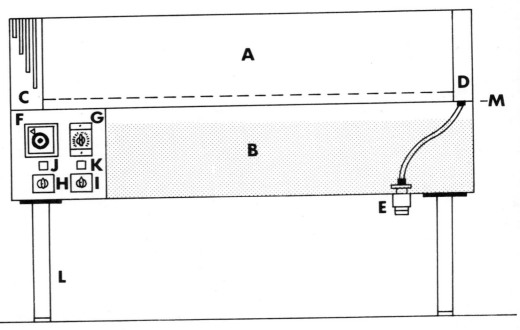

FIG. 43.
Florever Test 2500 Monoblok automatic office or house plant growing unit.

A: plant box
B: tank box
C: niveau (level) feeler
D: flowing pipe (to dam up)
E: pump
F: switch clock
G: short time limitation

H: elector, short time, long time
I: adjustment of flowing heat
J: working lamp (lamp which indicates that the installation is working)
K: trouble lamp
L: pedestal
M: dividing joint.

CHAPTER 21

Plantation and other crops

While it is unlikely that the majority of plantation and field crops will ever be grown generally on a large scale by means of soilless cultivation – since it is more profitable for hydroponicists to concentrate on producing vegetables, fruits, and flowers which have a higher unit value – nevertheless there may be certain times, like those of famine or destruction, when it would be extremely desirable to raise extra supplies of cereal foods and raw materials in particular areas without using soil. The contamination of a country's land after attack by an enemy using nuclear weapons is one case in point. As the world's population increases, local shortages of food are more than likely to occur. The further exploration of the Moon, and eventual landings by men on other planets, with the establishment of colonies in space would demand the setting-up of large scale hydroponica at such sites. Then again, soilless culture is a very valuable tool for investigations into the nutrient requirements of crops like rubber, certain fruits, tea, coffee, and tobacco. These plants can be more easily propagated in hydroponic troughs than in nurseries of soil beds, due to the reduction in the incidence of diseases and mortality of seedlings and cuttings.

Other plants that are suited to hydroponics include such varied species as strawberries, papayas, watercress, orchids, pyrethrum, and different fibres. The algae, which have so many possibilities both as a high-protein foodstuff and as sources of industrial raw materials, have responded well to artificial culture.

This chapter consists of a series of brief discussions about, and notes on, the propagation and growth of a number of different crops without soil.

Beverages and industrial plants

COCOA

Theobroma cacao

The seed, which must be sown fresh, can be propagated in beds of sand or litter trays. Germination takes place in about two-and-a-half weeks, and the seedlings should be planted out when they attain an approximate height of some 38 centimetres.

COFFEE
Coffea arabica, C. liberica, C. robusta
Seedlings can be produced quickly and easily in hydroponic troughs. There is usually less mortality than may be the case in soil nurseries. Young plants are healthier and in better condition for setting out when grown in soilless cultures, while the laborious and costly processes of sterilisation by heat or fire are obviated. The hard toil of carting dung or cow manure, and the preparation of slurry, are also eliminated. Coffee seed germinates in from four to six weeks, and the seedlings will be ready for planting out some eight months later. The absence of waterlogging and the properly controlled conditions of the cultures prevent the incidence and spread of diseases like *Hemelaia vastatrix*, and *Pythium* or 'damping-off'.

SUGAR-CANE
Saccharum officinarum
The cuttings or setts are usually selected from the upper joints of the canes, cut into lengths of 20 to 25 centimetres (including three or four joints), and placed in troughs filled with fine aggregate. Pre-soaking with a nutrient solution is often a good practice. The cuttings or 'plants' will sprout in about a week to ten days. The first sprout should be removed, so as to induce tillering. After a few weeks, the rooted setts may be transferred with a ball of substrate around them to their permanent sites in the fields. By starting sugar-cane plants in this way, quicker growth has been secured.

RUBBER
Hevea brasiliensis
Seed may be sown, or selected clones bud grafted, in hydroponic troughs. The young seedlings are afterwards transplanted at the rate of about 250 to the hectare. The advantages of the method are mainly to be found in the lower mortality rates, and the fact that selection and 'culling' become easier to carry out.

TEA
Camellia thea
Sowing takes place in sand cultures, carefully shaded from direct sun. After about eight to ten months, the young plants will be ready for removal to their permanent sites. Cuttings can also be rooted without difficulty in hydroponics. The method is very economical, since the establishment of permanent beds saves the labour of preparing new *bheties* (beds) each season.

TOBACCO
Nicotiana tabacum
Tobacco seedlings are normally subject to attacks by many diseases, especially those

caused by the parasitic and saprophytic fungi. In soil nurseries, this necessitates the sterilisation of the soil by burning or chemical means, often at considerable cost. Very good results have been obtained, with complete freedom from diseases, by raising seedlings in hydroponic beds. The seed, which is very small, should be mixed with a filler of fine sand, and sown carefully. After about six weeks, the young plants should be lifted into trays, and planted out in their permanent positions with a ball of sand around the roots. Hydroponic beds for tobacco seedling production should be filled with a fine aggregate, and be of sound construction, capable of lasting indefinitely.

Cereals

Wheat, barley, rye, and oats have all been grown without soil for experimental purposes. Work has also been carried out with crops such as pyrethrum, groundnuts, and similar economic species. Of more immediate concern, however, for hydroponic culture are maize and rice. These two cereals are both well adapted to soilless methods. Not only are they staple foodstuffs in many parts of the world, but their growth can be very profitable. Sweet corn, in particular, may be classed as a high grade horticultural crop.

MAIZE
Zea mays

Seed should be sown *in situ* in the main troughs, either alone or in combination with another crop. Ample irrigation is important, and care must be taken to ensure that the phosphorus concentration in the nutrient solution is adequate. Any deficiency of iron should be noted, and adjustment made accordingly. High winds may prevent effective pollination, in which case the silks on the ears will need to be fertilized by shaking the tassel over them. In hot areas maize grows at a phenomenal rate, and attains a height of 3.5 to 4 metres, so that a tall man on horseback can ride completely concealed through a stand of good quality corn. An increase of as much as 18 centimetres in height in growing maize during a period of twenty-four hours has been observed in Bengal. For table use, cobs should be picked fresh and lightly toasted, then spread with butter. The sooner green corn is eaten the better, since it loses its full taste two hours after picking.

RICE
Oryza sativa

Before sowing, the seed should be soaked in water or nutrient solution for twenty-four hours, and then covered with sacks for five days to allow it to commence germination. This process is very similar to the technique of vernalisation often used with wheat. As soon as initial germination has started, the seeds should be planted in the growing

medium at the correct spacing, care being taken to discard bad seed. The beds must be kept thoroughly irrigated during the growth period, the water level or degree of saturation being gradually dropped or lessened when ripening begins. Rice needs a damp atmosphere to pollinate well. It can utilise substantial quantities of the ammonium salts, and needs a greater supply of iron in bright light than in dull weather. The best temperature for good growth is about 33°C.

Fibres

Experiments have been carried out on the soilless cultivation of cotton, jute, flax, sisal, and other fibre-producing plants. Cotton is particularly susceptible to the effects of excess moisture. It needs a high level of calcium in the nutrient solution. This element appears to play a special part in protein synthesis, and its absence or deficiency greatly inhibits the growth of cotton plants. Boron and manganese are also important for proper development. Greater length of fibre may be obtained by using ammonium salts in the formulae. Jute (*Corchorus olitorious* var., and *C. capsularis* var.) has grown well in soilless cultures. It has long been recognised that for the successful cultivation of this crop, a high concentration of potassium is vital, and a level of not below 360 ppm of the nutrient is recommended in hydroponic work. Flax (*Linum usitatissimum*) responds well to soilless culture, and yields both seed and fibre. Sisal is another estate crop of considerable economic significance. Sand and aggregate troughs are ideal for the raising of bulbils and suckers of *Agave*.

Fruits

Seedlings of fruit trees may be grown in hydroponic troughs without difficulty. Some fruits, such as papayas, may be worth culturing in soilless beds in greenhouses in cold countries, especially where the product is considered a luxury, and is imported at high cost.

STRAWBERRIES.   Runners are most suitable for starting in the beds. They may either be forced for fruiting during the first season, or left in for three years, the best berries being then obtained in the second and third years. Strawberries need a good supply of phosphorus and potash. Care must be taken not to allow the plants to become water-

---

16. *(Plate opposite)* Root development in a plastic hydroponic layflat. Soilless grown plants have compact and well developed root systems.
(Dr. Cyril Pustan).

logged, nor should the lower leaves get saturated or rot will set in.

Several other soft fruits can be grown in hydroponics on whatever scale may be desired.

Watercress

For the most successful growth of this salad, watertight beds are desirable. The solution should be allowed to flow continuously through the aggregate by gravity from an elevated tank. It may be collected in a sump and returned to the reservoir at frequent intervals. Although seed is sometimes used, cuttings from selected plants give the best results. The temperature of the nutrient solution should be maintained at 15.5 to 20°C. The rate of flow should not be too quick; a speed of not much over one kilometre an hour is adequate.

Orchids

The best potting mixture for epiphytic orchids consists of equal parts of broken bricks, wood chippings, bark, or shavings, peat, and sphagnum moss (*Sphagnum zeylanicum*). For terrestrial orchids, charcoal, small pieces of bone, and some coarse sand may be added. The plants are usually propagated by means of cuttings or divisions of the rootstock or pseudo-bulbs, although expert growers do raise them from seed. The germinating medium should be infected with the appropriate microscopic fungus (mycorhiza) mycelium, pure cultures of which are available. In the absence of the fungus, orchid seeds seldom germinate, or if they do, the seedlings will not thrive. In order to grow orchids successfully, a knowledge of the climatic conditions under which they grow in their natural state is valuable. Some species grow well in humid surroundings, while others do best in dry places. Meristem cultivation of orchids has been carried out by F. Penningsfeld in Germany.

Mushrooms

Mushrooms cannot be grown in standard hydroponic cultures, since they require supplies of organic nutrients. The soilless cultivation of these fungi has been successful using compost of straw, sawdust and sand. The plants need dark and fairly dry surroundings. Another suitable form of culture would consist of a bed of agar-agar (a preparation of seaweed, chiefly *Gelidium*, called Japanese or Chinese moss) impregnated with organic compounds, which would supply the necessary nutrients. Normal fertilizing practice should be followed, and a solution of the appropriate concentrations made by dissolving quantities of the manures, sugars, and compounds in water, then straining off the liquor. This could then be used to dissolve the jelly, and the whole allowed to stiffen, before inserting the pieces of spawn.

Forestry

Hydroponics has proved of value in silvicultural work. Seeds which are normally difficult to germinate often do better in soilless beds. The advantage of having permanent units is obvious, while there is no danger of damage to young plants with delicate tap-roots when removing them for transplanting.

Algae culture

The artificial growth of algae on a large scale calls for a relatively simple programme of cropping. The container should have a transparent upper surface, there should be a means of circulating the culture medium within the apparatus so that the algae do not settle, and a method of controlling the temperature. Carbon dioxide and other nutrients have to be introduced continuously, at the same time as harvesting proceeds. It is also necessary to process the tiny plants as they mature, so that they may be preserved until required for consumption or industrial use. Specialised and simplified equipment are available in the market, or may be made up on the site. On removal from the centrifuge, which is generally employed for harvesting purposes, the algal cells form a thick paste, which contains about 75% water. In this condition, the material spoils quickly – in less than an hour in warm surroundings. Drying or freezing prevents deterioration.

For growing any given species of alga, it is necessary to provide favourable physical and chemical environments. The factors of light and temperature may show some variation, but in general it has been found that a minimum of 500 footcandles and a temperature range of from 15.5 to 22°C are a useful basis to work from. Carbon dioxide at 5% in ordinary air is normally adequate. The concentrations of the nutrient solutions do not differ materially from those of the ones employed for the growth of the higher plants. Water for mass cultures can be passed through a column containing cation and anion exchange resins, but there is no reason why natural waters of determined analysis cannot be employed directly, once the nutritional requirements of the organisms have been delineated, due allowance being made for the presence of any excess salts in the supply. With a satisfactory natural source available, only sterilization might be required.

Various crops

Essential oils, condiments, perfumery and medicinal plants of many kinds can be profitably grown in hydroponics. Rose geranium for scent is produced by soilless methods at Erevan in Armenia on a large scale.

Animal feed

Grasses and green forages produced by hydroponic methods are considered to possess valuable nutritional properties for farm livestock feeding purposes.

Many of the reports received over the past few years stress the advantages of using fresh green fodder in rations on a year-round basis. In particular, the protein content of grain or seed increased dramatically when it was germinated and grown to form young grass in hydroponic units. In the cases of oats, barley and other cereal grasses the protein values have been as much as 26 and 28%. Numerous farmers in different countries state that the milk yields of their dairy cows have risen substantially after the feeding of hydroponic forage has commenced. The system is especially valuable in arid or semi-arid regions, where there is little or no field grazing, in cold and harsh climates where stock must be kept inside much of the time, or at times of drought.

Feeding rates for soilless produced fodder vary from 5 to 10 or more kilos daily, according to the type of animal. The grass should be introduced slowly and the quantities supplied increased as the livestock become accustomed to it. In some instances, the forage is often employed as a ration ingredient, substituting for fresh grass, lucerne, and hay, but also allowing the level of concentrate feeding to be reduced, which constitutes a noteworthy economy.

Analyses of hydroponic grass and grain supplied by Hydroponics Inc., Indianapolis, read:

NUTRIENTS IN 45 KILOGRAMMES (100 LBS) OF OAT GRAIN AND 6-DAY OAT GRASS PRODUCED FROM THE OATS	*Seed*	*Grass*
Dry matter, lbs	89.24	84.80*
Protein, lbs	13.39	18.65
Ether extract (fat) lbs	3.76	4.41
Minerals, lbs	2.87	3.31
Calcium, lbs	0.056	0.202
Phosphorus, lbs	0.32	0.43
Carotene, mg	NIL	33,136**
Vitamin E, mg	1600	4,154
Riboflavin, mg	175	1,891
Thiamine, mg	280	1,091
Niacin, mg	640	8,818
Vitamin C, I.U.	NIL	370,356
Unknown growth factors	NONE	
Trace minerals	NIL	
Enzymes	NIL	

NOTE: 1 lb = 0.4536 kg

*Five per cent loss in dry matter occurred in these samples.
**Equivalent to 55,237, 712 I.U. of vitamin A.

COMPOSITION OF OAT GRAIN AND 6-DAY OAT GRASS*

| | OAT GRAIN | | 6-DAY OAT GRASS | |
	Per pound* as fed basis	Dry matter basis	Per pound* as fed basis	Dry matter basis
Water, %	10.76		90.77	
Dry matter, %	89.24	100	9.33	100
Protein, %	13.39	15.00	2.03	21.99
Ether extract (fat), %	3.76	4.21	0.48	5.20
Nitrogen free extract, %	58.77	65.86	3.95	42.79
Fibre, %	10.45	11.71	2.41	26.11
Ash, %	2.87	3.22	0.36	3.90
Calcium, %	0.056	0.063	0.022	0.238
Phosphorus, %	0.32	0.36	0.047	0.509
Carotene, mg **	NIL	NIL	3.645	39.067
Vitamin E, mg	16.0	17.95	4.56	48.87
Riboflavin, mg	1.75	1.96	2.08	22.29
Thiamine, mg	2.80	3.14	1.20	12.86
Niacin, mg	6.40	7.18	9.70	103.96
Vitamin C, I.U.	NIL	NIL	407.4	4366.5
Unknown growth factor	NONE	NONE		
Trace minerals	NIL	NIL		
Enzymes	NIL	NIL		

*Analyses by Wisconsin Research Foundation.
**Each milligram of beta carotene is equivalent to 1667 I.U. of vitamin A.

D. A. Harris, of Capetown, South Africa, has written: 'A farmer, with whom I had correspondence, summarised the position about soilless forage by saying that, as regards his Jersey cows, he is getting more financial return from them since introducing the hydroponic fodder. He has stopped using any form of dairy feed. He tells me that he is feeding only the recommended amount of hydroponic fodder produced from a commercial unit plus a certain amount of bulk which in his case consists of silage only.'

Still another report (Final Report ER 11.5.70 *Zero Grazing Trial with Dairy Cattle*) I have, shows that milk production in the Natal area was 0.89 litre per cow per day higher in a scientific trial conducted with groups of milk cows. The report concludes that 'the use of hydroponic units insofar as it reduced land requirements for fodder production would present a feasible solution to Zero Grazing dairy systems near urban areas.'

J. Muller Laboratories, Capetown, analysed barley green fodder, produced in a farm hydroponic unit, with the undernoted result:

HYDROPONIC BARLEY
GRASS

	Fresh basis	Dry basis
Moisture %	91.2	—
Protein (N × 6.25)	2.29	26.3
Fibre %	2.22	25.5
Ash %	0.42	4.81
Calcium %	0.033	0.38
Phosphorus %	0.073	0.84
Copper mg/kg	3.04	35.0
Zinc mg/kg	1.65	19.0
Manganese mg/kg	0.91	10.5
ß-carotene, mg/kg	20.6	237

The increase of ß-carotene in hydroponics is particularly notable, because in grains the content is virtually negligible.

PART FIVE

Chemical Control

17. The tower greenhouse erected at the Hydroponic Station, Erevan, of the Institute of Agrochemical Problems and Hydroponics of the Academy of Sciences of the Armenian SSR, in U.S.S.R.
(Professor G. S. Davtyan).

CHAPTER 22

Solution testing

The relative uptake by plants growing in hydroponica of the various nutrient ions is affected principally by local environmental conditions such as temperature, humidity, and light intensity. The type of crop and the stage of development also play an important part in the details of nutrition. It has long been known that this absorption of water and essential elements from the solution does not occur in the same proportion in which the components were supplied originally. In view of the existence of differential uptake of the different ions, the composition of the nutrient solution is continually changing, some of the elements being more rapidly depleted than others. The concentration may also be increased by the relatively greater absorption by the plants of water than of salts. In addition, the hydrogen ion concentration (pH) varies as a result of reactions with the aggregate and the unbalanced absorption of the anions and cations in solution. It is comparatively simple to replace the water which has evaporated from the growing medium, or has been absorbed by the plants, by the periodic replacement of the solution volume with fresh supplies. As far as the nutrient elements are concerned, however, the case is not so straightforward. Before adding extra amounts of chemicals, it is necessary to determine, at any rate in certain types of units, the existing concentrations of particular ions in the solution upon which the crops are feeding, by chemical methods of analysis. These also indicate the quantities of the elements that have been utilised. It is desirable to check the hydrogen ion concentration systematically, and to ensure that it stays within the proper range, influencing it when necessary by the addition of acid or alkali. Such determinations should be carried out regularly in commercial installations, and accurate records of the results, together with lists showing any additions of chemicals, must be kept. Apart from testing hydroponic solutions for any depletions of nutrients, it is often advantageous to ascertain whether accumulation of unused ions is occurring, or if excesses of toxic elements are present. Abnormalities in growth are sometimes indicators of a deficiency or an excess of nutrient ions. Tissue tests of plant leaves may be of great value in diagnosing troubles of this nature.

Equipment

In order to carry out chemical testing procedures efficiently in large commercial installations, it is necessary to have access to a well equipped laboratory. In many cases, it will be worthwhile to construct or adapt one of the service buildings for the purpose. The amateur grower does not, of course, require anything so elaborate.

A hydroponic laboratory should contain a refrigerator and a set of cabinets, together with supplies of the important reagents and glassware. It must be kept in first class condition at all times, and all unskilled workers should be excluded from it, only the technicians being permitted to enter. Glassware will require washing, and must be stored on shelves or in cabinets, each item being arranged in the most convenient position for general use. A still is essential, and this apparatus will need mounting above, and a little to one side of, the sink so that when in operation it will directly fill the distilled water bottle. For the drainage of washed glassware, a rack should be affixed just behind the sink. Heaters or Bunsen burners are placed on the bench. The window should preferably face north, so that it admits a good, clear light, but does not allow the rays of the sun to interfere with visual examinations. Corrosive chemicals are best stored near the sink, while strong acids and alkalis should be kept in stoppered bottles. Delicate equipment, like balances, microscopes, and conductivity apparatus, must not be left next to any corrosive acids. Centrifuges need oiling occasionally, and balances must be covered when not in use. It is a most undesirable practice to place dry chemicals on the balance pans – glass dishes (watch glasses) should always be employed, or else filter paper. Batteries of conductivity sets require periodic checking and replacement. Microscopes have to be covered up after use, and the eyepieces removed to prevent dust from collecting on the inner surfaces of the objectives. Comparators have to be kept clean, and well rinsed with distilled water before use. All containers must be clearly labelled.

Water

Pure distilled water is essential for all tests. Glassware must be well washed with distilled water each time it is used for any work in the laboratory, or when undertaking field tests. In order to check the purity of distilled water, the pH should be ascertained at regular intervals. Boiled distilled water has a pH of 7.0, and when freshly distilled, water ranges from pH 6.5 to 7.0. It is usually on the slightly acid side owing to the presence of dissolved carbon dioxide.

Preparing reagent and standard solutions

Certain general precautions should be observed in the preparation of these solutions. They are best made up in volumetric flasks. The solution in the flask has the volume indicated if the bottom of the meniscus coincides with the ring engraved at the stated volume. Solutes should be dissolved in solvents in a beaker, and the solution then transferred to the volumetric flask, adding enough of the solvent to bring it up to the final volume. Volumetric determinations must be made with all components at room temperature. Liquids, in particular, should be neither very hot nor very cold. Some substances expand on heating and contract on cooling, so it is impossible to undertake accurate determinations unless a relatively constant temperature is maintained. Pipetting of corrosive and poisonous chemicals also calls for some care, and the handling of sulphuric acid must conform to the recognised precautions. Many of the reagents are somewhat unstable and deteriorate with age. This can be accelerated by high temperatures, or exposure to strong sun. All reagents involving organic materials in water solutions should be stored in closed dark cupboards when not in use. Monthly tests may be run, using a standard nutrient solution, to check on reagents. It is essential in colormetric testing to have a constant light source, either north daylight, or fluorescent lamps.

Sampling

Samples of nutrient solutions for testing may be taken from the mixing tanks in solution cultures, or from the beds in other cases. Great care must be exercised when obtaining samples of solution from aggregates. Should it be necessary to squeeze the growing medium to extract any liquid, this should never be done with the bare hand. Instead, a rubber glove must be used, which has been well washed with distilled water. It should be carefully rinsed after each individual sampling. Enough solution should be secured each time to ensure an adequate amount for all the determinations that it is intended to make.

The concentration of the ions in the sample should always be within the range of the test, and not at either end. Dilution or concentration as necessary may be practised, in the case of the former with distilled water, and as far as the latter is concerned by boiling in the hot bath using glycerine at between 130 and 150°C. It is simplest to concentrate a sample more than necessary and then dilute it to the proper volume. For both dilution and concentration, the pH should be kept between 4.0 and 5.0 in order to prevent any precipitation.

Frequency of testing

This depends upon the experience of the operator and the rate of crop growth. As data is accumulated on the uptake of the various ions at the different periods of development, the frequency of the tests can be considerably reduced. With new installations the pH should be checked daily, and the concentrations of the major elements estimated twice weekly for the first month. Thereafter, checks at longer intervals are quite in order, unless visual symptoms of deficiencies or toxicities appear. While guessing, or haphazard 'hunches' are undesirable, unnecessary and over-meticulous testing are merely a waste of valuable time. At the first sign of any physiological un-balance or disturbance, chemical tests should be made for all the ions, and conductivity tests begun to ascertain whether the osmotic concentration has been raised to unduly high levels by accumulation of toxic elements under certain conditions.

Records

Complete and detailed records should be maintained of all tests undertaken. These may be of considerable value for future reference.

Test procedures

1. HYDROGEN ION CONCENTRATION OR pH

Testing kits, consisting of a comparator, tubes, and indicators with glass colour stan-dards may be purchased. The indicators are complex organic dyes, which change to distinctive colours through a specific pH range of the aqueous solutions. The ones most commonly employed in hydroponics are: bromocresol green, chlorophenol red, bromothymol blue, cresol red, and methyl red.

Usually, comparators are supplied with two 10 ml Nessler tubes. Both should be filled with the water or the nutrient solution to be tested, and placed in the apparatus. Into one of the tubes 0.5 ml of the selected indicator is then pipetted, the glass standard is inserted in the comparator, and the colour read off. With a two dye series, the indica-tors are added to different tubes, in a modified comparator.

Indicator ranges are as follows:

Indicator	pH range	
Bromocresol green	3.6–5.2	
Chlorophenol red	4.8–6.4	
Bromocresol purple	5.2–6.8	
Bromothymol blue	6.0–7.6	
Diphenol red	7.0–8.6	
Cresol red	7.2–8.8	*Only suitable for very approximate
Thymol blue	8.0–9.5	estimations, or quick field tests.
B.D.H. universal	4.0–11.0*	**Chiefly employed to indicate the
B.D.H. 678	5.0–10.0**	points pH 6.0, 7.0, and 8.0.

Standard Lovibond discs, containing permanent colour standards are available for these indicators, with full instructions for use, and may be purchased from any sup-plier of chemical apparatus.

If desired, indicators may be prepared without difficulty in the laboratory, as follows:

Bromocresol green. Dissolve 0.04 gm of bromocresol green in 5 ml of 95% ethyl alcohol. Add 95 ml of distilled water, and adjust pH to 4.6.

Chlorophenol red. Dissolve 0.04 gm of chlorophenol red in 5 ml of 95% ethyl alcohol. Add 95 ml of distilled water, and adjust pH to 5.6.

Bromothymol blue. Dissolve 0.04 gm of bromothymol blue in 5 ml of 95% ethyl alcohol. Add 95 ml of distilled water, and adjust pH to 6.6.

Phenol red. Dissolve 0.04 gm of phenol red in 5 ml of 95% ethyl alcohol. Add 95 ml of distilled water, and adjust pH to 7.4.

For adjustment of pH, very dilute sodium hydroxide should be added drop by drop. Comparisons may be made with the usual colour charts. Very dilute hydrochloric acid solution will re-adjust pH point if it should be by-passed accidentally.

Indicators prepared as suggested above respond to the following ranges:

Bromocresol green	4.0–5.4
Chlorophenol red	5.2–6.8
Bromothymol blue	6.0–7.6
Phenol red	6.8–8.4

Methyl red. Dissolve 30 mg of methyl red in 2.22 ml of 0.05 normal NaOH, and make up to 100 ml volume with alcohol (95%).

Bromothymol blue. Dissolve 0.05 gm of bromothymol blue in 4.0 ml of 0.02 normal NaOH, and make up to 125 ml volume with distilled water.

NOTE: pH meters may be purchased from suppliers of chemical apparatus and are well worthwhile for large units.

2. NITRATE NITROGEN

Measure a 1.0 ml sample of nutrient solution with a pipette into a pyrex ignition tube, and add a drop or two of 0.2 potassium permanganate until a persistent pink coloration remains. Then evaporate to dryness at 150°C, in the hot bath. Now add 2.0 ml of phenoldisulphonic acid reagent to the dry residue, and rotate the tube until all the residue is dissolved. Add 3.0 ml of distilled water and mix, finally pouring 12 N potassium hydroxide very slowly and with careful shaking into the tube until a maximum yellow colour is obtained. This reaction is violent with evolution of heat, unless the potassium hydroxide is added slowly. It should be permitted to stand until cooled to room temperature. Then filter the contents, using Whatman paper No. 40 or 42, and with small quantities of distilled water wash the ignition tube and the solid potassium sulphate on the paper free of the yellow colour. Make up the solution in the flask to the 50 ml mark, mix by inversion, and read off the colour, with the standards.

The test is colormetric, and is based upon the nitration of phenoldisulphonic acid by the nitrate ions present in a nutrient solution. The tripotassium nitrophenol disulphonate salt is formed by the addition of strong potassium hydroxide. This tripotassium salt has a bright yellow colour, the intensity of which is proportional to the amount of nitrate nitrogen present in the nutrient solution analysed.

Standards for colour comparison should be prepared by putting up solutions of known concentration, testing them, and preserving the results either in flasks, or by copying the exact shades produced onto charts.

Reagents: *Phenoldisulphonic acid*
Dissolve 25 gm of pure white phenol in 150 ml of pure concentrated sulphuric acid. Add 75 ml of fuming sulphuric acid (15% free SO_3), stir well, and heat for 2 hours at about 100°C.

Potassium hydroxide solution
Prepare an approximately 12 N solution by dissolving 672 gm of potassium hydroxide in approximately 500 ml of distilled water. Then cool, and make up to 1 litre.

Potassium permanganate
Dissolve 6.3 gm of potassium permanganate in distilled water, making up to 1 litre, to obtain an approximately 0.2 N solution. Keep in a dark bottle.

3. AMMONIUM NITROGEN
Pour 25 ml of nutrient solution into a large Nessler tube, adding 2.5 ml of gum arabic solution, and fill to 50 ml mark with distilled water. Now add 2.0 ml of the Nessler solution, in a series of 0.7 ml drops, mixing each time by inversion of the tube. Allow the mixture to stand for two minutes, and compare with the standards.

Standards for colour comparison should be prepared by putting up solutions of known concentration.

Reagents: *Gum arabic solution (protective colloid)*
Add 10 gm of gum arabic to 190 ml of distilled water, and stir until dispersed fully. Now drop in 4 gm of permutit powder, and shake at intervals for ten minutes. Then decant the slightly turbid supernatant liquid for use, discarding the permutit. A crystal of thymol should be placed in the solution to stop the growth of moulds and bacteria.

Nessler solution
Dissolve 72 gm of NaOH (A.R.) in 450 ml of distilled water. After the solution has cooled, add 25 gm of HgI_2, and dilute to 500 ml with distilled water. Then mix thoroughly and allow to settle for two days. Use the supernatant liquid.

4. POTASSIUM

Measure 10 ml of unfiltered nutrient solution into a test tube, and add 0.25 gm of magnesium oxide. Place the tube in the hot bath for about three-quarters of an hour, and evaporate to dryness. Then filter through a No. 42 Whatman paper, and make up to 10 ml with distilled water. Now measure 1 ml of the treated solution in a 15 ml centrifuge tube, put the tube in the hot bath, and evaporate contents to dryness. Cool to the room temperature, and add 1 ml of freshly filtered lithium dipicrylaminate with an Ostwald pipette. Shake gently, so that all the residue comes into contact with the reagent then allow to stand at room heat for about two hours. After this lapse of time, centrifuge the sample, and withdraw 0.2 ml from it with care. Place this in a 50 ml Nessler tube, dilute to the mark with distilled water, allow to stand for half-an-hour, and compare with the standards. As lithium dipicrylaminate is a vesicant, care should be taken when handling it.

The test is based upon the fact that the potassium ion reacts with dipicrylamine to form a potassium salt insoluble in water. The unfiltered solution is treated with magnesium oxide to remove ammonia and phosphates, and is then filtered. The two hour period of waiting is estimated for the average small laboratory room temperature of about 26°C.

Standards for colour comparison should be prepared by putting up solutions of known concentration.

Reagents: *Magnesium oxide*
Solid compound, must be chemically pure (C.P.).

Lithium dipicrylaminate
This is a 0.6% solution in water, saturated with potassium dipicrylaminate. Dissolve 0.55 gm of lithium carbonate (A.R. or C.P.) in 100 ml of distilled water, and add 3 gm of dipicrylamine. Heat this solution to 50°C and stand for twenty four hours, then filter into a 500 ml volumetric flask, and make up to the mark with distilled water. Now heat again up to 50°C and add moist potassium dipicrylaminate until no more will dissolve. Allow the saturated solution to cool at room temperature. Do not filter from the deposited crystals. To prepare potassium dipicrylaminate, add a few ml of dipicrylamine (3%) to about 10 ml of 1% potassium chloride or sulphate, washing and centrifuging the precipitate several times with distilled water.

5. PHOSPHORUS

Measure 1 ml of filtered nutrient solution with a pipette into a 50 ml Nessler tube, and 7.6 ml of 0.32 N hydrochloric acid. Mix well. Now add 1 ml of molybdic sulphuric acid reagent, and then 0.4 ml of amino naptholsulphonic reagent, mix everything together well, and allow it to stand for ten minutes. Compare with the colour standards, which should be prepared by testing solutions of known concentrations. The test is based upon the reaction of inorganic phosphorus with molybdic sulphuric acid to give phosphomolybdate, which is then reduced selectively with amino naphtholsulphonic acid to produce a blue colouration.

Reagents: *0.32 hydrochloric acid*
Add 27 ml of concentrated hydrochloric acid to about 500 ml water in a 1 litre volumetric flask, then dilute to the mark, and mix well.

Molybdic sulphuric acid
Dissolve 25 gm of ammonium molybdate in 200 ml of distilled water. Rinse into a volumetric flask containing 300 ml of 10 N sulphuric acid. Dilute to the mark, and mix. 10 N sulphuric acid is prepared by adding 225 ml of concentrated sulphuric acid to 650 ml of distilled water.

Amino naphtholsulphonic acid
Dissolve 30 gm of sodium bisulphite and 1.0 gm of sodium sulphite in 200 ml of distilled water. Add 0.5 gm of amino naphtholsulphonic acid, and stir well. It should be freshly made each month, and must be stored in a dark bottle.

6. MAGNESIUM

Measure 1 ml of filtered nutrient solution into a 50 ml Nessler tube and add 6 ml of distilled water, mixing well together. Now add 1 ml of titan yellow solution and 2 ml of 16% sodium hydroxide, stopper the tube and mix by inversion. If there is any tendency to precipitation, a drop (0.25 ml) of glycerine may be added. Read off the colour by matching with the standards.

Standards for colour comparison should be prepared by putting up solutions of known concentrations.

When analysing solutions for magnesium, the amount of magnesium present as magnesium carbonate should be noted, since this information is needed in the determination of calcium. It is obtained by multiplying the ppm of the magnesium present by 3.46.

This test rests upon the reaction of magnesium ions in alkaline solution with titan yellow dye. The red colouration produced is directly proportional to the concentration of magnesium in the solution.

Reagents: 0.05% *titan yellow solution*.
Weigh out 50 mg of titan yellow, and dissolve it in 100 ml of distilled water. This solution will remain stable for two weeks if kept in a dark bottle in a closed cupboard.

16% *sodium hydroxide solution*
Dissolve 16 gm of sodium hydroxide in 100 ml of distilled water. Keep the bottle containing the solution tightly closed.

7. CALCIUM

Place 25 ml of the nutrient solution to be tested into a 250 ml glass stoppered bottle, and add 25 ml of distilled water, Add the standard soap solution, shake vigorously, and for a constant interval after each addition, until a strong lather is obtained, which remains unbroken for five minutes when the bottle is laid on its side. This is the end-point.

The test is titrimetric, and determines the total hardness by the soap method. It actually measures the soap-consuming power of the nutrient solution, and approximates the total amount of calcium and magnesium in solution. The total hardness is estimated, and to find the calcium concentration, the amount of magnesium carbonate present must be subtracted from the figure arrived at. This content of magnesium should be estimated by the magnesium test given in (6) above.

Reagent: *Standard soap solution*
The stock solution is made by dissolving 100 gm of pure powdered castile soap in a litre of 80% alcohol. It should stand overnight and then be decanted. This is approximately ten times the strength of the dilute standard soap solution. Dilute a portion of the stock solution with 80% ethanol until, when titrated with standardized $CaCl_2$, 1.0 ml of the soap solution is equivalent to 1 ml of standard $CaCl_2$ solution, which in its turn is equivalent to 1 mg of $CaCO_3$. $CaCl_2$ solution consists of 0.5 gm of pure $CaCO_3$ dissolved in diluted hydrochloric acid, and made up to 500 ml with CO_2 free water. Allowance has to be made for the lather factor of the adjusted soap solution. This is the amount of standard soap solution required to produce a permanent lather of five minutes minimum in the same amount of distilled water. 1.0 ml of the final solution, after substracting the lather factor, equals 1 mg $CaCO_3$. Pre-standardized soap solutions can be made up on this prescription by any qualified chemist, and supplied with a stated lather factor.

Calculation: The final burette reading, after deducting the lather factor, and multiplying by 40, gives the total hardness as Ca and Mg carbonates in ppm. Correction must be made for magnesium, as mentioned. If 1.0 ml of the standard soap solution is equivalent to 1 mg $CaCO_3$, it is also equivalent to 1.2 ppm $MgCO_3$, consequently the ppm of $MgCO_3$ divided by 1.2 equals the ml of soap solution to deduct from the final burette reading (after it has been multiplied by 40) to correct for magnesium. The corrected reading times 0.4 equals the ppm of calcium. For example, if the burette reading on a 25 ml sample of nutrient solution is 12.4 ml of standard soap solution, and the lather factor for this solution is 0.4 ml, then 12.4 − 0.4 = 12.0,

and 12.0 × 40 = 480 ml soap solution per litre

or 480 ppm $CaCO_3$ (including $MgCO_3$)

As the test for magnesium indicated that 20 ppm was present so:

20 × 3.46 (see 6) = 69.2 ppm $MgCO_3$

Since 1.0 ml of soap solution is equivalent to 1.2 ppm $MgCO_3$ then,

$\dfrac{69.2}{1.2}$ = 57.5 ml to deduct for Mg correction,

with the result that

480 − 57.5 = 422.5 ml

and   422.5 × 0.4 = 169 ppm calcium.

8. CHLORINE

The result is expressed in terms of the chloride ions present in the solution.

Pipette 10 ml of the filtered nutrient solution into an evaporation dish, and add 5 ml of standard silver nitrate solution, stirring thoroughly. Then add 5 ml of nitric acid, mix, and allow it to stand for five minutes. Flocking out of silver nitrate will occur. Now using a spatula, place 0.3 gm of ferric ammonium sulphate in the mixture, and titrate with standard thiocyanate solution until a salmon red colour persists for at least ten seconds in spite of stirring. The test is based on the precipitation of the chloride ions from a solution by the addition of silver nitrate, with the formation of insoluble silver chloride.

Reagents: *Standard silver nitrate*

Dissolve 4.791 gm of reagent silver nitrate in distilled water, and make up to 1 litre. Mix thoroughly, and store in a brown bottle. 1.0 ml of this solution corresponds to 1.0 mg of chloride. The solution is an N/35.46 one.

Standard potassium or ammonium thiocyanate solution
Dissolve 3 gm of KCNS or 2.5 gm of NH_4CNS in 1 litre of distilled water. The solution is an $N/35.46$ one.

Concentrated nitric acid

Powdered ferric ammonium sulphate

Calculation: ml of silver nitrate minus ml of thiocyanate equals ml of silver nitrate utilized in precipitating the chloride. 1.0 ml of standardised silver nitrate solution is equivalent to 1 mg of chloride. Multiply by 100 to give ppm with a 10 ml sample of solution.

9. IRON

Measure 50 ml of the nutrient solution into a 125 ml Ehrlenmeyer flask, add 5 ml of 6 N nitric acid and several glass boiling beads, then boil for ten minutes, adding three drops of 0.2 normal potassium permanganate. The resultant pink colour will persist for about 5 minutes. Cool the mixture to room temperature, and then pour the contents of the flask in a 50 ml Nessler tube, washing the flask out with a small quantity of distilled water. Make up to the 50 ml mark, and add 5 ml of 2% potassium thiocyanate, mix well by inversion and read off the colour.

Standards for colour comparison should be prepared by putting up solutions of known concentration.

In this test, the ferrous iron is oxidized to ferric iron, rendered soluble by a strong nitric acid solution, and after the addition of a thiocyanate, a pink colour of varying intensity develops. This colour is proportional to the amount of ferric iron in solution.

Reagents: *6 N nitric acid*
Dilute 382 ml of concentrated nitric acid (specific gravity 1.42) with distilled water to 1 litre.

Potassium or ammonium thiocyanate (2%)
Dissolve 2 gm of the thiocyanate in distilled water, and make up to 100 ml volume. Store in a dark bottle.

0.2 potassium permanganate solution
see (2) above.

10. COPPER

Measure 40 ml of the sample of nutrient solution into a 50 ml Nessler tube. Add 5 ml of ammonium hydroxide reagent, and filter only if a precipitate forms, then add 5 ml of sodium diethyldithiocarbamate. The resultant colouration should be compared with the standards within a hour.

The organic chemical compound, sodium diethyldithiocarbamate, gives a brown colour in the presence of copper.

Reagents: *Ammonium hydroxide solution*
Dilute one part ammonium hydroxide (specific gravity 0.9) A.R. or C.P., with five parts of distilled water.

Sodium diethyldithiocarbamate
Dissolve 1.0 gm of this salt in 1 litre of distilled water, and keep in a dark glass bottle away from the light. The solution will be stable for about six months.

11. MANGANESE

Pipette 2.0 ml of nutrient solution into a Nessler tube, and add 0.2 ml of sulphuric acid, exercising considerable care. Cool to room temperature, and then add 0.1 gm of bismuthate powder. Shake the mixture for half a minute, and afterwards allow the excess sodium bismuthate to settle. Leave for half an hour, and then compare with colour standards.

Standards for comparison may be prepared by putting up solutions of known concentrations.

Reagents: *Concentrated sulphuric acid* (specific gravity 1.84)

Sodium bismuthate

12. SULPHUR

The result is calculated as ppm of sulphate ions.

Measure 5 ml of nutrient solution in a 125 ml Ehrlenmeyer flask, and add 20 ml of distilled water and 25 ml of 95% ethyl alcohol. Allow the mixture to stand until room temperature is attained, then add 0.2 gm of potassium chloride disodium tetrahydroxyquinone indicator. Having filled a burette with barium chloride solution, add about 0.5 ml of this solution to the flask, and also 0.5 ml of silver nitrate reagent. Continue the titration with swirling until the appearance of a red orange colour is obtained. The end point should be sharp.

Reagents: *Potassium chloride disodium tetrahydroxyquinone*
solid mixture

Ethyl alcohol
95%

Silver nitrate
standard, as used for chloride determinations.

Barium chloride solution
Weigh out 3.053 gm of barium chloride, dissolve it in distilled water, and make up to 1 litre, for a 0.025 N solution.

Calculation: A subtraction of a blank value for phosphate ions present is necessary. A mean blank value of 0.15 ml barium chloride is adequate for 15–60 ppm P.
Using a 5 ml sample of solution,

total ml of barium chloride − 0.15 ml × 240 = ppm SO_4

The technique of this test is to titrate directly with a standard solution of barium chloride. The colour change is from yellow to red orange.

In addition to the tests listed above, a number of others may be undertaken if desired. Details of analyses for additional micro-nutrient estimations will be found in chemical literature. However, no really satisfactory or accurate tests have yet been evolved, which could be undertaken in the hydroponic laboratory, for the estimation of the amounts of many of the trace elements. Several manufacturing firms are now producing special apparatus and equipment for the chemical testing of plant nutrient solutions. These include both pH testing outfits, and more advanced laboratory kits. In particular, The Tintometer Ltd., Salisbury, England, produce a useful range of apparatus, together with a book giving the details of a number of tests. (*The Chemical Testing of Plant Nutrient Solutions,* by G. S. Fawcett and R. H. Stoughton.) Other suppliers include the La Motte-Morgan Chemical Co., Baltimore, Maryland; W. A. Taylor and Co., 7300 York Road, Baltimore, Maryland; the Edwards Laboratory, Lansing, Michigan; and Charles C. Gilbert & Co., San Diego, California. Local dealers can usually order direct from these manufacturers.

Electrical pH meters of convenient size are available from W. G. Pye & Co., Ltd., Granta Works, Cambridge, England. These instruments weigh only 2 kg, and are portable, being battery operated. They are accurate to within +0.1pH. Another supplier is Baird & Tatlock Ltd., Chadwell Heath, Essex, England and U.S.A. agents.

Standards

It is often convenient to make up standards in the laboratory, using only one salt for each solution, and diluting a stock solution to make an operating standard as desired. This saves the labour of mixing up a number of formulae for comparative purposes.

The following tables give details of the quantities of salts needed to prepare different standards.

STOCK STANDARDS

Element	ppm	Salt	Quantity gm	Amount of distilled water ml
Nitrate nitrogen	200	potassium nitrate	0.326	1000
Ammonium nitrogen	200	ammonium chloride	0.594	1000
Potassium	200	potassium chloride	0.382	1000
Phosphorus	200	potassium phosphate	0.877	1000
Magnesium	200	magnesium sulphate	2.028	1000
Calcium	200	calcium chloride	0.555	1000
Sulphate	800	magnesium sulphate	2.028	1000
Chloride	400	ammonium chloride	0.594	1000

OPERATING STANDARDS

Element	Amount of stock solution to give 10 ppm ml	Distilled water ml
Nitrate nitrogen	3.0	57
Ammonium nitrogen	3.0	57
Potassium	3.0	57
Phosphorus	3.0	57
Magnesium	3.0	57
Calcium	3.0	3.0
Sulphate	0.75	14.25
Chloride	1.5	58.5

To prepare a ferrous iron standard solution, dissolve 0.007 gm ferrous aluminium sulphate in 1000 ml of distilled water containing 0.1 ml concentrated sulphuric acid. This gives a 1 ppm solution. A ferric iron solution of the same concentration requires the addition of 0.0048 gm of ferric chloride to 1000 ml of distilled water.

0.004 gm of manganese sulphate dissolved in 1000 ml of distilled water produces a concentration of 1 ppm, while 0.195 gm of copper sulphate in 1000 ml H_2O gives a stock solution for general work. This latter may be diluted at the rate of 1.0 ml of the stock solution to 1000 ml of water to form a concentration of 0.05 ppm.

CHAPTER 23

Tissue test procedures

The information obtained by means of regular chemical testing of nutrient solutions can be usefully supplemented with periodic checks carried out on the leaves and stems of plants growing in soilless cultures. Tissue tests are qualitative, and give indications only as to the presence or absence of the essential elements. They are primarily of value in diagnosing nutritional diseases when the normal chemical analyses of the solution in the beds or the tanks does not yield complete data. Sometimes, root injuries and low temperatures in the aggregate or growing medium will reduce the capacity of crops to absorb nutrients. In such cases, tissue tests may be of considerable value to the operator.

Nitrate and phosphorus tests are the most important. The starch test is of help only to the experienced grower who has used it consistently on a number of plants under varying conditions, and who consequently knows how to interpret the results.

Nitrate nitrogen

There are two methods for carrying out this test.
(a) Take the sample of tissue from near the middle of the plant, in the case of tall crops, or from a leaf blade in smaller ones. Using a clean knife, squeeze a drop of sap from a petiole or vein onto a microscope slide or a watch glass. Add three drops of diphenylamine reagent.

(b) Make a diagonal cut across the petiole, and add one drop of diphenylamine reagent to the cut surface.

The test is based in the reaction of the nitrate ion with diphenylamine in a strong acid to give a deep blue to purple colour. This colouring develops quickly, and fades within a few minutes. The reagent should not come into contact with the hands, or clothing. All glassware and knives should be kept absolutely clean. Diphenylamine reagent must be stored in a dark bottle.

A normal healthy condition in the plant gives a dark blue to blue black colour. Pale blue to green indicates a shortage of nitrate. Brown to brown black colouring is indicative of no nitrate. In case of any doubt as to whether the colouring is blue black or brown black, add several drops of pure concentrated sulphuric acid to another sample. If the black colour develops, this is simply the carbon produced by the action of the acid, and there is no indication of the presence of nitrates.

Reagent: *Diphenylamine solution*
Dissolve 1.0 gm of diphenylamine in 100 ml of concentrated sulphuric acid. Store in a dark bottle away from high temperatures, or direct sunlight.

Phosphate

Take 5 gm of the leaf petiole from the middle of the plant, or else the same amount of leaf blades. Chop up the tissues, and macerate them with a glass rod, then extract with 25 ml 0.32 N hydrochloric acid. Centrifuge, and test the clear extract, employing the procedure recommended for the estimation of phosphorus in nutrient solutions (Chapter 22, page 295).

This test determines the presence or otherwise of inorganic phosphate in a dilute acid extract of the plant tissues.

Starch

Remove some young but mature leaves from as near to the top of the plant as possible, and extract most of the chlorophyll by boiling the foliage in alcohol. If the process is too slow, the leaves may be killed with boiling water before the extraction is commenced. After this treatment has been completed, transfer them to the iodine solution, and watch the colour development.

This test determines the presence or absence of starch (carbohydrate) reserves in the leaves. Iodine reacts with the starch grains in the cells to produce a deep blue to purple coloration. The deeper the colour the larger will be the starch reserves, while a brown to light tan stain is indicative of a deficiency of starch.

Reagents: *Methyl, ethyl, or isopropyl alcohol*

Iodine solution
Dissolve 1.5 gm of potassium iodide in 100 ml of distilled water, add 0.3 gm iodine crystals, then stir until completely dissolved.

Other deficiency tests

Tissue tests for elements other than nitrates and phosphates are not usually of much value. However, extracts can always be made from plant leaves or stems, and the procedures laid down for routine solution estimations followed. In the case of chlorosis on foliage, a solution of the salt which is suspected to be deficient may be made up and sprayed onto, or injected into, the leaves. For foliar treatments, the solution strength should not exceed 0.01 to 0.1%, otherwise scorching and burning may arise. Responses to such applications should appear within a few days if the right diagnosis has been made.

PART SIX

Ecology and Economics

18. Soilless culture of the Aloe arborescence (medicinal plant) at the hydroponic open-air station of the Institute of Agrochemical Problems and Hydroponics of the Academy of Sciences of the Armenian SSR, at Erevan, U.S.S.R.
(Professor G. S. Davtyan).

* I. Reviews of Research on Arid Zone Hydrology.
  II. Proceedings of the Ankara Symposium on Arid Zone Hydrology.
  III.Directory of Institutions engaged in Arid Zone Research.
  IV. Reviews of Research on Problems of Utilization of Saline Water.
  V. Plant Ecology, Proceedings of the Montpellier Symposium.
  VI. Plant Ecology, Reviews of Research.
     United Nations Educational, Cultural, and Scientific Organisation, place de Fontenoy, Paris 7e, France.

CHAPTER 24

The influence of hydroponics

The basic aim of all hydroponic cultural practice is to provide each plant with the optimum conditions for its successful growth and development. Cultivated plants, as we know them today, are essentially a human creation, left to themselves they could not survive in competition with wild species. Much study has been given during recent years to the investigation of the intimate relations that exist between plants or groups of plants and their environment. A knowledge of the origin, development, and structure of vegetation, and the various factors of the habitat, whether natural or modified by cultivation, are of importance to any production programme. The field of ecology is unique in its fundamental contributions to a general understanding of the different influences that, by processes of interaction, eventually constitute an environment favourable or unfavourable for the growth of particular plants. Vegetation is more than the mere aggregation of individual species. It is the result of the interplay of numerous factors. The effects of plants upon the place in which they grow and their influence upon each other are especially significant. The appearance of vegetation in a particular area may greatly modify the local conditions, often causing the habitat to become wetter or drier. The force of the wind may be lessened, or perhaps evaporation may be checked.

Man's influence upon the climate and vegetation of large parts of the world has been profound. In India, there is historical evidence to show that about 4000 B.C. the present Rajputana desert was well-wooded and even marshy in parts, and was the grazing ground of elephants and rhinoceroses. By 1000 A.D. desert conditions had become evident, due mainly to human settlement and the wholesale destruction of the forests. The irreparable havoc wrought to the great irrigation systems of Mesopotamia by the Mongol invasions of the 12th century is well known. During Roman times, northern Africa was the granary of Europe; today little may be seen except barren ground and the ubiquitous goat. In medieval England the vine grew profusely where now stand squalid slums and dreary suburbs. The United Nations Educational, Scientific, and Cultural Organisation decided in 1951 to commission experts to prepare reports* upon the research carried out on plant ecology in the arid and semi-arid regions as a matter of high priority. These documents, together with further papers dealing with conditions in other areas, show clearly the need for intensive efforts to reclaim and rehabilitate the productivity of such places. The ecological studies carried out embrace a wide field and include investigation into agriculture, botany, forestry, horticulture, plant physiology, plant pathology, and other connected subjects.

The paucity of published work upon the biocoenosis of crop plant communities is a striking feature of contemporary ecology. Much scope exists for examination of the close relationship subsisting between the natural and artificial conditions of nutrition and climate, on the one hand, and the totality of the organism in culture on the other. Only in the cases of single components, besides the crop plant itself, have extensive research programmes been carried out. Crop ecology, as it relates to hydroponics, can conveniently be divided into a number of sub-headings:

      (i)   Irrigation ecology,
     (ii)   Unit ecology,
   (iii)   Introduction ecology,
   (iv)   Plant protection,
    (v)   Production ecology,
   (vi)   Historical aspects,
  (vii)   Hydro-engineering,
 (viii)   Climatology,
   (ix)   Planning.

Irrigation ecology

The supply of water to hydroponic installations is free from many of the dangers that are inherent in the establishment of large scale conventional field cultures, where problems like those of the alkali soils of the Punjab, and waterlogging in the irrigated areas of Sind, can become acute. Important contributions to applied ecology have resulted from studies carried out on the water requirements of various crops growing in hydroponics. The different systems of bed construction, and the method adopted in each case of supplying water or solution, such as sub-irrigation, surface watering, sprinkling, flume, or other means, represent not only substantial alteration in technique, but also amount to ecologically dissimilar kinds of water supplies.

Unit ecology

The decisive influence of the nutritional status of cultures upon the size of harvests is well known. In soilless cultivation the ecology of the unit or environment is especially significant. Hydroponics may be said to represent the hemerarch series. Human disturbance has reached its maximum limits in the hydroponicum, culminating in the creation of an artificial environment more favourable to the growth and development of cultivated species than can be found elsewhere in nature. Viewed logically, how-

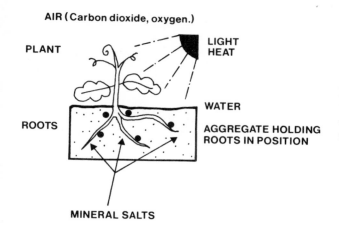

AIR (Carbon dioxide, oxygen.)

PLANT

LIGHT
HEAT

WATER

ROOTS

AGGREGATE HOLDING
ROOTS IN POSITION

MINERAL SALTS

FIG. 44.
Unit ecology in hydroponics. Soilless techniques ensure that all the main essentials for good plant growth are supplied — air, light, heat, water, support for the roots, and mineral salts, in balanced and adequate manner to maintain optimum environmental conditions.

ever, the growth of crops in artificial media is no more than the predetermined outcome of the civilising of man himself. Having abandoned the barbaric state for the comforts of civilisation, mankind would sooner or later obviously desire to impose some element of progressiveness upon the life of the plants vital to existence.

Co-operation between hydroponic research institutions and individual growers in different areas will greatly facilitate the advancement of ecological studies of the unit environment and its influence upon plants.

Introduction ecology

Ecological research is extremely important for the successful introduction of new plants, especially from one hydroponic environment to another in widely separated regions. The most significant factor in the ecology of introduction, in so far as it concerns out-of-door installations, is climate. Only in the second place is it necessary to consider nutrition. The use of indicator plants has many advantages. Homoclimatic maps prepared for different areas can be of considerable use in hydroponic work and planning. In all cases, it is desirable to know as many details as possible of the natural climax vegetation, if any, of a particular area. The suitability of a certain species for introduction to a new unit may be in large part dependent upon the correct choice of variety. Ecological institutions usually undertake the distribution of seed lists, and are able to give valuable advice upon the selection of plants for given localities.

Plant protection

The problems of plant protection and plant pathology are a scientific field of their own.

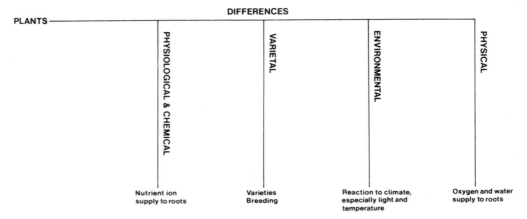

FIG. 45.
Diagrammatic representation of the main differences apparent in ecological terms between plants grown without and with soil. *Physiological and chemical:* in hydroponics, the most important factor is the total ion concentration, expressed as osmotic pressure. As light intensity becomes lower, the osmotic pressure rises; conversely with high light intensities a low osmotic pressure is generally desirable. *Varietal:* some varieties of plants do better in hydroponics and others thrive most effectively in soil. *Environmental:* plants growing in hydroponics often react differently in given climatic conditions than do the same species and varieties cultivated in soil. *Physical:* oxygen supply to the roots in hydroponics is vital, even more so than in soil, because the root system is normally small and finer.

Hydroponics is virtually free from the soil-borne diseases. However, many plant diseases are closely connected with ecological phenomena. For example, mildew has been shown to be related to dew magnitude, while liability to the attacks of pests may be greater in a hydroponic unit than in the surrounding habitat when both are open to the same climatic influences. This is attributable to the easier feeding conditions obtaining in soilless cultures than in wasteland. Sanitation and hygiene are therefore matters of the utmost importance to successful soilless crop growth.

Production ecology

A field of endeavour where ecology has an especially vital contribution to make is the search for economically valuable sites for hydroponic culture in regions unsuited to normal soil operations. These may be deserts, waste or barren lands, and sterile areas. The proper utilisation of such places, and the choice of the right crops to grow in them, without using soil, is a subject for ecological research. In towns, cities, and urban districts, large and convenient sites exist on rooftops, along roadsides, in yards, and similar localities, for extensive crop growing by hydroponic methods. Additionally, many plants constitute potential sources of essential raw materials, but may not be economic to cultivate conventionally outside their existing habitats. In these cases, selection of convenient hydroponic sites would probably encourage their development as commercially exploitable crops.

Historical aspects

Research into the history of soilless cultivation often reveals facts that have important bearing upon certain specific problems of crop cultivation. The field of study is wide, and a considerable amount of literature has accumulated during the past one hundred years.

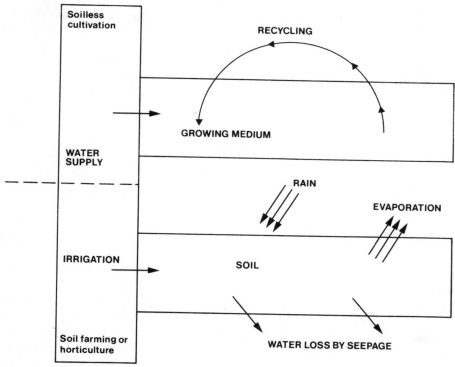

FIG. 46.
Water economy in hydroponics. Hydro-engineering aspects of soilless culture are largely based on the fact that scarce water supplies can be conserved through the recycling and re-use of water, whereas in soil irrigation much of the water is lost in evaporation and seepage.

Hydro-engineering

Soilless culture has an intimate connection with hydro-engineering and hydrology. Methods of plant ecology, as applied to these subjects, are mainly valuable for the quantitative determination of geophysical values relating to the establishment of hydroponic units in particular areas. These include investigations into water supply, mean annual rainfall, evapo-transpiration, correlation between growth and climate and other matters. The engineering aspects of installing hydroponic apparatus are of much significance.

Climatology

The fundamental concept in plant ecology is that the vegetation of an area taken as a whole is the result of a long period of adaptation to the environment – water supply, evaporation, humidity, wind, insolation, temperatures, and other factors. The habitat in nature is the reflection of the climate. Ecology is the key to the correct understanding of the relations between plants and their environments. In hydroponics, the object of the grower must be to create optimum conditions of climate, whether artificially or by selection of sites and varieties, so that the plants are provided with surroundings of the most favourable type from the start.

Planning

In soil culture, the grower has first of all to study the existing environment, and then, guided by the recommendations of the ecologists, to choose certain plants that will probably suit the habitat in question. With hydroponics, the procedure is rather different. There, as a rule, the producer selects the crops that it is felt will prove economically advantageous for the place, and afterwards creates at the desired site a set of surroundings designed to secure optimum results. It is quite possible to provide any crop with the right environment, no matter how unfavourable the locality chosen may turn out to be for its culture, provided that the necessary apparatus and protective devices are available and can be erected. In practice, however, the question of costs must necessarily enter into the picture. It would be obviously uneconomic to plan for a large capital expenditure which would not be fully recoverable from profit within a reasonable period. Nevertheless, there are many instances where high initial outlay is justified. R. H. Stoughton (1957) has forecast the future of horticultural development in cold areas in the following words: 'The greenhouse will be a sealed structure, perhaps of transparent plastic, into which air is blown automatically, conditioned to the right temperature, humidity, and carbon dioxide content. The plants will be grown in an artificial medium with automatic control (by computers) of their water and nutrient supply and a strictly regulated temperature regime. Natural daylight will be supplemented by artificial light, and harvesting and packing of the plants will be done by automatic machines.'

The planning and siting of large hydroponic installations, whether built out-of-doors in the tropics, or under shelter in the colder zones, offers considerable scope for a sustained programme of ecological investigations and research. The influence of such constructions upon the local environment may prove of great interest.

Future developments

The spread of hydroponics in towns is a feature of recent years. Much use has been made of rooftop units. In so far as the introduction of soilless cultivation results in the creation of vegetation in places where none previously grew, the field of ecological investigation has been widened. It is more than likely that in time to come the implications of this urban farming and gardening, and its influence upon the local environment, will receive the constant attention of architects, planners and research workers. Similarly, in deserts and arid regions, the establishment of soilless units may well point the way to the reclamation of such areas. Up to now, the various plant associations and formations of a country, and its vegetation provinces, have been set off from one another by differences in environmental factors due to natural and geophysical factors. Within each province, unless the land is covered by a climax association, exist series, related successionally, leading towards the climax. To have succession under natural conditions requires migration or the spread of the plants that are to bring about succession, together with ecesis. If ecesis does not follow migration, succession cannot take place in the conventional manner. All these processes are dependent upon the existence of the right natural environment. In the absence of favourable conditions for establishment and growth, an area remains barren or sterile. The attention of ecologists has so far been mainly concentrated upon the investigation of operative environments, and the often scanty vegetation that may subsist there. The condition of the region examined is too often regarded as predetermined and practically unchangeable, at any rate for the foreseeable future. This conception has undergone a significant revision, following the discovery of large-scale methods of soilless culture of plants. The ecologist now has a tool that will enable him to create to a greater or a lesser degree environments favourable for the growth of specific economic crops in what were formerly thought to be hostile habitats. The introduction of plants in to new areas has been greatly simplified. Hydroponics provides ecology with the means to establish footholds for exotic species in unfavourable surroundings. The initial success so attained may, in many cases, result in still greater achievements thereafter. It requires little imagination to envisage the profound effects upon, say, the climate and population of the Sahara, that the planned establishment of a large number of hydroponic units would have. By utilizing the vast underground supplies of water available in that area, and piping them into soilless cultures, a close coverage of vegetation could be rapidly established. This might well result in substantial climatic improvement, with the consequent possibility of the early introduction of forests and grasslands, initially using the surplus irrigation water from the hydroponica, and later the induced natural rainfall.

The field today

The expansion of soilless culture as a practical method of crop production has continued steadily during the past few years. Obviously many new developments have still to come, and further research will undoubtably result in the introduction of yet more improvements. The trend today is towards simplification in so far as the routine operation of units is concerned, with an emphasis upon automatic working at low cost. To present a clear picture of the present position it is necessary to define briefly the various fields of activity. These may be divided into:

(a)   The production of commercial greenhouse crops in cold and temperate zones, especially in off-season periods. This aspect is particularly important in highly industrialised countries where labour is very expensive.

(b)   The growth of good quality vegetables and flowers in tropical and sub-tropical regions in the vicinity of profitable markets, or for rapid transport to consuming centres.

(c)   The raising of food plants in desert areas or in famine districts, such as exist in the underdeveloped countries. Owing to foreign exchange difficulties or other international restrictions, it is vital that food should be produced in the places where it is actually needed, particularly in view of population increases.

(d)   The supply of military forces stationed at isolated bases or in countries where the local vegetable stocks are insufficient. This can be equally significant in time of war, when shipment is affected by hostile surface action or aerial bombardment.

(e)   The introduction of plants producing materials of strategic value in areas where they would not normally grow owing to the unsuitability of the local soil or environment.

(f)   The cultivation of crops in barren regions where exploration may be taking place, such as the Antarctic, or in arid places of high commercial productivity including oilfields, mines, and other complexes.

(g)   The investigation of problems in plant nutrition on a large scale, in the field. Hydroponics used in this connection is, of course, merely an extension of the laboratory methods well known to plant physiology.

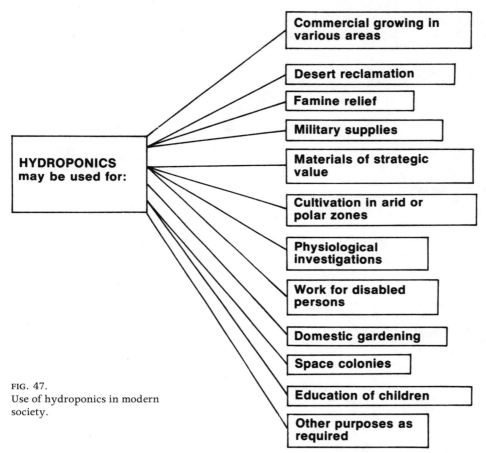

FIG. 47.
Use of hydroponics in modern
society.

(h) The provision of work for incapacitated persons, interested in horticulture, but
     unable to cope with the hard manual labour of soil gardening.

(i) The growing of vegetables and ornamentals by the householder, either as a hobby
     or for providing the family with fresh salads. In overcrowded towns, where
     fresh greenstuff is hard to get, hydroponics can be a great boon to the busy house-
     wife or flat-dweller.

(j) Production of food and amenity plants in space colonies.

(k) The education of children in the fundamentals of plant life. Botany, as taught in
     schools, is often a rather boring subject, but it can be made far more interesting if
     illustrated in a practical way by the working of a hydroponicum.

1. Netherlands. Secretariat of International Working-Group on Soilless Culture, Wageningen.
2. British Columbia; Saanichton.
3. France; Versailles.
4. Kuwait; Ministry of Public Works.
5. Italy; Pisa.
6. France; Antibes.
7. Canary Islands; Las Palmas, Tenerife.
8. California; Berkeley.
9. Zambia; Kitwe.
10. Spain, Barcelona.
11. India; Sibpur, Calcutta.
12. Texas; Grapevine.
13. New Mexico; Las Cruces.
14. Armenia; Erevan.
15. Sardinia; Sassari.
16. Israel; Lev Hasharon, Bet Dagan, Ramat Gan, Eilat.
17. Brazil; Sao Paulo.
18. East Germany; Berlin.
19. England; Stonehouse, Gloucestershire.
20. Morocco; Agadir.
21. Mexico; Mexico City.
22. Poland; Wroclaw.
23. Colorado; Fort Collins.
24. South Africa; Capetown.
25. England; Bristol.
26. Japan; Sendai and Kanagawa.
27. Sweden; Stockholm.
28. West Germany; Hanover, Freising.
29. Philippines; Rizal.
30. Spain; Madrid.
31. Italy; Perugia.
32. Arizona; Phoenix.
33. Italy; Florence.
34. South Africa; Johannesburg, Transvaal.
35. Austria; Ort im Innkreis, Vienna.
36. Western Samoa; Apia.
37. England; Peel, Blackpool.
38. Seychelles; Mahé.
39. India; Bombay.
40. India; Mirik, Darjeeling.
41. Guatemala.
42. New Zealand; Marlborough.
43. Nebraska.
44. Pennsylvania.
45. England; Middlesex.
46. St. Croix; U.S.V.I.
47. Belgium; Ghent.
48. Bahama Islands; Grand Bahama.
49. New York.

FIG. 48.
Location of hydroponic consultancies throughout the world. Centres marked indicate presence of a member of the International Working-Group on Soilless Culture (I.W.O.S.C.). A detailed list of names and addresses of official representatives and members of I.W.O.S.C. may be obtained from Dr A. A. Steiner, Secretary, Post Box 52, Wageningen, The Netherlands. (List subject to periodic changes.)

CHAPTER 25

Costs and returns

American growers have always claimed that hydroponics is cheaper than soil. Experiments in other countries have also shown this to be the case. Trials at the Colorado A. & M. College, Fort Collins, U.S.A., showed that expenses were 28 per cent less in hydroponics than in soil culture. It must be borne in mind when making any comparison that if fair contrasts are to be drawn, the cost of building a hydroponicum of a certain size from scratch should be likened to the expense of bringing a similar area of *virgin* soil under cultivation. Secondly, once the troughs have been erected they will require little or no attention for many years. Soil, on the other hand, has to be cultivated regularly at considerable outlay. Economy in labour is another big point. Forty hours monthly is ample to allow for looking after $\frac{1}{2}$ hectare under hydroponics. Casual workers have, of course, to be engaged for extra operations such as plucking, picking and packaging of produce, but just the same applies to the ordinary market garden or farm. Again, far smaller quantities of fertilizers are required, since the whole of the nutrient supply is available to the plants without waste, whereas in normal soil cultivation much of the manure is used by micro-organisms in the ground and quite a lot is leached out and lost by watering. In hydroponics, wastage of nutrients is most unlikely to occur. There much less water is used, and in sterilising gravel a smaller quantity of chemicals is necessary for a given area than for soil.

A soilless growing medium gives up all its water to the crops, but in earth a very high percentage of the moisture present is not available to plants. The amount of this non-available water, which is of little use, is often as high as 16 per cent in a clay soil, where fine colloidal particles are abundant. It is also important to remember that in normal soil irrigation practices, a large proportion of the water run on to fields is lost by seepage and evaporation. In hydroponics, there will be no such seepage losses in properly managed units, re-cycling of solutions may be arranged, and evaporation can be reduced to a minimum.

Average figures

Owing to the considerable variations that exist in different regions of the world, it is not possible to give any universal pattern of expenses, incomes and profits in hydro-

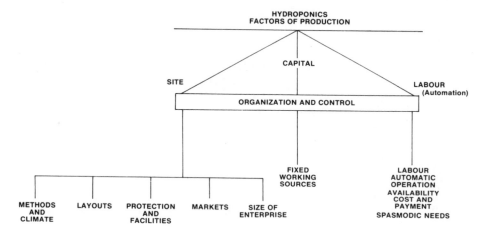

FIG. 49.
Factors governing the planning and design of soilless culture projects.

ponic cultivation. Moreover, any estimates prepared now may soon be overtaken by the effects of global or local inflation.

Normally, the capital cost of installing a hydroponic unit should be amortized within one-and-a-half to two years by operating profits. In India, it has been found that maintenance, taxes, and running expenses absorb some two-thirds of the returns from a commercial soilless farm or garden, leaving the grower with one-third of the takings as net income. This profit can, at present money standards, amount to about the equivalent of US $5000 per hectare per annum, which is low by international standards but very good for India.

Figures prepared from actual operating returns by a Colorado hydroponic installation show that a soilless unit, producing just over sixty tonnes of tomatoes yearly in the United States, will bring in a total net profit of $21,895 at 1968 rates. Maintenance was carried out by two persons, including upkeep, mixing of nutrients, harvesting, packing, and other tasks. In arriving at this figure, a gross income of $44,000 was considered as average and typical from an installation of the size in question, while the cash expenses and nominal depreciation amounted to some $22,000 a year.

In sheep farming work in southern Africa, using Gordon hydroponic fodder producing units for providing the livestock with fresh grass rations, it was found that the following profit could be secured:

*NOTE: R = rand, South African unit of currency 1 Rand = about US $ 1.25 in 1974

CAPITAL COSTS	'Gordon' machine	R	3033.00
	Housing (9 × 4.8 × 3.6 m) supplied and built by farmer plus seed storage	R	1000.00
	7 Sheep pens (12.2 × 6.1 m) to house about 35 ewes of 70 kg body weight, R 800 each	R	5600.00
	250 Ewes. R 25 each	R	6250.00
	5 Rams. R 60 each	R	300.00
		R	16,183.00

EXPENSES (BASED ON 250 SHEEP PER YEAR)	Barley/oats 20,075 kg, 6.17 c/kg (1,36 kg green fodder per ewe per day at a conversion rate of 6 to 1 = 0.22 kg seed per day)	R	1238.62
	Balance of made-up ration, R 9.89 per ewe/year	R	2472.50
	Labour for above	R	700.00
	Water, electricity, nutrients	R	150.00
		R	4561.12

RETURNS (BASED ON 250 SHEEP PER YEAR AND LAMBING RATE OF 150%)	1.5 lambs (mass 27 kg) per ewe for slaughter, 70 c/kg	R	4725.00
	Wool from mother, R 3.00 per ewe	R	750.00
	Manure, free of sand and containing urine for fertilizer, R 7.50 per ewe	R	1875.00
		R	7350.00
	Profit	R	2789.00
	Profit on capital		17.2%

One very interesting point that emerges from this study is that on the pen or battery system for sheep, 250 animals can be raised in an area of some 520 m² whereas by conventional South African standards 1 sheep per 2.5 ha is the norm.

The manufacturers of the 'Groenvoer 365' hydroponic grass unit summarise the economics of the process for dairy cattle feeding as follows:

CONVENTIONAL FEEDING

Cost of
100 cows
per year

Veld hay: 13.5 kg per cow/day
(R 0.011 per kg)   R   5420.25
Concentrate: 4.0 kg per cow/day
(R 0.053 per kg)   R   7738.00

R 13,158.25

GROENVOER 365

Cost of
100 cows
per year

10 unit System, capital cost R 6600,
5 year lease at 11% interest   R   2046.00
Housing, capital cost R 1000, deprecia-
tion over 5 years   R   200.00
Temperature control, capital cost
R 300, depreciation over 5 years   R   60.00
Seed: 600 bags (90 kg), R 5.00 per bag,
per year   R   3000.00
Labour: 365 days, R 2.00 per day   R   730.00
Electricity   R   100.00
Veld hay: 11 kg per cow per day,
R 0.011 per kg   R   4416.50

R 10,552.50

ADDITIONAL
PROFITABILITY   Estimated annual milk yield increase
                           (approx. 5%)   R   1277.50

From the above it would appear that the hydroponic system is if anything cheaper to run than conventional feeding.

However, we must bear in mind the fact that we are not making a comparison with raising milk cows in unlimited good pastures but in a situation where either poor pasture or no pasture is available. This is a very usual position in Africa.

Returns

Allowing for cost differences and income levels in separate countries, it is safe to say that generally speaking anyone investing in hydroponics may reasonably expect to receive in gross income, from high quality vegetable growing or floriculture, about double what annual expenses and write down of equipment amount to. This means

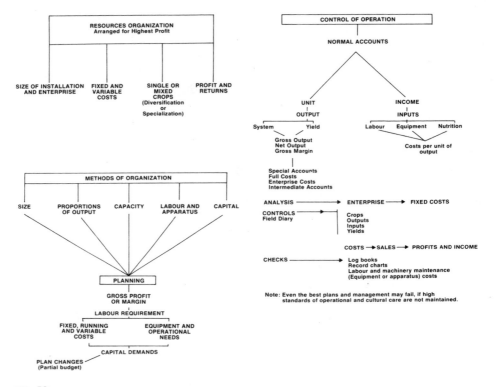

FIG. 50.
Organization and control in hydroponics. Main points to watch in
checking costs and profits.

that the return on investment, after reckoning on normal amortization of capital,
should be between 25 and 40 per cent.

Construction costs of hydroponic units will depend on the materials employed and
the use made of local supplies. Growers should therefore always make every effort to
utilise whatever materials and facilities may be close at hand, instead of relying on
expensive imported apparatus.

Marketing, too, is highly important. In the United States, during the off-season,
when field grown imports of tomatoes from California and Mexico are absent from the
shops, hydroponically produced tomatoes command a premium price. A wholesale

carton of about 10 kilos of such fruits sold for $6.00 at 1972 figures, with a retail value of 59 to 69 cents per $\frac{1}{2}$ kilo. All soilless grown tomatoes are labelled with a sticker when they are packed to identify them as 'Hydroponically grown, vine-ripened tomatoes'. This is a major marketing factor in selling the fruits, which are extremely popular amongst buyers because of their excellent flavour, good colour and perfect shape.

An interesting recent development in soilless cultivation in the United States has been the establishment of a hydroponic tomato industry in Utah. K. D. Gurgel has commented on its future prospects as follows:

Hydroponic tomato production will remain one of the most technical and intensive segments of contemporary agriculture. Utah's hydroponic tomato industry has gone through the first stage of development. Some growers experienced financial setbacks because expertise was absent in Utah during the early years of hydroponic tomato production. Growers have learned how to combat and overcome technical problems in growing a good tomato. Every tomato marketed is of superior quality when compared to the competitive tomatoes on the market shelf. Hydroponic tomatoes, therefore, enjoy a high popularity in Utah where demand exceeds supply at the present time.

Future expansion will be slow, which may be a healthy sign. Initial capital investments will have to be reduced to make expansion easier. Diversification from strictly tomato production into other vegetables and cutting flowers will have to be considered. New, higher-yielding tomato varieties must be developed. Better engineering methods, such as fully computerized feeding systems, must be introduced at a reasonable cost to improve growing methods.

As a neighbour of Arizona, the Utah grower will have to watch the current developments taking place at Glendale, near Phoenix, Arizona. There, Hydroculture Inc., operates 210 greenhouses on a 5 hectare commercial area with main emphasis on tomato production. It is estimated that these greenhouses have the capacity to produce around seven million pounds* of tomatoes annually.

---

*1 pound = 0.4536 kilogramme.

Suggested Books for Further Reading

Proceedings of the Second and Third International Congresses on Soilless Culture at Las Palmas, 1969, and Sassari, 1973. International Working-Group on Soilless Culture (I.W.O.S.C.) Post Box 52, Wageningen, The Netherlands.

Collings G. H. *Commercial Fertilizers, Their Sources and Use.* McGraw-Hill Publishing Co., New York and London 1955.

Davtyan G. S. *Hydroponics as an Industrial Achievement of Agrochemical Science.* Armenian Academy of Sciences, Erevan, Armenia, U.S.S.R., 1969.

Ellis C. and Swaney M. W. *Soilless Growth of Plants.* Reinhold Publishing Corporation, New York. Revised by T. Eastwood, 1947.

Fawcett G. S. and Stoughton R. H. *The Chemical Testing of Plant Nutrient Solutions.* The Tintometer Ltd., Salisbury, Wiltshire, 1944.

Gericke W. F. *The Complete Guide to Soilless Gardening.* Prentice-Hall Inc., New York, 1940.

Hewitt E. J. *Sand and Water Culture Methods used in the Study of Plant Nutrition.* Commonwealth Bureau of Horticultural and Plantation Crops, Maidstone, Kent, England, 1966.

Nutriculture. United States War Department Technical Manual, 1946.

In cases where books are out of print, it may be possible to obtain copies on loan from public and scientific libraries. Detailed bibliographies listing technical papers and other works on hydroponics are available from the Secretariat of the International Working-Group on Soilless Culture (address above).

Index